ESSAYS ON THE
ETHNOGRAPHY OF THE ALEUTS

The Rasmuson Library
Historical Translation Series
Volume IX
Marvin W. Falk, Editor

All titles listed are available from the University of Alaska Press.

ESSAYS ON THE ETHNOGRAPHY OF THE ALEUTS

(AT THE END OF THE EIGHTEENTH AND THE FIRST HALF OF THE NINETEENTH CENTURY)

Roza G. Liapunova
Academy of Sciences USSR
N. N. Miklukho - Maklai Institute of Ethnography

translated by Jerry Shelest
with the editorial assistance of
William B. Workman and Lydia T. Black

University of Alaska Press
Fairbanks

Library of Congress Cataloging-in-Publication Data

Liapunova, R. G. (Roza Gavrilovna)
 [Ocherki po etnografii aleutov. English]
 Essays on the ethnography of the Aleuts : at the end of the
eighteenth and the first half of the nineteenth century / Roza G.
Liapunova ; translated by Jerry Shelest, with the editorial
assistance of William B. Workman and Lydia T. Black.
     p. cm.v. -- (Rasmuson Library historical translation series,
ISSN 0890-7935 ; v. 9)
     Includes bibliographical references and index.
     ISBN 0-912006-85-4 (alk. paper)
     1. Aleuts. 2. Ethnology--Alaska--Aleutian Islands. 3. Ethnology-
-Russia (Federation)--Commander Islands.   I. Title. II. Series.
E99.A34L5213   1996
979.8'4--dc20   96-16064
                                                                              CIP

*Originally published in Russian in 1975 by
Publishing House "Nauka," Leningrad Branch.*

*International Standard Series Number: 0890-7935
International Standard Book Number: 0-912006-85-4
Library of Congress Catalog Card Number: 96–16064
English Translation © 1996 by The University of Alaska Press.
All rights reserved. Published 1996.
Printed in the United States of America
by BookCrafters, Inc.
on recycled and acid-free paper.*

*This publication was printed on acid-free paper that meets the minimum
requirements of American National Standard for Information Sciences-
Permanence for Paper for Printed Library Materials, ANSI Z39.48-1984.*

*Publication coordination by Deborah Van Stone
with production by Kate Sander with assistance from D. Van Stone.*

*Cover: Woman of Unalaska Island in a fur seal skin parka.
Beside her are wooden bowls, bone spoons, and a dancing belt.
Drawing by M.D. Levshov. TsGAVMG.*

CONTENTS

LIST OF ILLUSTRATIONS

LIST OF ABBREVIATIONS*

AGO   Archive of the Geographical Society of the USSR. (Leningrad)

ALOII   Archive of the Leningrad Department of the Institute of History of the Academy of Sciences of the USSR. (Leningrad)

AVPR   Archive of the Foreign Policy of Russia. (Moscow)

GIM   The State Museum of the Estonian SSR. (Tallin)

GME   The State Museum of the Ethnography of the Peoples of the USSR. (Leningrad)

LOAAN   Leningrad Branch of the Archives of the Academy of Sciences of the USSR. (Leningrad)

MAE   The Museum of Anthropology and Ethnography in the name of Peter I of the Academy of Sciences of the USSR. (Leningrad)

TsGADA   Central State Archives of Ancient Acts. (Moscow)

TsGAVMF   Central State Archive of the Navy of the USSR. (Leningrad)

TsVMM   Central Naval Museum. (Leningrad)

---

* The names and abbreviations listed here are those that were in use at the time of the original publication.

EDITOR'S NOTE FOR THE ENGLISH EDITION

This was one of the first titles selected for publication when the Rasmuson Library Historical Translation Program started in the early 1980s. It was considered to be the best available ethnography from a Russian scholar at that time and remains a valuable contribution to the literature today.

The initial translation was completed by Jerry Shelest, an engineer who worked on irrigation projects in Soviet Central Asia before he emigrated to Canada. At the time of translation he was engaged in graduate level research on the Russian-American Company as a part of a Ph.D. program in history. The initial translation was completed by the end of 1982. A number of questions raised in the manuscript needed to be clarified, but given the state of international relations at the time, direct and substantive contact with Roza Liapunova was not feasible. Clarification and thus publication, had to wait.

As international relations improved during the last years of the old Soviet Union, the project was once again taken up. Liapunova attended the "Russian America: The Forgotten Frontier" lecture series held in Anchorage in 1990, where she was given the draft English translation of her book. She was subsequently able to edit the translation herself, working with Bill Workman, a professor of anthropology at the University of Alaska Anchorage. Following Roza Liapunova's death, Professor Lydia Black at the University of Alaska Fairbanks read the manuscript and has provided useful editorial advice and a number of explanatory footnotes. Katherine Arndt has lent her copy-editing expertise to the book as well.

—*Marvin W. Falk*
Editor

A BRIEF BIOGRAPHY OF ROZA G. LIAPUNOVA
WITH SELECTED BIBLIOGRAPHY OF WORKS

The work translated here is *Ocherki po etnografii aleutov (konets XVIII-pervaia polovina XIX v.)* (Leningrad: Nauka, 1975), the earlier of Roza G. Liapunova's two monographs on the Aleuts of Alaska. It treats Aleut origins as hypothesized by archaeologists, Aleut life as documented in early historical sources, and Aleut material culture as documented both in historical sources and in the ethnological collections found in various museums. Though twenty years have passed since its original publication, it remains a valuable synthesis of English- and Russian-language sources on these topics. It also showcases the wide-ranging interests and broad expertise of a Soviet scholar whose work deserves to be much better known to an English-speaking audience.

Roza (Ol'ga) Gavrilovna Liapunova, nee Tabakova, was born in 1928 in the village of Kash-Elga, Bizhbuliak region, Bashkir ASSR, in the USSR. She was raised and received her early education in Cheboksary, Chuvash ASSR, where her father taught Russian language and literature. In 1946 she began studies at the Leningrad Wood Technology Academy and a year later transferred to the Ethnography Department of the Eastern Faculty at Leningrad State University. In 1950 she transferred to the History Faculty, where she was the last student of the venerable Russian folklorist and ethnologist Dmitrii K. Zelenin, and graduated with a specialist's degree in ethnohistory two years later. She defended her candidate's dissertation in historical sciences in 1970.

From 1952 until her death forty years later, Liapunova was engaged in research in the American sector of the Institute of Ethnography of the Academy of Sciences, Leningrad (St. Petersburg), advancing from senior scientific-technical fellow to junior scientific fellow, and finally to senior scientific fellow. She was one of the leading Soviet specialists in the ethnography of the peoples of northwestern North America, and the only Soviet ethnographer who specialized in Aleut culture.

Roza Liapunova in conversation with Captain A. N. Timon'kin. Photograph by A. N. Anfert'ev, 1976.

Many of her publications focus on various aspects of Aleut material culture, based on analysis of collections in the Museum of Anthropology and Ethnography in Leningrad (now the Peter the Great Museum of Anthropology and Ethnography, St. Petersburg). Much of her early research on this topic is synthesized in the monograph translated here. In later years her expertise in this field made her a valued participant in preparation of two major exhibitions of ethnological materials collected in Alaska in the eighteenth and nineteenth centuries: the "Crossroads of Continents" exhibit, organized by the (U.S.) National Museum of Natural History, and the Etholen collection exhibit, "Gifts from the Great Land," organized by the National Museum of Finland. She contributed articles to the publications that accompanied both exhibits, as well as to the symposium proceedings accompanying a third exhibition, "Russian America: The Forgotten Frontier," organized by the Washington State Historical Society and the Anchorage (Alaska) Museum of History and Art (Black and Liapunova 1988, Liapunova 1990a, 1990b, 1994).

Her second major area of endeavor was the search for and publication and analysis of primary sources on the eighteenth- and nineteenth-century history and ethnography of Alaska, the "Russian American" period. Her works in this sphere include analysis and publication of the archival materials of I. G. Voznesenskii, captains Krenitsyn and Levashov, and others. In 1979, together with Svetlana G. Fedorova, she published one of the most important sources on the history and ethnography of Russian America: *Russkaia Amerika v neopublikovannykh zapiskakh K. T. Khlebnikova* [Russian America in the unpublished notes of K. T. Khlebnikov]. Much of her research in this field is synthesized in her second monograph on the Aleuts, *Aleuty: Ocherki etnicheskoi istorii* [The Aleuts: Essays on ethnohistory], published in 1987.

Liapunova did not confine her research to museums and archives. A talented field worker, she spent a number of seasons among the Aleuts of the Commander Islands, where she was much beloved and is still well remembered. There she gathered material for her unpublished monographs *Ocherki dukhovnoi kul'tury aleutov* [Essays on the spiritual culture of the Aleuts] and Transformatsiia kul'tury korennogo naseleniia Aliaski (Russkaia Amerika - sovremennost') [Transformation of the culture of the native population of Alaska (Russian America to the contemporary period)], and various articles on the ethnic history of the Commander Islands Aleuts.

Nor was she a stranger to the Aleut people of Alaska, who are quite familiar with her work. In August of 1991 she visited Unalaska, where she felt very much at home. She took back with her many fond memories of the people she met and of at least one glorious afternoon of salmonberry picking. Until stricken with the illness that ended her life, she was eagerly planning a return visit to the Alaskan Aleut communities. Following her death in December of 1992, she was remembered during services at the St. Innocent of Irkutsk Cathedral in Anchorage and at the Orthodox church in Unalaska.

Selected Bibliography of Works by Roza G. Liapunova

Black, Lydia T., and Roza G. Liapunova. 1988. Aleut: Islanders of the North Pacific. In: *Crossroads of Continents: Cultures of Siberia and Alaska*, edited by William W. Fitzhugh and Aron Crowell, pp. 52-59. Washington, D.C.: Smithsonian Institution Press.

Liapunova, Roza G. 1963. Muzeinye materialy po aleutam: Orudiia okhoty aleutov [Museum materials relating to the Aleuts: Hunting implements of the Aleuts]. *Sbornik Muzeia antropologii i etnografii* 21:149-171.

————. 1964. Aleutskie baidarki [Aleut baidarkas]. In: 250 let Muzeiia antropologii i etnografii imeni Petra Velikogo [250 years of the Peter the Great Museum of Anthropology and Ethnography], pp. 223-242. *Sbornik Muzeia antropologii i etnografii* 22.

————. 1967a. Zoomorfnaia skul'ptura aleutov [Zoomorphic sculpture of the Aleuts]. In: Kul'tura i byt narodov Ameriki [Culture and life of the peoples of America], pp. 38-54. *Sbornik Muzeia antropologii i etnografii* 24.

————. 1967b. Rukopis' K. T. Khlebnikova "Zapiski o koloniiakh v Amerike" kak istochnik po istorii i etnografii Aliaski i Aleutskikh ostrovov [K. T. Khlebnikov's manuscript "Notes on the colonies in America" as a source on the history and ethnography of Alaska and the Aleutian Islands]. In: *Ot Aliaski do Ognennoi Zemli* [From Alaska to Tierra del Fuego], pp. 136-141. Moscow: Nauka.

————. 1967c. Ekspeditsii I. G. Voznesenskogo i ee znachenie dlia etnografii Russkoi Ameriki [I. G. Voznesenskii's expedition and its significance for the ethnography of Russian America]. In: Kul'tura i byt narodov Ameriki [Culture and life of the peoples of America], pp. 5-33. *Sbornik Muzeia antropologii i etnografii* 24.

————. 1971. Etnograficheskoe znachenie ekspeditsii kapitanov P. K. Krenitsyna i M. D. Levashova na Aleutskie ostrova (1764-1769 gg.) [Ethnographic significance of the expedition of captains P. K. Krenitsyn and M. D. Levashov to the Aleutian Islands (1764-1769)]. *Sovetskaia etnografiia* 1971(6):67-80.

————. 1975a. *Ocherki po etnografii aleutov (konets XVIII-pervaia polovina XIX v.)* [Essays on the ethnography of the Aleuts (end of the 18th through first half of the 19th century)]. Leningrad: Nauka.

————. 1975b. Pletenye izdeliia aleutov [Aleut woven work]. In: Iz kul'turnogo naslediia narodov Ameriki i Afriki [From the cultural heritage of the peoples of America and Africa], pp. 36-51. *Sbornik Muzeia antropologii i etnografii* 31.

————. 1976. O proiskhozhdenii obriadovykh golovnykh uborov aleutov [On the origin of Aleut ritual headgear]. In: *Pervobytnoe iskusstvo* [Aboriginal art], pp. 157-165. Novosibirsk: Nauka, Sibirskoe otdelenie.

————. 1979a. Traditsionnye ukrasheniia aleutov (k voprosu ob etnokul'turnykh sviaziakh v tikhookeanskom basseine) [Traditional ornamentation of the Aleuts (toward the question of ethnocultural ties in the Pacific basin)]. In: *Drevnie kul'tury Sibiri i Tikhookeanskogo basseina* [Ancient cultures of Siberia and the Pacific basin], ed. by R. V. Vasil'evskii, pp. 201-210. Novosibirsk: Nauka, Sibirskoe otdelenie.

———. 1979b. "Aleutskaia problema" v noveishikh amerikanskikh issledovaniiakh [The "Aleut problem" in the latest American research]. In: *Aktual'nye problemy etnografii i sovremennaia zarubezhnaia nauka* [Pressing ethnographic problems and contemporary science abroad]. Leningrad: Nauka.

———. 1979c. Novyi dokument o rannikh plavaniiakh na Aleutskie ostrova: ("Izvestiia" F. A. Kul'kova, 1764) [A new document about early voyages to the Aleutian Islands: (F. A. Kul'kov's "News," 1764)]. *Strany i narody Vostoka* 20(4):97-105.

———. 1979d. Zapiski ieromonakha Gedeona (1803-1807)—odin iz istochnikov po istorii i etnografii Russkoi Ameriki [Notes of Hieromonk Gedeon (1803-1807), one of the sources on the history and ethnography of Russian America]. In: *Problemy istorii i etnografii Ameriki* [Problems of the history and ethnography of America], pp. 215-229. Moscow: Nauka.

———. 1979e. K etnicheskoi istorii komandorskikh aleutov [Toward an ethnic history of the Commander Islands Aleuts]. In: *Kratkie soderzhaniia dokladov na XIV Mezhdunarodnom tikhookeanskom kongresse* [Abstracts of papers at the 14th International Pacific Congress]. Moscow.

———. 1980. Kollektsiia severo-vostochnoi geograficheskoi ekspeditsii Billingsa-Sarycheva v sobranii MAE [Collection of the Billings-Sarychev northeastern geographical expedition in the collection of the Museum of Anthropology and Ethnography]. *Sbornik Muzeia antropologii i etnografii* 35:173-177.

———. 1984. Voron v fol'klore i mifologii aleutov [Raven in the folklore and mythology of the Aleuts]. In: *Fol'klor i etnografiia: U etnograficheskikh isstokov fol'klornykh siuzhetov i obrazov* [Folklore and ethnography: At the ethnographic sources of folkloric subjects and forms]. Leningrad: Nauka.

———. 1985a. K probleme etnokul'turnogo razvitiia amerikanskikh aleutov (so vtoroi poloviny XVIII v. do nashikh dnei) [Toward the problem of ethnocultural development of the American Aleuts (from the second half of the 18th century to the present day)]. In: *Istoricheskie sud'by amerikanskikh indeitsev: Problemy indeanistiki* [Historical fates of the American Indians: Indianist studies]. Moscow: Nauka.

———. 1985b. Golovnye ubory aleutov v sobranii MAE [Aleut headgear in the collection of the Museum of Anthropology and Ethnography]. In: Kul'tura narodov Ameriki [Culture of the peoples of America], pp. 4-49. *Sbornik Muzeia antropologii i etnografii* 40.

————. 1987a. *Aleuty: Ocherki etnicheskoi istorii* [The Aleuts: Essays on ethnohistory]. Leningrad: Nauka.

————. 1987b. Relations with the Natives of Russian America. In: *Russia's American Colony*, ed. by S. Frederick Starr, pp. 105-143. Durham, North Carolina: Duke University Press.

————. 1990a. The Aleut. In: *The Etholen Collection*, by Pirjo Varjola, pp. 136-139. Helsinki: National Board of Antiquities of Finland.

————. 1990b. The Aleuts before contact with the Russians: Some demographic and cultural aspects. *Pacifica* 2(2):8-23.

————. 1992. Prazdnestva eskimosov ostrova Kad'iak [Festivals of the Eskimos of Kodiak Island]. In: *Fol'klor i etnograficheskaia deistvitel'nost'* [Folklore and ethnographic reality], pp. 71-87. St. Petersburg: Nauka.

————. 1994. Eskimo masks from Kodiak Island in the collections of the Peter the Great Museum of Anthropology and Ethnography in St. Petersburg. In: *Anthropology of the North Pacific Rim*, ed. by William W. Fitzhugh and Valerie Chaussonnet, pp. 175-203. Washington, D.C.: Smithsonian Institution Press.

Liapunova, Roza G., and Svetlana G. Fedorova, compilers and annotators. 1979. *Russkaia Amerika v neopublikovannykh zapiskakh K. T. Khlebnikova* [Russian America in the unpublished notes of K. T. Khlebnikov]. Leningrad: Nauka. (Available in translation as *Notes on Russian America, Parts II-V: Kad'iak, Unalashka, Atkha, the Pribylovs*, by Kiril T. Khlebnikov, compiled, with introduction and commentaries by, R. G. Liapunova and S. G. Fedorova, transl. by Marina Ramsay, ed. by R. A. Pierce, Kingston, Ontario and Fairbanks, Alaska: Limestone Press, 1994.)

This brief biography and selected bibliography was prepared by Dr. Chuner M. Taksami, Deputy Director of Kuntkamera Museum of Peter the Great, Russian Academy of Sciences, St. Petersburg and Dr. Lydia Black, Professor of Anthropology, University of Alaska Fairbanks.

EDITOR'S NOTE FROM THE RUSSIAN EDITION

This book presents a series of essays about the Aleuts, the inhabitants of the islands in the northern part of the Pacific Ocean. The essays are based on studies of museum collections, written sources, and illustrative material gathered by Russians in the late eighteenth and in the first half of the nineteenth century in Alaska and the Aleutian Islands.

Ethnographic evidence, together with information drawn from archaeological, anthropological, and linguistic sources, is used to formulate conclusions about the origins of the Aleuts. These data also shed light upon a number of questions related to the Eskimo-Aleut problem, the date and routes for the peopling of the American North.

This work is intended for ethnographers, archaeologists, historians, and also for teachers of history and students of local lore.

—*I. S. Vdovin*
Editor-in-chief

FOREWORD

This work is dedicated to the traditional culture of the Aleuts, a people occupying the territory between the Old and the New World. Ethnographic materials are examined here as data for the study of the ethnogenesis of this people. Therefore, the essays on ethnography proper are preceded by an introduction characterizing the present state of the art in respect to the problem of the origin of the Aleuts, and by a chapter dealing with the history of the "Aleutian Problem." The separate essays also contain ethnogenetic conclusions.

One of the principal sources for analysis of the ethnography of the Aleuts at the end of the eighteenth and the first half of the nineteenth century is the very rich collections of the Museum of Anthropology and Ethnography of the Academy of Sciences of the USSR (MAE) gathered in that period, the period of the discovery and mastery of the Aleutian Islands by Russian navigators, pioneer explorers [*zemleprokhodtsy*], and scientific explorers.

Other sources of information are old publications and archival materials. Among the latter, the most valuable are the materials of the expeditions to the Aleutian Islands in the second half of the eighteenth century, which contain information about the Aleut culture not yet touched by colonization. These consist of the "accounts" [*skazki*] and "reports" of Russian merchants and *promyshlenniki* (fur hunters/traders) who set out for furs to the then little-known Aleutian Islands, the materials of the government expeditions of 1765–1769 (Krenitsyn-Levashov) and 1785–1793 (Billings-Sarychev), and the notes of the first chief manager of Russian America, A. A. Baranov, which date back to 1790. Among the sources perused are both published and unpublished ones, the latter extracted by the author from various archives, the Archive of the Foreign Policy of Russia (AVPR), the Archive of the Geographical Society of the USSR (AGO), the Archive of the Leningrad Department of the Institute of History of the Academy of Sciences of the

USSR (ALOII), the Leningrad Branch of the Archives of the Academy of Sciences of the USSR (LOAAN), the Central State Archive of Ancient Acts (TsGADA), and the Central State Archive of the Navy of the USSR (TsGAVMF). From the latter unpublished archival sources, information has been drawn from the manuscripts of K. T. Khlebnikov, an employee of the Russian-American Company, "old-timer and chronicler of Russian America" (AGO, ALOII, LOAAN), and also from materials from the archives of I. G. Voznesenskii (LOAAN), who was engaged in assembling collections in Russian America and Northeast Asia for a ten-year period (1839–1849) for the museums of the Academy of Sciences.

The book is illustrated with materials from the collections of the MAE, with little-known drawings from publications about the early voyages to the Aleutian Islands and, finally, with drawings from archival sources which are being published for the first time.

The illustrations for this work were executed by T. L. Iuzepchuk and A. S. Fateev.

The author expresses gratitude to the employees of the above-mentioned archives for their cooperation and assistance.

The author expresses her thanks to Professor W. S. Laughlin (USA) for publications he has sent and for consultations during his stay in the USSR.

The author thanks Academician A. P. Okladnikov, Doctors of Historical Science S. V. Ivanov, Iu. P. Averkieva, and R. V. Kinzhalov, and Doctor of Philological Science G. A. Menovshchikov for consultations and valuable advice.

INTRODUCTION

The native inhabitants of the Aleutian Islands, the Aleuts, belong to a single group of peoples of the North Pacific basin and the American Arctic whose ethnic history draws the intense attention of contemporary researchers. Together with questions of the initial settlement and subsequent formation of population groups of Northeast Asia and the North American continent, it [ethnic history] involves questions of ancient contacts among the peoples in this region, movement of population streams from Asia to America, and the settlement of America as a whole. All the enumerated questions still contain many uncertain propositions linked both with the time of settlement and with the process of adaptation to this region, and with the character of migrations which took place here and which, to a great extent, determined the ethnic picture. Resolution of the question of the place of Aleut culture among all the regional cultures and of the problem of their ethnogenesis has important significance for clarifying the problem of the ethnic history of that region.

Ethnographic information about the material culture of the Aleuts can serve as an important source for the study of their ethnic history, and, together with archaeological, anthropological, and linguistic data, can help to reconstruct the ethnic processes which took place in the distant past.

The peculiarity of the territory occupied by the Aleuts is its insular character and its intermediate location between Northeast Asia and northwestern America. The Aleutian Island chain curves to the south in an arc from the Alaska Peninsula almost to Kamchatka, linking northwestern America with Northeast Asia and separating the Bering Sea from the Pacific Ocean. It consists of 110 large and a great number of smaller islands with a total area of 37,840 square kilometers (Figure 1). In accordance with the history of discovery and by geographical features, the islands are divided into four groups. Next to Kamchatka are the Near Islands (Attu, Agattu, Semichi, etc.), then come the Rat Islands

1

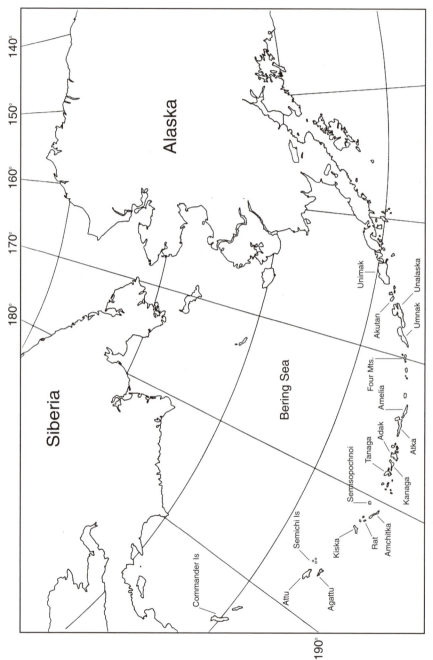

Figure 1. The Aleutian Islands.

2

(Kiska, Rat, Amchitka, Semisopochnoi, etc.). Beyond the Rat Islands stretches the Andreanof chain of islands (Tanaga, Kanaga, Adak, Atka, Amlia, etc.). Next are the Fox Islands, the largest group, which also includes the largest islands in the chain (Four Mountains, Umnak, Unalaska, Akutan, Unimak, etc.).

These islands are basically volcanic in origin, mountainous, with extinct and still active volcanoes and hot springs. Arboreal vegetation is absent on them, the predominant landscape being tundra. According to climatic conditions, the Aleutian Islands belong to the region of oceanic tundra. The average winter temperature here ranges from 0° to 1°, and the average summer temperature from 6.4° to 9.3° [Celsius]. Strong winds, frequent storms and constant fog add to the severe nature of the archipelago's character.

Though inhospitable in appearance, this region was rich in sea mammals (whales and pinnipeds), in fish (including seasonal ones entering the rivers at the time of spawning), and in sea birds (which formed bird colonies on the countless rocky islands). A significant source of means for subsistence was the tidal zone, abundant in invertebrate animals (echinoderms and mollusks), and seaweed. Here sea mammals and fish, and also driftwood, were found washed ashore. From ancient times, people inhabited these islands.

The first of the Europeans who visited the Aleutian Islands and the northwestern part of North America (1741), were members of the Second Kamchatka Expedition headed by V. Bering and A. I. Chirikov. The merit of the Russians during the second half of the eighteenth and the first half of the nineteenth century was the discovery, exploration, and economic assimilation of the Aleutian Islands and the northwestern part of North America (Alaska) as a whole, and also the initial study of the peoples of those territories, which were Russian land at that time. From 1799 the Russian-American commercial company was active here, right up to 1867, when Alaska and the Aleutian Islands were sold to the United States by Russia.

Prior to the coming of the Russians, the Aleutian Islands, especially their eastern part, were densely populated and the number of Aleuts living there approached sixteen to twenty thousand.[a]

---

a. In later publications, Liapunova revised the estimate downward to about eight to nine thousand—L. B.

3

According to [physical] anthropological and ethnographic features, the Aleuts are divided into two groups, the eastern and the western. Accordingly, there existed two dialects in the language of the Aleuts: the eastern, or Unalaska (among the Aleuts of the Fox Islands and the Alaska Peninsula); and the western, or Attu (among the Aleuts of the western half of the chain). On the boundary of these two dialects there existed a mixed sub-dialect called Atka. The eastern group of Aleuts was numerous and outnumbered the western group by more than two to one.

"Aleuts" was not the name they called themselves. This term appeared and became firmly established after the first sailing (on the return of the Bering-Chirikov expedition) of merchants and promyshlenniki to the islands (from 1747). The question of the origin of the name "Aleuts" is still under discussion. Most convincing is the opinion expressed by I. S. Vdovin, that it has a Chukotka-Koriak base.[1] The name the Aleuts called themselves is considered to be "Unangan," but it is known for certain only that the eastern group of Aleuts called themselves by this name.[b]

As a result of colonization and the exploitation of the natural resources of the islands (initially by the Russians, and later by the Americans), their population diminished considerably. The traditional economy of the Aleuts decayed and the ancient original culture was almost entirely destroyed. Capitalism did not give the Aleuts a new basis for subsequent economic and cultural development in lieu of that which they had lost, and that inevitably led to their degradation. At the beginning of the twentieth century, the Aleut population numbered only two thousand people. At the present time the remaining Aleuts on the Aleutian Islands number about a thousand. They share the fate of the other representatives of the aboriginal peoples of America, the Eskimos

---

b. In subsequent publications, on the basis of new archival data and linguistic work by Menovshchikov, Liapunova accepted the term "Aleut" as the autonym of the Attuans (R. G. Liapunova, "Novyi dokument o rannikh plavaniiakh na Aleutskie ostrova ("Izvestiia" Fedora Afanas'evicha Kal'kova, 1764 g.)" [A new document on early voyages to the Aleutian Islands ("News" of Fedor Afanas'evich Kal'kov, 1764)] in *Strany i narody Vostoka* [Lands and peoples of the East], vol. 20, book 4, Moscow: Nauka, 1979, pp. 97–105; idem, *Aleuty: Ocherki etnicheskoi istorii* [Aleuts: Sketches of ethnic history], Leningrad: Nauka, 1987, p. 9)—L. B.

4

and Indians, living in conditions of social and national [ethnic] discrimination.

A small group of Aleuts, resettled by the Russian-American Company from the Aleutian to the Commander islands (Bering and Mednyi) at the beginning of the nineteenth century, found itself within the Soviet Union after 1917. Those Aleuts (now numbering about four hundred people) have an entirely different fate. They, together with other small ethnic groups of the North, enjoy equal rights as citizens of our [Soviet] state. The Commander Islands comprise the Aleutian region [*raion*] of the Kamchatka district [*oblast'*]. Here Lenin's principles of national (ethnic) policy are realized. A contemporary economy and culture are successfully being developed in the region.

Similarities among the peoples of the North Pacific and the American Arctic are not limited to economic-cultural types.[c] Numerous investigators have noted that, together with the common character of economic life which conditioned the common cultural elements, there is a similarity in the ancient cultural traditions and in the [physical] anthropological and linguistic characteristics of the inhabitants on the Asiatic coast of the Pacific Ocean (the northeastern Paleo-Asiatics—the Chukchi, Koriak, and also the Itel'men and Eskimo) and on the American coast (Eskimos and Aleuts). This allowed the posing of the problem of the genetic and historical ties of the above-named peoples and of the common origin of their coastal way of life.

But there is still no generally accepted view as to the origin of the economy of the sea hunters and fishermen of the northern part of the Pacific basin. The question of those migrations, which determined the formation of the peoples of that region, remains unclear. Therefore, investigation of the region's ancient cultures and their interrelations, as well as investigation of ethnographic materials about the peoples inhabiting it in the period recorded in historical sources, now attract close attention.

The question of the origin of the coastal cultures of the North Pacific and the American Arctic has been advanced considerably in the last decade by the work of Soviet archaeologists on Kamchatka, on the coast of the Sea of Okhotsk, on Sakhalin, on the Kuril Islands, on Chukotka

---

c. "Economic-cultural type" is an analytical category proposed by Levin and Cheboksarov and widely utilized in Soviet ethnographic literature—L. B.

5

and in Yakutiia, and by American, Canadian, Danish, and Japanese archaeologists in Alaska, the Aleutian Islands, the Canadian Arctic, Greenland, and northern Japan.

In 1962 the American archaeologist Chester Chard, on the basis of a summation of archaeological, anthropological, and linguistic investigations, formulated the hypothesis that the type of coastal economy in the North Pacific basin was connected with the generalized Eskimo cultural tradition (and that its carriers were connected with a physical anthropological type close to that of the Eskimo), and that [this economic type] appeared in southwestern Alaska (in the region of Bristol Bay) about 2,000 B.C. From there it spread to the north, to Bering Strait and as far as Puget Sound, on the one hand, and to the south along the shores of the Pacific Ocean to the island of Hokkaido on the other, laying the foundation for the future cultural development of that territory in its entirety.[2]

But this hypothesis encounters first of all serious objections to the idea of a single center of the chain of cultures of sea mammal hunters from the islands of Japan to the coast of northwestern America.

As early as 1958, M. G. Levin expressed his point of view that there were two formative centers of the cultures of this region. In his opinion, the area of the original settling and formation of the northeastern Paleo-Asiatics was the northern part of the Okhotsk Sea littoral, including the coastal regions of both the [Asiatic] mainland and Kamchatka, while the lengthy and complicated process of the formation of the Eskimos took place in the area adjoining the Bering Sea.[3] This concept was developed by R. S. Vasil'evskii on the basis of archaeological study of the Old Koriak culture of the northern part of the coast of the Sea of Okhotsk. He determined that while there are sharp differences in all the diagnostic features between the Old Koriak culture and the main cultures of the Eskimos of the Bering Sea, similarity is revealed between the earliest Old Koriak bone and stone inventories and those of the Paleo-Eskimo cultures of southwestern Alaska (Kachemak I in Cook Inlet, Kiwak [Kiavak?] and Rolling Bay on Kodiak Island), including also the culture of the Paleo-Aleuts. He notes the similarity between the Old Koriak, the Okhotsk (found on northern Hokkaido, Sakhalin, and the Kuril Islands), and the Paleo-Aleutian cultures, and outlines a single sphere of cultures of sea mammal hunters, which encompasses northern Hokkaido,

Sakhalin, the Kuril Islands, the Okhotsk Sea littoral and the coast of southwestern Alaska. He considers the Eskimo cultures of Northeast Asia and northern and northwestern Alaska to be different from the cultures of that sphere, and to have had another center of formation, namely, southwestern Alaska.[4]

Thus, we see that the solution of the problem of Eskimo origins, closely linked to the problem of Aleut ethnogenesis, plays an important role in shedding light on the ethnic history of the North Pacific. Those two peoples are in a very close relationship: according to [physical] anthropological features they are distinguished as being within the arctic type, a special variant of the Pacific Ocean branch of the Mongoloid race; the languages of the Aleuts and Eskimos constitute one Eskimo-Aleut linguistic family. Their cultures, too, are similar in many ways—not long ago many researchers viewed the Aleuts as being a Pacific Eskimo group.

The Eskimo problem—a complicated problem of their origin, language and culture—has a long (almost two-hundred-year) history of study and an exceptionally rich literature.[5] But up to now there are still many unclear points concerning both the center of Eskimo formation, and the interrelationships between their numerous cultures scattered throughout a vast area. Very far from any solution derived from broad concrete materials (rather than from isolated finds) are questions of the sources of the deep ties of Eskimo culture with the ancestral Paleolithic cultures of Asia.

Special attention is now drawn to the question concerning the center of Eskimo formation. And although there is still no unity of opinion with regard to a concrete region, the views of concerned scholars are approaching agreement that the formation took place on a local base. Thanks to research by M. G. Levin and G. F. Debets, the migrational theories of the origin of the Eskimos which held sway for a long time have changed. The theoretical view that the formation of the Eskimos, their culture, and language, took place in the areas along the Bering Sea coasts has become firmly established.

Numerous investigators believe that the center of Eskimo development was in southwestern Alaska. This is supported first of all by archaeological materials. Excavations conducted mainly in the postwar decades singled out southwestern Alaska as the territory with the

7

most ancient finds of Eskimo cultures. As far back as 1931, F. de Laguna discovered on Cook Inlet the ancient Eskimo culture Kachemak I, which was then dated to the eighth century B.C.[6] Its later stages, Kachemak II and III, were found on the coast of Prince William Sound.[d] That culture, according to well-known ethnographic data, was subsequently transformed into the culture of the Pacific Eskimos: Chugach and Koniag [Alutiiq]. The most ancient of the cultures of that region that have been brought to light were discovered by W. S. Laughlin. At the source is the culture of the multi-level site of Chaluka on Umnak Island. The age of the lower levels was determined to be 2,000 B.C., and the upper levels demonstrated the transition to the culture of the Aleuts that was found by the Russians on their arrival in that area in the middle of the eighteenth century.

As far back as 1952 Laughlin advanced the proposition, which was accepted by the majority of scholars, that the culture of the lower Chaluka levels was close to the Proto-Eskimo-Aleut culture or was even part of it.[7] At the same time, he substantiated the point of view that southwestern Alaska was the place of formation of the Eskimo, their culture and language, in view of the fact that precisely this area demonstrated the greatest concentration of population, and the greatest variety of dialects close to the Aleutian language and the language of the Siberian Eskimo. An important argument was that this region was ecologically the most benevolent in comparison with the adjacent ones.

The concept of southwestern Alaska as the homeland of the Eskimo was developed in the works of Chard, Laughlin, and other American authors.

But, not all scholars share this opinion. S. A. Arutiunov and D. A. Sergeev believe that the origin of the Eskimo took place on the Asiatic and American shores of Bering Strait.[8] N. N. Dikov opposes the search for a single origin of Eskimo culture, pointing out the possibility of the existence of an intricate cultural complex arising in the north (the shores of Bering Strait) from the middle of the first millennium B.C., and a more ancient one (second to first millennium B.C.) coming from the south,

---

d. Kachemak II and III are not present in Prince William Sound, though there are some similarities to Kachemak III as defined for Kachemak Bay on the Kenai Peninsula—W. W.

from the direction of Kamchatka and the Aleutian Islands, as well as the possibility that some Eskimo cultures of Canada and Greenland originated on a local Neolithic base.[9]

Linguistic data confirm the ancient commonality of the Aleuts and Eskimos, but also point out the possible time of their separation. Thus, in the 1950s the American linguist M. Swadesh, using the method of glottochronological analysis that he had created, showed that four thousand years ago the Proto-Eskimo language split into Eskimo and Aleut proper. In this process, the Aleut language preserved more features of the Proto-Eskimo language.[10] The works of D. Hirsch[11] and K. Bergsland[12] confirmed the same.[e]

The discovery by W. S. Laughlin of a site considerably more ancient than Chaluka on the small island of Anangula, located near the southeastern [*sic*; southwestern] end of the island of Umnak, served as the foundation for the advancement of a new hypothesis concerning the ancient presence of the Aleuts in the New World and the routes by which they reached that territory. The materials from the Anangula site were initially dated to the sixth millennium B.C. (8,425 ±275, 7,600 ±300, and 7,990 ±230 years), and later to an even earlier time.[f] According to geological data, its age is 10,000 B.C.[13] The culture of that site was determined to be one which was developing in the direction of the Proto-Eskimo-Aleutian. All this permitted Laughlin to advance a hypothesis according to which the Proto-Eskimo-Aleuts appeared in the New World in great antiquity (about eleven thousand years ago) and to speak of the Aleuts as descendants of the ancient inhabitants of Beringia (which served as a bridge for the settlement of the New World from Asia). Thus, if all previous hypotheses placed the ancestors of the Eskimo-Aleuts very recently within the process of the settlement of America (even close to our era), the new studies permitted movement of the date back considerably. This hypothesis in our day receives ever-growing evidential support and proponents among scholars. This

---

e. The view of Bergsland is misinterpreted here. He does not believe in glottochronology—L. B.

f. The age of the Anangula site is still debatable (L. T. Black, "Some problems in interpretation of Aleut prehistory," *Arctic Anthropology* 20, no. 1, 1983, pp. 53, 55)—L. B.

hypothesis is also in full agreement with the contemporary hypothesis of the settlement of the American continent by man.[g]

The hypothesis of the settlement of America is now based on geological, paleogeographic, and biogeographic investigations of latter years. It substantiates the settlement of the American continent from Asia in the period up to 38,000 years ago in several waves along the land bridge that replaced Bering Strait and part of the Bering and Chukchi seas during glaciations. The sea level during the glacial periods was lower than at present—up to 150 meters lower—and rose in the intervals, forming Bering Strait between the Old and New Worlds. According to Iu. A. Mochanov,[14] for example, there were three stages of the settlement of northwestern America: the first, 35,000–22,000 years ago; the second, 22,000–10,000 years ago; and the third, 10,000–6,000 years ago.[h]

In light of such archaeological evidence as the Anangula site, one may accept the possibility that the migration of peoples with a coastal culture along the coastal strip of the Bering Land Bridge took place in the period of the second stage of the settling of America (22,000–10,000 years ago).[15] This migration proceeded parallel to the migration of the ancestors of the Indians—hunters of land animals—along the interior part of the same [land] bridge.[16]

The paleogeographic situation in that period was conditioned by the following factors. Approximately 22,000 years ago the maximum cold of the Sartan Glaciation began in Siberia, and in America, the Wisconsin Glaciation began in its classic form. The regression of the world ocean then reached 420 meters, and as a result the Bering Land Bridge—Beringia—extended into part of the Bering Sea, and the Pribilof Islands and the eastern part of the Aleutian Islands, including Umnak Island, formed a peninsula of the American mainland. The width of the bridge here was approximately 1,500 kilometers. About 11,000 years ago, as a result of the thaw, the sea level began to rise quickly and Beringia was

---

g. For a discussion of alternative interpretations of Aleutian prehistory, see L. T. Black, "Some problems in interpretation of Aleut prehistory," *Arctic Anthropology* 20, no. 1 (1983), pp. 49–78—L. B.

h. There is no widely accepted evidence in North America supporting Mochanov's hypothesized first stage of settlement (35,000–22,000 years ago)—W. W.

submerged. From 10,000 to 4,500 years ago the sea level fluctuated approximately ten to fifteen meters lower than the present level, and approximately 4,500 years ago the outline of the land finally attained its present form.[17]

The location of the Anangula site under Beringian conditions represented the coastline of the land bridge. The site was located seventeen to twenty meters above sea level (the descent to the water was steep) and because of such a unique topographical location this site was not flooded, as all other sites of that time were. In Laughlin's opinion, there exists a continuity between the stone tools of Anangula and those of the lower strata of Chaluka. According to Laughlin's hypothesis, the Aleuts lived in the given territory from the time of the existence of Beringia, later finding themselves on the islands formed on the site of the peninsula. At the time of the flooding of Beringia, the ancestors of the present-day Eskimos, occupying the land adjacent to the coastal territories, had to migrate considerably farther, into the Subarctic and Arctic with their colder climate. Consequently, after the separation of those two peoples from a common stem, the Aleuts remained almost in the same territory and in the same conditions, but in a more isolated insular situation. Archaeological evidence provides a picture of the subsequent rather stable development of the Aleut culture.

The discovery of the Anangula site, revealing the most ancient layer of the coastal cultural traditions and, moreover, of an Asiatic appearance (as shown by its comparison with the Paleolithic cultures of Kamchatka, Primor'e and the pre-ceramic complexes of Japan), gives evidence that the ancestors of the present-day Aleuts reached those territories during the existence of Beringia. Given the present geological land formation, there are no sites which can indicate that there were migrations through the region of Bering Strait. In 1962 Chard noted that archaeology, anthropology, and linguistics do not offer any evidence for the movement of inhabitants from Asia into America in the last 5,000 years (although some diffusion in both directions has been observed).[18] The route of the settlement of America through the chain of the Aleutian and Commander islands is not supported by archaeological investigations.[19]

It should be noted that not all investigators are inclined to consider the Anangula site as the origin of Aleut culture proper, though the Chaluka site is recognized as being unquestionably Paleo-Aleut.

The discovery by N. N. Dikov of Paleolithic cultures in Kamchatka near Ushki Lake (Ushki I, II and IV, levels V, VI and VII, with an absolute date of 10,360 ±350 to 14,300 ±200 and 14,300 ±250 years) had great significance for the questions under discussion. The artifacts of the Paleolithic strata of those multi-level sites, according to Dikov's testimony, are similar in many features to the southern Siberian Late Paleolithic and the pre-ceramic cultures of Japan on the one hand, and, on the other hand, to the Late Paleolithic and Early Mesolithic complexes in Alaska (Anangula, Onion Portage, Healy Lake and others), and also to the Early Mesolithic points of the Cordilleran sites and to the oldest sites in the south of America, found in Fell's Cave and Palli Aike Cave. All this allowed Dikov to state that the Paleolithic of Kamchatka possessed relics of the most ancient Proto-Indian and Proto-Eskimoan cultures. In the Ushki sites, clothing decorations of stone circles [beads], of a type with Indian wampum,[i] and red ocher in association with burials were also found. Found in the Neolithic levels were stone labrets—lip ornaments—which are typical among the Eskimos of Alaska, the Aleuts, and the Indians of the northwest coast of North America, the Tlingits.[20]

The material of the Anangula site reveals closest similarity to the Paleolithic levels of the Ushki sites on Kamchatka. This circumstance became an important point in resolving the question of the ties of Aleut culture with the ancient cultures of Asia. A summary of the data connected with this question appears in the recently published book by R. S. Vasil'evskii.[21] Let us dwell on these data briefly. The similarity of the stone implements of Alaska, Japan, and mainland Asia leads one to consider the materials of the Paleolithic and Mesolithic cultures of the Baikal and Angara regions. Laughlin particularly pointed out the similarity between the artifacts from the Anangula site and those of the Baikal-region site of Budun.[22] The latter site is linked with the other pre-ceramic complexes of the Baikal area (Kharilgai, Sarma), which in turn compare well with the Mesolithic remains of the Angara region (Ust'-Belaia, Badai, Cheremushnik, and Verkholenskaia Gora). Burins of the Verkholensk type are found not only in Transbaikalia and in Mongolia, but also on the islands of Japan (burins of the Araya type). The

---

i. Wampum is a particular kind of shell bead from the historic period of the northeastern United States. The term cannot be used to describe shell beads in Alaska and Northeast Asia—W. W.

invariable companions of the Verkholensk burins are cores of the Gobi type. The area of distribution of similar cores in the Upper Paleolithic and Mesolithic periods includes Angara, Transbaikalia, Aldan, Amur, Primor'e, northern China, Japan, Kamchatka, and Alaska.[23] The original centers whence those implements spread are believed to be the basins of the Angara and Amur. But broader analogies of the stone industry of Anangula are in other locations: the islands of Japan and regions of the Soviet Far East. Analogies with the materials of Sakkotsu and Araya are frequently traced among Japanese sites. But, in the opinion of Japanese archaeologists, the blade technique typical of those cultures was brought from the north of the Asiatic mainland. They believe, as does A. P. Okladnikov,[24] that the center of those cultures is located somewhere in the steppe region of Asia. The excavations made by A. P. Okladnikov at the sites of Khere-Uul in the valley of the river Khalkhin Gol in eastern Mongolia have great significance for the study of the sources of the Upper Paleolithic and Mesolithic cultures of Primor'e and Japan, and consequently, of Kamchatka and Anangula. It is precisely in the complex Khere-Uul that all the salient elements are concentrated: cores of the Gobi type, burins of the Araya type, scrapers and knives of the Verkholensk type, and others appeared in various combinations in the Baikal region, in the Far East (Ustinovka), in Japan, in Kamchatka (Ushki) and on the Aleutian Islands (Anangula). Consequently, eastern Mongolia was that center from which cultural impulses were spreading to the north and east. At the end of the Paleolithic, the Far East and the north of Japan apparently formed the "Pacific Ocean" ethnocultural region, encompassing the Lower Amur, Primor'e, Hokkaido, Sakhalin and Kamchatka. The Anangula site gravitates toward that "Pacific Ocean" cultural region.

Thus, the Anangula site allowed the opening, in a very real way, of questions about the Asiatic ancestors of the Aleuts. Laughlin's hypothesis regarding the continuity between the Anangula and Chaluka sites and, accordingly, about the Aleuts as inhabitants of those locations from the time of the existence of the ancient Bering Land Bridge, extraordinarily raised the interest in the Aleuts' culture and its correlation with the cultures of the Eskimos, Paleo-Asiatics and Indians.

We have seen that questions connected with the routes and time taken by the Aleuts to settle the Aleutian Islands are at present being actively discussed. These questions are also helping to shed light on a series of questions connected with the Eskimo problem. One of them is the question of the time and place of separation of the Proto-Eskimo-Aleuts. In this matter, the studies of G. A. Menovshchikov are of great interest.[25] A comparative analysis of the vocabulary of the Eskimo and Aleut languages led him to the conclusion that during the time when they belonged to a single [common] speech community, the Proto-Eskimo-Aleut led a continental way of life. The evidence for this is in the names of sea hunting implements and of sea mammals, which are common to the entire Eskimo horizon (from Bering Strait to Greenland), but not one of those names agrees with the corresponding Aleut ones. Moreover, Menovshchikov points out the presence of ancient foreign substrata (presumably Paleo-Asiatic languages) in the Aleut language. Therefore, he does not exclude the possibility that in the pre-Beringian epoch, the Eskimo-Aleutian languages followed parallel development out of a common grammatical system base and, consequently, the separation of those two peoples could have taken place still in Asia.

R. S. Vasil'evskii also indicates that the latest archaeological data have considerably extended the date of the separation of the Aleuts and Eskimos backward in time. He places it back to eight or ten thousand years ago, to the time of the existence of the ancient Bering Land Bridge. The "substratum" of those cultures, he writes, must be sought in Asia.[26]

Besides the problem connected with the establishment of the early history of the Aleuts (and Eskimos), interest is drawn to the question of the relationship of the cultures of the Eskimo-Aleuts and the Indians of the northwest coast of America (determining their common features, which either ascend to a common substratum, or reflect cultural-historical ties). In this context, we will only briefly mention Chard's opinion that the main roots of all populations of the New World are in the coastal zone of the Pacific Ocean.[27] Laughlin, on the other hand, expresses the supposition that the common features of the Eskimos and the Indians may have their origin in an early Proto-Eskimo-Aleut population.[28] In our opinion, the hypothesis of S. I. Rudenko about the migration of Eskimos at a comparatively late date from the southeast insular portion of Asia, although it cannot be accepted as a theory of their origin, deserves attention concerning the southern elements of the Eskimo culture. M. G. Levin, who justifiably subjected Rudenko's theory to criticism, pointed out at the same time that the southern elements exist not only in Eskimo culture. Southern ties of various historical depths are evident also in the cultures of the northeastern Paleo-Asiatics and particularly of the Indians of northwestern America.[29] This allows us to consider the southern elements of those cultures as possibly common and most ancient components which point to a common habitation in former times.

Further, Chard, following Laughlin, points out that opinions that the great richness and variety of the culture of the southern Bering Sea Eskimos is the result of the influence of the culture of the Indians of the Northwest Coast, and that the Pacific Eskimos penetrated into those former Indian territories comparatively recently, have been completely disproved.[30]

The opinion is expressed that the contiguity of the Proto-Eskimo and Proto-Wakashan peoples[31] deserves discussion.[32]

The well-known American investigator of the northwestern Indians, P. Drucker, sees in their culture the presence of an ancient Eskimo substratum. He speaks of an Eskimo-Aleut base in the culture of the Northwest [Coast] Indians. Drucker believes that the northern part of the Northwest Coast could have been populated only by people who were already well adapted to life by the sea, while the archaeological data of that region do not indicate a great antiquity for its settlement.[33,j] At the same time, on the southern Northwest Coast, on the lower course of the Fraser River, the Canadian archaeologist C. E. Borden discovered an old coastal culture similar to that of the Eskimo and dating back approximately to 475 B.C.[34] Its similarity with the culture of the Kachemak I and Chaluka sites and the relative date permitted one to speak of the possibility of the spread of Eskimo-Aleut culture along the American coast of the Pacific Ocean to the south as far as the Fraser River. This supported Drucker's hypothesis of an Eskimo-Aleut base of the culture of the northwestern Indians. This point of view was also supported by Chard.[35] Consequently, the question of the genetic and historical ties of the Eskimo-Aleuts and the Indians demands further discussion.

---

j. New evidence presents a very different view of the prehistory of the Northwest Coast, occupied for the last 10,000 years. Many ideas advanced by Drucker are now considered out of date. See K. Fladmark, *British Columbia Prehistory* (Ottawa: National Museums of Canada, 1986), and *Handbook of North American Indians,* vol. 7, *Northwest Coast,* ed. Wayne Suttles (Washington: Smithsonian Institution, 1990)—W. W.

As we see, the ancient history of the Aleuts and the Eskimos at the present stage of our studies is the subject of thorough archaeological, anthropological, and linguistic investigation and a series of its phases is gradually becoming clearer. But, the ethnographic study of the Aleuts, which could help in solving a variety of important questions, remains far from satisfactory.

Literature on the ethnography of the Aleuts consists first of all in publications containing the observations of the early Russian travelers and investigators. Outstanding among them, by far the most complete and generalized information is the work of I. Veniaminov, published in 1848 [1840]. Studies pertaining to some questions of Aleut ethnography appeared also at a later time (W. H. Dall, S. V. Ivanov, G. I. Quimby, and W. S. Laughlin). A summarized account of existing ethnographic information on the Aleuts has been given in several foreign publications (V. I. Iokhel'son [W. I. Jochelson], A. Hrdlička, and W. S. Laughlin). But on the whole, one can agree with the great American archaeologist and ethnographer H. B. Collins, who said "... it cannot be said that we possess a detailed or rounded picture of Aleut ethnology."[36]

The insufficiency in the ethnographic study of the Aleuts may be explained by the fact that their original culture was quickly destroyed as a result of the colonization of the islands. Owing to historical reasons, the most complete collection of materials on which ethnographic study of the Aleuts can be based in our time is located in the museums and archives of our country. To some extent, this also pertains to old Russian publications.

Meanwhile, the ethnographic material on the Aleuts can play an important role in solving ethnogenetic questions since, thanks to the discovery and analysis of the Chaluka and Anangula sites, it is possible to speak of the uninterrupted history of the Aleuts on the Aleutian Islands in the course of ten thousand years, and moreover, in conditions of insular isolation.

The essence of the differentiation of the Eskimo and Aleut cultures, the time and place of their separation—these questions, although posed by investigators, are not completely resolved to this day. All these matters are closely interrelated. Therefore, determination of the specifics of Aleut culture is of great importance. However, the entire series of features can be ascertained only on the basis of ethnographic materials, for only they provide the means to appreciate most fully the achievement of this people in the field of material and spiritual culture and social relations.

In the study of the material culture of the Aleuts, our attention was drawn to the difference of this culture from the culture of the Eskimos, a difference that is clearly apparent despite their similarity. At the same time, an interesting question arises about the similarity of Aleut culture with that of the Indians. This singular feature of the Aleuts has already been pointed out by both Russian and foreign scholars (W. H. Dall, V. I. Iokhel'son, S. V. Ivanov, and G. I. Quimby). On the other hand, the investigation of traces of Eskimo-Aleut culture among the northeastern Paleo-Asiatics—the Chukchi, Koriak, and Kamchadal (I. S. Vdovin)—opens broad perspectives.

Exposure of the specifics of the material culture of the Aleuts and its difference from that of the Eskimo appears sufficiently important for the resolution of questions pertaining to the early history of the Eskimo-Aleuts, and also for the conclusion that there is a possible common ancient component in the culture of the Eskimo-Aleuts and that of some Indians. Such a formulation was not excluded by B. O. Dolgikh, who dealt with problems of the ethnography and anthropology of the Arctic: "Probably, the Indians of both the Americas represent a branch of those early inhabitants of Beringia who could also have contributed one of the components of the original nucleus of the Eskimos."[37]

Laughlin's conclusion that the difference between Eskimo-Aleut and Indians may not have existed four to six thousand years ago[38] also speaks to the very deep common ethnogenetic roots of their ancestors. He notes the curious fact of the existence of a very rare blood group, N, in both the Eskimos and the Indians.[39] As far as the difference in the various anthropological features of those peoples is concerned, the latest investigations of Soviet and American anthropologists assume that development of the Mongolian features of the Arctic race took place comparatively late. V. P. Alekseev suggests the following possible date: "… the Eskimo, or Arctic, type is a separate variant of the Pacific branch of the Mongolian race. It was formed within a two-thousand-year period from the beginning of the first millennium B.C. to the boundary of our era."[40] And, this took place already in Arctic and Subarctic conditions under the influence of adaptation to the environment.[41] Laughlin estimates the appearance of the Mongoloidness in general [to have occurred] within the last 15,000 years.[42] It is appropriate to mention here that the racial type of the American Indians is defined as a type preserving the ancient form of the Mongolian race. The Eskimos, by a series of anthropological features, occupy an intermediate position between the American Indians and Asiatic Mongoloids.[43]

It is very interesting also to trace, when the material allows, the differences according to ethnographic data between the eastern and the western Aleuts. The reasons for the emergence of these subdivisions of Aleuts are not clear up to this time. In previous years, the presence of the several groups gave cause (as we shall see below) for suppositions about two waves of settlement to the islands and even by peoples with a culture different from that of the Aleuts. At the present time, the questions of the relationship of the archaeological cultures of the eastern and western part of the Aleutian chain, and also the reasons for the anthropological differences of those population groups, draw the ever greater attention of archaeologists and anthropologists.[44]

CITATIONS AND NOTES

1. I. S. Vdovin, "K voprosu o proiskhozhdenii nazvaniia 'aleut'" [On the question of the origin of the term 'Aleut'], in *Strany i narody Vostoka* [The countries and peoples of the East], vol. 6 (Moscow, 1968), pp. 101–105.

2. C. S. Chard, "Proiskhozhdenie khoziaistva morskikh okhotnikov severnoi chasti Tikhogo okeana" [The origin of the economy of the maritime hunters of the northern part of the Pacific Ocean], *Sovetskaia etnografiia*, 1962, no. 5.

3. M. G. Levin, *Etnicheskaia antropologiia i problemy etnogeneza narodov Dal'nego Vostoka* [Ethnic anthropology and problems of the ethnogenesis of the peoples of the Far East] (Moscow, 1958), pp. 225, 228, 302.

4. R. S. Vasil'evskii, "O pervonachal'nom formirovanii drevnekoriakskoi kul'tury v severnoi chasti Okhotskogo poberezh'ia" [On the initial formation of the Old Koriak culture on the northern part of the Okhotsk coast], in *Voprosy istorii sotsial'no-ekonomicheskoi zhizni Sibiri i Dal'nego Vostoka* [Questions of the history of the socio-economic life of Siberia and the Far East], vol. 1 (Novosibirsk, 1968), pp. 312–320; idem, *Proiskhozhdenie i drevniaia kul'tura koriakov* [The origin and ancient culture of the Koriak] (Novosibirsk, 1971).

5. A historical survey of theories connected with the Eskimo problem is most thoroughly elucidated in the works of M. G. Levin *(Etnicheskaia antropologiia...)*, L. A. Fainberg *(Obshchestvennyi stroi eskimosov i aleutov* [Social structure of the Eskimos and Aleuts], Moscow, 1964), and C. S. Chard

("Arctic anthropology in America," *Philadelphia Anthropological Society Papers Presented on its Golden Anniversary,* ed. J. W. Gruber, New York: Columbia University Press, 1967, pp. 77–106). See also S. I. Rudenko, *Drevniaia kul'tura Beringova moria i eskimosskaia problema* [The ancient culture of the Bering Sea and the Eskimo problem] (Moscow and Leningrad, 1947); N. A. Beregovaia, "Drevneishie kul'tury Aliaski i vopros o zaselenie Ameriki" [The most ancient cultures of Alaska and the question of the settling of America], *Sovetskaia etnografiia,* 1948, no. 4, pp. 204–219; S. A. Arutiunov and D. A Sergeev, *Drevnie kul'tury aziatskikh eskimosov* [Ancient cultures of the Asiatic Eskimos] (Moscow, 1969); N. N. Dikov, *Drevnie kostry Kamchatki i Chukotki* [Ancient hearths of Kamchatka and Chukotka] (Magadan, 1969); idem, "Chukotka ot epokhi pervobytnoobshchinnykh otnoshenii do Velikoi Oktiabr'skoi sotsialisticheskoi revoliutsii" [Chukotka from the epoch of primitive communal relations to the great October socialist revolution], in *Ocherki istorii Chukotki s drevneishikh vremen do nashikh dnei* [Essays on the history of Chukotka from ancient times to the present] (Novosibirsk, 1974), pp. 18–75.

6. After the discovery by Laughlin of more ancient sites, and on comparison with them, de Laguna revised the date of the Kachemak I culture considerably back in time (F. de Laguna, "Intemperate reflections on Arctic and Subarctic archaeology," in *Prehistoric Cultural Relations Between the Arctic and Temperate Zones of North America,* ed. J. M. Campbell, Arctic Institute of North America Technical Papers, no. 11, Montreal, 1962, pp. 164–169). [Initially, de Laguna dated Kachemak I to after A.D. 1. Later this dating was revised to 800 B.C.—W. W.]

7. W. S. Laughlin, "Contemporary problems in the anthropology of southern Alaska," *Science in Alaska* (Washington, 1952), pp. 66–84.

8. S. A. Arutiunov and D. A. Sergeev, *Drevnie kul'tury....*

9. N. N. Dikov, *Drevnie kostry...,* pp. 155–158, 207–213.

10. M. Swadesh and G. Marsh, "Eskimo-Aleut correspondences," *International Journal of American Linguistics* 17, no. 4 (1951), pp. 209–216; M. Swadesh, "Linguistic relations across Bering Strait," *American Anthropologist* 64, no. 6 (1962), pp. 1262–1291.

11. D. Hirsch, "Glottochronology and Eskimo-Aleut prehistory," *American Anthropologist* 56, no. 5 (1954), pp. 825–838.

12. K. Bergsland, "Aleut demonstration and the Aleut-Eskimo relationship," *International Journal of American Linguistics* 17, no. 3 (1955), pp. 167–179.

13. R. F. Black and W. S. Laughlin, "Anangula: A geological interpretation of the oldest archeological site in the Aleutians," *Science* 143, no. 3612 (1964), pp. 1321–1322.

14. Iu. A. Mochanov, "Drevneishie etapy zaseleniia Severo-Vostochnoi Azii i Aliaski" [The most ancient stages of the peopling of Northeast Asia and Alaska], *Sovetskaia etnografiia*, 1969, no. 1, pp. 79–86.

15. Mochanov dates the migration of the ancestors of the Aleut-Eskimo into America to the very latest period, already after the three stages indicated, but this view of Mochanov's does not seem well-founded to us.

16. W. S. Laughlin, "Human migration and permanent occupation in the Bering Sea area," in *The Bering Land Bridge,* ed. D. M. Hopkins (Stanford: Stanford University Press, 1967), pp. 409–450. [For recent thinking on Beringia, see D. M. Hopkins et al., eds., *Paleoecology of Beringia* (New York: Academic Press, 1982)—W. W.]

17. D. M. Hopkins, "Quarternary marine transgressions in Alaska," in *The Bering Land Bridge,* ed. D. M. Hopkins (Stanford: Stanford University Press, 1967), pp. 47–90; idem, "The Cenozoic history of Beringia, a synthesis," ibid., pp. 451–484.

18. C. Chard, "Arctic anthropology...," p. 71.

19. A. Hrdlička, *The Aleutian and Commander Islands and their Inhabitants* (Philadelphia: Wistar Institute of Anatomy and Biology, 1945), pp. 277–287, 381–397; N. N. Dikov, *Drevnie kostry...*, pp. 98–102.

20. N. N. Dikov, "Otkrytie paleolita na Kamchatke i problema pervonachal'nogo zaseleniia Ameriki" [Discovery of the Paleolithic in Kamchatka and the problem of the initial peopling of America], in *Istoriia i kul'tura narodov severa Dal'nego Vostoka* [History and culture of the peoples of the north of the Far East] (Moscow, 1967), pp. 16–31; idem, *Drevnie kostry...*, pp. 102–119; idem, *Drevnie kul'tury Kamchatki i Chukotki* [Ancient cultures of Kamchatka and Chukotka], Synopsis of doctoral dissertation (Novosibirsk, 1971).

21. R. S. Vasil'evskii, *Drevnie kul'tury Tikhookeanskogo Severa* [Ancient cultures of the North Pacific] (Novosibirsk, 1973).

22. W. S. Laughlin, "Eskimos and Aleuts: Their origins and evolution," *Science* 142, no. 3593 (1963), pp. 633–645.

23. M. P. Askenov, "Kompleks nizhnego kul'turnogo gorizonta stoianki Makarova na Lene" [The complex of the lower cultural horizon of the Makarovo site on the Lena], in *Sibir' i ee sosedi v drevnosti* [Siberia and its neighbors in antiquity] (Novosibirsk, 1970), pp. 43–52.

24. A. P. Okladnikov and V. N. Goregliad, "Novye dannye o drevneishei kul'ture kamennogo veka na severe Iaponii" [New data on the most ancient culture of the Stone Age in northern Japan], *Sovetskaia arkheologiia,* 1958, no. 3, pp. 246–150; A. P. Okladnikov, *Dalekoe proshloe Primor'ia* [The distant past of Primor'e] (Vladivostok, 1959); idem, "Drevnee poselenie na r. Tadushi u der. Ustinovki i problema dal'nevostochnogo mezolita" [Ancient settlement on the Tadusha River near the village of Ustinovka and the problem of the Far Eastern Mesolithic], in *Chetvertichnyi period Sibiri* [The Quarternary period of Siberia] (Moscow, 1966), pp. 352–372.

25. G. A. Menovshchikov, "Eskimossko-aleutskie iazyki i ikh otnoshenie k drugim iazykovym sem'iam" [Eskimo-Aleut languages and their relation to other language families], *Voprosy iazykoznaniia,* 1974, no. 1, pp. 46–59.

26. R. S. Vasil'evskii, *Drevnie kul'tury...,* p. 124.

27. C. S. Chard, "The Old World roots: Review and speculations," *Anthropological Papers of the University of Alaska* 10, no. 2 (1963), pp.115–121.

28. W. S. Laughlin, "Contemporary problems...," p. 79.

29. S. I. Rudenko, *Drevniaia kul'tura Beringova moria...;* M. G. Levin, [Review of] S. I. Rudenko, *Drevniaia kul'tura Beringova moria i eskimosskaia problema, Sovetskaia etnografiia,* 1949, no. 1.

30. C. Chard, "Arctic anthropology...," p. 87; W. S. Laughlin, "Contemporary problems...," p. 79.

31. The peoples of the northwest coast of North America are subdivided into three groups: the northern—Tlingit, Haida, and Tsimshian; the central—Wakashan, consisting of two subgroups, the Kwakiutl and the Nootka; and the southern—Salish and Chinook. The Protowakashan group is the most ancient inhabitant of these places (distinguished from the other groups, which came here at a later time).

32. W. S. Laughlin, "Bering Strait to Puget Sound: Dichotomy and affinity between Eskimo-Aleuts and North American Indians," in *Prehistoric Cultural Relations Between the Arctic and Temperate Zones of North America,* ed. J. M. Campbell, Arctic Institute of North America Technical Papers, no. 11 (Montreal, 1962), pp. 113–125.

33. P. Drucker, "Sources of Northwest Coast culture," in *New Interpretations of Aboriginal American Culture History* (Washington: Anthropological Society of Washington, 1955), p. 68.

34. C. E. Borden, "West coast crossties with Alaska," in *Prehistoric Cultural Relations Between the Arctic and Temperate Zones of North America,* ed. J. M.

Campbell, Arctic Institue of North America Technical Papers, no. 11 (Montreal, 1962), pp. 9–19.

35. C. S. Chard, "Proiskhozhdenie khoziaistva...," p. 98.

36. H. B. Collins, A. H. Clark, and E. H. Walker, *The Aleutian Islands: Their People and Natural History* (Washington, 1945), p. 21.

37. B. O. Dolgikh, "Problemy etnografii i antropologii Arktiki" [Problems of the ethnography and anthropology of the Arctic], *Sovetskaia etnografiia*, 1964, no. 4, p. 86.

38. W. S. Laughlin, "Generic problems and new evidence in the anthropology of the Eskimo-Aleut stock," in *Prehistoric Cultural Relations Between the Arctic and Temperate Zones of North America,* ed. J. M. Campbell, Arctic Institute of North America Technical Papers, no. 11 (Montreal, 1962), p. 125.

39. W. S. Laughlin, "The Alaska gateway viewed from the Aleutian Islands," in *Papers on the Physical Anthropology of the American Indian,* ed. W. S. Laughlin (New York: Viking Fund, 1951), pp. 98–126.

40. V. P. Alekseev, "Antropologicheskoe svoeobrazie korennogo naseleniia Aliaski i bipoliarnye rasy" [The anthropological distinction of the aboriginal population of Alaska and bipolar races], in *Ot Aliaski do Ognennoi Zemli* [From Alaska to Tierra del Fuego] (Moscow, 1967), p. 214.

41. V. P. Alekseev, "K kraniologii aziatskikh eskimosov (material k etnogenezu)" [Toward a craniology of the Asiatic Eskimos (Material on ethnogenesis)], *Zapiski Chukotskogo kraevedcheskogo muzeia*, v. 4 (1967), pp. 22–26; idem, "Antropologicheskoe svoeobrazie korennogo naseleniia Aliaski...."

42. W. S. Laughlin, "Eskimos and Aleuts...," p. 12.

43. G. F. Debets, "Proiskhozhdenie korennogo naseleniia Ameriki" [Origin of the aboriginal population of America], in *Proiskhozhdenie cheloveka i drevnee rasselenie chelovechestva* [Origin of man and the ancient settling of mankind], *Trudy Instituta etnografii*, n.s., t. 16 (1951), pp. 534, 538.

44. A. P. McCartney, "A proposed western Aleutian phase in the Near Islands, Alaska," *Arctic Anthropology* 8, no. 2 (1971), pp. 92–142.

I. A HISTORY OF ALEUT STUDIES
"The Aleutian Problem"

The history of the study of the Aleuts begins with the discovery of the Aleutian Islands by the members of the Second Kamchatka Expedition (1733–1743), who sailed to America on the packet-boats *St. Peter* and *St. Paul* under the command of V. Bering and A. I. Chirikov.[1] The beginnings of such study are linked to the Russians' advance eastward following the discovery and investigation of the huge expanse of Northeast Asia and their emergence onto the coast of the Pacific Ocean. It is also connected with the development of Russian science. It was the time when the young Petersburg Academy of Sciences conducted systematic expeditions of exploration to the little-known regions of the vast Russian state. And although ethnography at that time was not yet an independent branch of science, the ethnographic study of peoples, naturally, was included in the range of investigations.

Professors and adjuncts of the Academy of Sciences were among the members of the Second Kamchatka Expedition. One of the participants in this expedition, the historian G. F. Müller, drafted detailed instructions for the collection of information about the population which stipulated both ethnographic and anthropological investigations.[2]

Members of the Bering-Chirikov expedition—G. W. Steller, adjunct of the Academy of Sciences, Chirikov himself, and the naval officer Sven Waxell—collected the earliest information about the Aleuts.

Steller and Waxell were on the *St. Peter*, which reached the coast of America on the twentieth of July 1741 and stood off Kayak Island. Here Steller made several observations (including ethnographic ones, although he did not see the inhabitants, the Eskimos). On the return voyage, the Shumagin Islands were discovered. Near the largest islands of that group—Unga and Nagai—stops were made. The first meeting with the Aleuts took place here. Steller describes his observations in detail.[3] Waxell's observations are briefer, but they complement Steller's information about the Aleuts.[4]

The vessel *St. Paul*, having reached the shores of America on the fifteenth of July 1741 at Prince of Wales Island, approached Adak Island (Andreanof island group). Here the Aleuts approached the vessel in *baidarka*s [kayaks]. This meeting was described by Chirikov.[5]

Steller, Waxell, and Chirikov simply call the Aleuts "Americans." Although not extensive, their information about the Aleuts is extremely valuable, for it was obtained at the time of the very first contact of those people with Europeans. Steller, being a scholar-naturalist and an attentive observer, compiled the most complete and interesting records. He was the first who raised the question of the origin of the Aleuts. Thus, he expressed the possibility that the settlement of the islands was from Asia, basing his supposition on the likeness of certain cultural elements of the Aleuts with those of the Kamchadal and Koriak.[6] In another work, Steller noted the physical similarity of the Kamchadal and Koriak with the "Americans" and expressed the supposition that the natives of America were migrants from Asia.[7]

The Second Kamchatka Expedition, which pioneered a route to the Aleutian Islands and northwestern America, was the beginning of a new epoch of voyages in the second half of the eighteenth century by enterprising Russian merchants, seafarers and promyshlenniki to the Aleutian Islands. Bering's companions brought valuable sea otter furs and information about the abundance of furs in the newly discovered lands which served to stimulate the organization of artels [*arteli*, hunting parties], and later of larger commercial and mercantile companies for expeditions to the Aleutian Islands. On those trade voyages new islands were discovered one after another, until the entire chain of the Aleutian Islands, the Alaska Peninsula and Kodiak Island became known to the Russians.[8]

The first voyages (1743–1747) were organized by a sergeant of the Okhotsk Port command, E. Basov. Basov and his companions visited the Commander Islands and sailed past some of the Aleutian Islands. A detachment of promyshlenniki with the navigator M. Nevodchikov and the *peredovshchik* [foreman] Ia. Chuprov wintered on the Near Islands of the Aleutian chain in 1745–1746. Here (on Agattu Island and later on Attu Island), for the first time since Bering and Chirikov, the Russians encountered the Aleuts.

The Andreanof Islands were investigated in detail during the voyage of the merchant Andreian Tolstykh (1747–1764), after whom they were eventually named. Tolstykh was not only an excellent navigator, but also a gifted explorer who strove to describe thoroughly the lands he visited, their natural setting, and the inhabitants' mode of life. Unfortunately, returning on his last voyage, his ship was wrecked near the shores of Kamchatka. Among the lost articles was a chest in which was kept the description of this last voyage, the islands, and their inhabitants. It was only possible to save an Aleut baidarka, a hat, and fishing gear which were brought from Adak Island. Those items were sent to the office in Bol'sheretsk. Information about this expedition was preserved in the written statements by Tolstykh and his companions, the cossacks Vesiutinskii and Lazarev. Based on those testimonies, a description of the islands was made and presented to Catherine II by the governor of Siberia, D. I. Chicherin. To his account Chicherin appended a map of the Andreanof Islands and several Aleut artifacts.

In 1753 [1752], a vessel sailed under the navigator P. Bashmakov, a merchant, and with the peredovshchik A. Serebrennikov, also a merchant.[9] This *shitik* [sewn boat] was cast ashore on Adak Island. Besides a detailed account of the voyage, information about the natural environment and about the way of life of the island's inhabitants has been found among the documents.

Credit for the discovery of the Fox Islands belongs to the navigator S. Glotov, peredovshchik I. Solov'ev, and the *iasak* [tribute] collector S. Ponomarev (1759–1762). Glotov received the assignment to search for new islands and not to put in at those already known. Glotov and Ponomarev visited various islands of the Fox Island group. Ponomarev, together with the promyshlennik P. Shishkin, drew a map of the Aleutian Islands.[a] The "news" [*izvestiia*] of Ponomarev and Glotov about the islands discovered by them, and the map, were sent to Petersburg after their return. The voyage of Glotov was one of the most significant of that time: he sailed farther than others along the whole of the Aleutian chain, discovered many new islands, compiled their description, facilitated the drawing of the map and, besides all that, established friendly relations with the inhabitants.

---

a. The ascription of this map to Ponomarev is disputed by Grekov and many other Russian specialists (V. I. Grekov, *Ocherki iz istorii russkikh geograficheskikh issledovanii v 1725–1765 gg.* [Essays from the history of Russian geographical investigations in 1725–1765], Moscow, 1960)—L. B.

During these voyages (their total number was seventy) navigators, merchants and promyshlenniki encountered the island's inhabitants, the Aleuts; relations with them were both extremely strained and friendly. Information about the life of the native inhabitants was brought home and submitted to the Bol'sheretsk office in the form of *skaski, raporty,* and *doklady* [accounts, reports, and memoranda]. Publication of a number of these interesting documents occurred only in our time. L. S. Berg published the "report" of P. Vasiutinskii and M. Lazarev, and the "descriptions" by A. Tolstykh.[10] A. I. Andreev published the reports of S. Ponomarev and S. Glotov,[11] S. Cherepanov, I. Korovin, I. Solov'ev and V. Shilov.[12]

The works of A. S. Polonskii (a member of the Council of the Main Office for the Administration of Eastern Siberia in Irkutsk), dating to the 1850s and 1860s, are based to a considerable degree on the materials in the files of Kamchatka's offices [*prikaznye kantseliarii*] and of the office of the Port of Okhotsk, including materials on the history of the expeditions of Russian promyshlenniki in the Pacific Ocean in the second half of the eighteenth century. These manuscripts are in the archives of the Geographical Society of the USSR[13] and are very interesting and reliable sources, although they unfortunately do not contain references to the documents on which they are based. One of them, "Promyshlenniki na Aleutskikh Ostrovakh" [Promyshlenniki on the Aleutian Islands], contains a considerable amount of ethnographic information about the Aleuts.

All these early materials about the Aleuts constitute an extremely valuable collection of data about their culture. They reflect it as it was prior to contact with the Europeans.

Information about the new discoveries of the Russian promyshlenniki in "the Eastern Ocean" reached the government and got to the Senate and the Admiralty College.

Those in Petersburg attentively monitored the events taking place on the shores of America. The tsarist government approved and encouraged the activities of the Russian merchants and promyshlenniki, and at the same time gained considerable profits for itself.[14] Eventually, the government initiated attempts to secure the rights of Russia to the lands discovered by Russian seafarers. In 1764 the Admiralty College decided to dispatch a hydrographic expedition to the East under the command of

Captain P. K. Krenitsyn and Lieutenant Levashov. This government expedition of 1764–1769, kept secret for political reasons, concluded the stage of discoveries and opened a new stage of systematic investigations and explorations, in which the main role belonged to the Russian navy. The Krenitsyn-Levashov expedition brought back, for the first time, valuable material intentionally gathered about the geography, hydrography, environment and inhabitants of the Aleutian Islands. Levashov's journal contains four independent sections: "A Description of the Island of Unalashka," "About the Inhabitants of that Island," "About Iasak" and "About the Gathering of Various Species of Foxes on the Island of Unalashka by Russian People." The section "About Inhabitants..." was published by A. P. Sokolov together with other materials of the expedition,[15] but part of the expedition's ethnographic materials have remained unused until now. Levashov's album of excellent ethnographic sketches (for example, see Figure 2) is in the Hydrography collection [*fond*] of the Central State Archives of the Navy. Besides that, a number of important observations concerning the history and social organization of the Aleuts are in Levashov's journal. Thus, the Krenitsyn-Levashov expedition gives us a considerable amount of material indicative of the original culture of the Aleuts, still untouched by European influence.[16]

The growing ethnographic information about the peoples of the newly discovered islands was reflected also in the literature of the time. The work of I. I. Georgi, *Opisanie vsekh v Rossiiskom gosudarstve obitaiushchikh narodov* [Description of all the peoples inhabiting the Russian state], appeared in 1776–1777. The chapter entitled "The Inhabitants of the Eastern Islands" contains generalized information available at that time about the Aleuts.

Individual works of a popular-scientific character, containing information about the newly discovered islands and their inhabitants, appeared in the historical and geographical *Mesiatseslovy* [Almanacs] issued by the Academy of Sciences beginning in 1726. There were also publications in the journal *Ezhemesiachnye sochineniia k pol'ze i uveseleniiu sluzhashchiie*, also published by the Academy of Sciences (1755–1764). Information about Russian voyages and discoveries in northwestern America appeared in the journal *Neue Nordische Beitrage*,[17] published by the academician P. S. Pallas in 1781–1788 and 1793–1796.

27

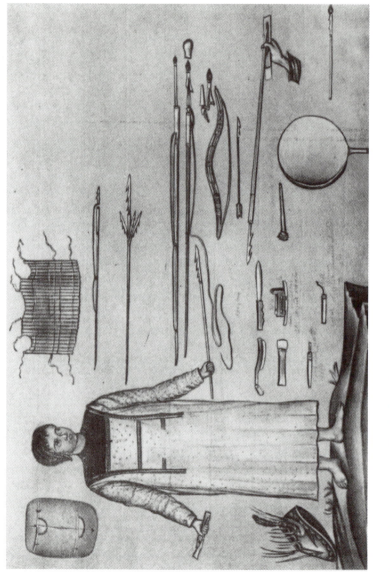

Figure 2. An Aleut of Unalaska Island and items connected with men's activities. Drawing by M. D. Levashov. TsGAVMF.

The works of Pallas, devoted to the Russian discoveries on the shores of America, were published here, as were documents pertaining to the voyages of the promyshlenniki.

But even earlier than in Russia, materials about Russian discoveries in northwestern America began to appear abroad. Among them it is necessary to mention the work of W. Coxe[18] based on data received from the historiographer of the Academy of Sciences, G. F. Müller.[19] Some information about the Krenitsyn-Levashov expedition and an "extract" from the journals of the expedition were published for the first time in Coxe's work.

Of foreign expeditions, the third round-the-world voyage of James Cook (1776–1780) provided rich material on the ethnography of the Aleuts.[20]

A new governmental secret expedition under the command of Captains I. I. [Joseph] Billings and G. A. Sarychev (1785–1793) was organized for the investigation of Bering Strait and the northwestern shores of North America during the reign of Catherine II. During this expedition Sarychev compiled descriptions of the Chukchi Peninsula, the shores of the Sea of Okhotsk, the Aleutian Islands, the shores of North America up to Kal'ka [?] Island, and also of the way of life of the peoples inhabiting these regions.[21] At the same time, a great number of artifacts were collected for museums, including Aleut ethnographic collections. Sarychev's ethnographic notes about the Aleuts have great value.

The results of the investigations of that expedition were published also in the works of Sauer, Billings's secretary and interpreter.[22]

C. H. Merck took part in the expedition in the capacity of physician. He collected valuable material on the ethnography of the Chukchi, Eskimo, and Aleut.[23] Extracts from the manuscript, devoted to the Aleuts and Eskimos, were published only in 1937.[24]

Permanent Russian settlements began to appear in Alaska beginning in 1784. The initiator of this enterprise was the Russian merchant G. I. Shelikhov, head of the largest commercial and mercantile company. Out of it, in 1799, the Russian-American Company was established, receiving from Paul I a monopoly for carrying on trade in all lands discovered by the Russians in northwestern America and for managing those possessions of Russia (which received the name "Russian America").

The subsequent study of Russian America and the accumulation of ethnographic knowledge about its peoples was then linked with the activity of the Russian-American Company. Scientific guidance for most of those studies was provided, as before, by the Academy of Sciences.

During the circumnavigating voyages at the beginning of the nineteeth century, organized with the aim of establishing a more convenient and cheaper route for communication with Russian possessions in America, extensive geographic, oceanographic and natural scientific studies were also carried out. The significance of those voyages for international scholarship, as is known, was enormous.

The first round-the-world voyage was completed by the ships *Nadezhda* and *Neva* under the command of Captains I. F. Kruzenshtern and Iu. F. Lisianskii (1803–1806).[25] The leaders of this expedition, N. P. Rezanov and I. F. Kruzenshtern, were elected as corresponding members of the Academy of Sciences and received instructions concerning the gathering of natural science collections for the Kunstkamera. Among the information collected about peoples of Russian America and collections of their cultural artifacts, the expedition delivered Aleut material.[26] G. H. Langsdorff took part in this first voyage around the world in the capacity of naturalist. His ethnographic description of the Aleuts is of considerable interest.[27]

In 1817–1819 a round-the-world voyage was undertaken under the command of V. M. Golovnin[28] on the sloop *Kamchatka*, and in 1826–1829 the ships *Seniavin* and *Moller* made a circumnavigation under the command of F. P. Litke and M. I. Staniukovich.[29] On these voyages Aleut collections and information about Aleut culture were acquired.[30]

It is particularly necessary to note the value of such an ethnographic source as the pictorial material which was brought back by these expeditions. Drawings by members of the expeditions or artists specially included, excellently supplement the ethnographic information about the inhabitants of the places visited.[31]

Particular observations and notes of an ethnographic nature are also to be found in the works of employees of the Russian-American Company. The most significant is the work of "the old-timer and chronicler of Russian America" K. T. Khlebnikov, *Zapiski o koloniiakh v Amerike* [Notes on the colonies in America], which largely remained unpublished.[32] Khlebnikov lived in Russian America from 1818 to 1832. Besides materials of an ethnographic character, his work contains a considerable amount of information on the history of the Aleuts for the period indicated above.

At approximately the same time (the years 1824–1839 [1834]) there resided in the Aleutian Islands the outstanding scholar of the culture and lifeways of the peoples of Russian America, the missionary I. E. Veniaminov (later Metropolitan Innokentii), a self-taught ethnographer, linguist, and biologist.[33] His main work, *Zapiski ob ostrovakh Unalashkinskogo otdela* [Notes on the islands of the Unalaska district], presents an interesting description of the Aleuts.[34] He was one of the first who foresaw the growing need not for fragmentary ethnographic observations, but for serious comprehensive studies of separate peoples. Veniaminov himself stated that: "The accounts of our travelers Messrs. Sarychev, Lisianskii, Kotzebue, Litke and others, aside from the nautical part, contain only brief sketches of this region, and these are not always accurate, due to unavoidable reasons: a short-term stay, ignorance of the native language, and various important undertakings did not allow them to gather information either sufficiently detailed or reliable."[35] The importance of Veniaminov's work lies not only in the gathering of interesting ethnographic information. It lies also in the systematization of an enormous accumulation of material, in approaching it through contemporary scientific methodology, and in the use of anthropological, linguistic, and folkloric data for his conclusions. It is also necessary to note such valuable traits in his study as historicism, which included the reconstruction of the aboriginal culture of the Aleuts and their social organization in the first half of the eighteenth century (prior to contact with the Russians).[36]

Veniaminov's work on the Aleut language is a source of exceptional value.[37] It is the principal basis for linguists, including foreign ones, for the study of the Aleut language.

Veniaminov raises and resolves the question of the origin of the Aleuts on the basis of language data, physical type, and folkloric material. He takes into account all the information known to him relative to the length of time the Aleuts inhabited their islands, and investigates the question of whence the Aleuts could have come—from America (from the east) or from Asia (from the west)—and inclines toward the conclusion that they originated in Asia. Veniaminov believed that the ancestors of the Aleuts may have sailed to the islands from Kamchatka, where they might have landed from Japan.

In the eighteenth and the beginning of the nineteenth century, that is, the period when study of the Aleuts originated, collections were also made. These were later concentrated mainly in the Kunstkamera (now the Museum of Anthropology and Ethnography of the Academy of Sciences of the USSR).[b] Early voyagers and later explorers of the islands brought back individual articles and large or small collections, but a considerable part of the collections relating to the Aleuts (as well as to some of the other peoples of northwestern America) was gathered by the preparator of the Zoological Museum, I. G. Voznesenskii.[38] He was specially sent by the Academy of Sciences to Russian America (and to the northeastern part of Russia's Asiatic possessions) to gather collections on zoology, botany, mineralogy and ethnography. During the ten years from 1839 to 1849, Voznesenskii accomplished by himself the tasks of an entire complex expedition. He enriched all the museums of the Academy of Sciences with the most valuable materials. Voznesenskii's collection on the Aleuts, in conjunction with the previous museum accessions, constitutes a collection of artifacts which characterizes with sufficient completeness the culture and way of life of the Aleuts at the end of the eighteenth and the first half of the nineteenth century. An excellent supplement to the collections are Voznesenskii's ethnographic notes that are housed today in the Leningrad branch of the Archive of the Academy of Sciences of the USSR.

But already by the end of the 1840s, interest in the ethnographic study of Russian America began to decline noticeably in Russia. In 1867 the Russian possessions in the western hemisphere—Alaska and the Aleutian Islands—were sold to the United States of America.

The initial period of the study of the Aleuts, sketched above, connected with the discovery and initial study of the Aleutian Islands and their inhabitants by Russians, constitutes the most important epoch in the history of Aleut studies—the accumulation of ethnographic materials which at a later time were almost impossible to supplement, as the Aleut culture with time was losing more and more of its original

---

b. Now returned to its former name, the "Kunstkamera," Museum of Peter the Great—L. B.

features. But for that period, it was typical not merely to accumulate materials. Attempts were also made to systematize them, to interpret, and the problem of the origin of the Aleuts was posed (Steller and Veniaminov). Particular note should be made of the enormous significance of the collections on the Aleut culture and way of life that were gathered during that period and which are preserved mainly in the museums of our country.

In regard to the question of Aleut origin, the opinion expressed by Veniaminov about the settlement of the islands from the west through Kamchatka was predominant in Russian scholarship of that and a much later time. L. Shrenk, on the strength of this assumption, numbered the Aleuts among the Paleo-Asiatics.[39] S. Patkanov followed Shrenk.[40] This point of view was also accepted by the majority of foreign scholars at that time.

* * *

Beginning with the end of the eighteenth century, the study of the Aleuts assumes the character of an investigation of the question of their origin. Investigation of the "Aleutian Problem" ranks with study of the origin of the northeastern Paleo-Asiatics and Eskimos, and also with the problem of the settlement of northwestern America. The first American student of the Aleutian Islands was W. Dall.[41] The sphere of his interests was extremely broad: geography, geology, paleontology, anthropology, history, ethnography, and archaeology.

Dall devoted two works specifically to the tribal composition of the aboriginal population of Alaska.[42] In them, he summarizes the information from many Russian sources as well as the results of his own investigations. Dall was one of the first to carry out systematic archaeological excavations on the Aleutian Islands.[43] He excavated caves (on the islands of Attu, Amchitka, Adak, Atka, Unalaska, and Shumagin), where he found the remains of ancient burials, and [also excavated] at the sites of ancient settlements.[c]

During the investigations of the burial caves, Dall gathered a large collection of mummies, skeletal parts, and articles of material culture. Those collections were described and published together with folklore materials also collected by him.[44]

---

c. Dall did not conduct all these excavations himself. Others collected mummies as well and are credited in Dall's publications—L. B.

A result of the excavations of the ancient Aleut settlements ("shell-heaps") was Dall's conclusion concerning three periods of development in the culture of the Aleuts on the Aleutian Islands.[45] Every period, in his opinion, corresponded to a definite cultural stratum. Dall isolated three such strata: a stratum of mollusk shells *(Echinus);*[d] a stratum of fish bones with implements and means of fishing; and a stratum of sea mammal bones with implements and the means for sea hunting. The first stratum, the earliest according to Dall's conclusion, belonged to the littoral period in the culture of the Aleuts, when the main source of food was the products gathered along the seashore. The second stratum, a later one, corresponded to the fishing period, and the third, a still later period, belonged to the hunting period, when the main occupation of the Aleuts became the hunting of sea mammals.

Dall speaks of the antiquity of Aleut settlement on the islands (up to three thousand years ago) and expresses the opinion that they belong to the Eskimo (Inuit) stock, and that they settled the islands from the east, from the American continent.[46]

In his work on the origin of the Eskimos, Dall energetically opposes the theory of the settlement of America via the Aleutian Island chain, believing that the original settlement of the American continent took place via the region of Bering Strait.[47] He argues that the distance from Kamchatka to the Commander Islands and from the Commander Islands to Attu Island is too great for the people of such a cultural level to overcome. Moreover, the Commander Islands were never inhabited (Dall did not find traces of man there).[e] In his opinion, the native land of the Eskimos was located in America (in its interior). From here, from the east, the Aleutian Islands were populated by one group of Inuit who were the ancestors of the Aleuts. The rest of the Eskimo tribes, pressed by the Indians, settled the Arctic. Speaking of the Asiatic Eskimos, he advances arguments of their rather later migration to Chukotka.

In his work devoted to masks and facial decorations (labrets), Dall examines the question of the existence of these traditions among the

---

d. Echinoderms are sea urchins, not mollusks—W. W.

e. Dall himself did not visit the Commander Islands. His article "Remarks on the origin of the Innuit," here cited by Liapunova, states that Vitus Bering and his crew did not find any inhabitants on the Commanders—L. B.

aboriginal populations of America (including the Aleuts) and raises the question of the origin of these artifacts.[48]

For support of his thesis about the settling of America from Asia via the region of Bering Strait, Dall uses the data of geological investigations.[49] He advances the hypothesis of the possibility of the existence in ancient epochs of a land bridge to the north of Bering Strait.

Dall's theory of three periods of development in the culture of the Aleuts was refuted by V. I. Iokhel'son [W. Jochelson in American usage].

In 1900–1902, in the capacity of leader of the Siberian section, Iokhel'son participated in the North Pacific Expedition, organized by the American Museum of Natural History and financed by Jesup (the Jesup Expedition) for the study of the cultural-historical relations among the peoples of Northeast Asia and northwestern America.[50] A result of that investigation was the theory of the "Eskimo wedge," put forward by the participants (Boas, Iokhel'son, and Bogoraz), about an American-Asiatic chain of kindred peoples that was broken by incoming Eskimos. They considered the Aleuts to have been the point of this "wedge." Boas and Iokhel'son named the Arctic regions of America as the home of the Eskimos, while Bogoraz defended the idea of their Asiatic origin. The Paleo-Asiatics, according to Boas and Iokhel'son, were re-emigrants to Asia.[51]

In 1909–1911 Iokhel'son conducted investigations, organized by the Russian Geographical Society, on Kamchatka and the Aleutian Islands. He based the necessity of studying the Aleuts—"the sharp point of the Eskimo wedge"—on the fact that the "Aleutian Problem" was elucidated very poorly (the work of the Jesup Expedition did not touch upon them [the Aleuts]) and that the Aleuts constituted one of the missing links in the chain of Asiatic and American tribes.

Considering the main task of the investigation to be the elucidation of the early history of the Aleuts, Iokhel'son devoted his primary effort to archaeological excavations.[52] He conducted these on the islands where Dall had already dug (Attu, Atka, Amaknak) and on the islands of Umnak and Uknadak [Hog], believing that Dall's conclusions merited testing. In all, Iokhel'son excavated thirteen ancient settlement sites and investigated fifty-seven depressions of various sizes, three burial caves, and three caves with traces of human occupation. He confirmed many of Dall's observations, but sharply criticized the theory of three cultural periods in the development of the Aleuts. According to Iokhel'son, all strata of kitchen midden, even the lowest, contain items of a much higher culture. In all strata he discovered stone and bone lamps, fire drills, traces of ash, stone griddles, and bones of sea mammals (including whales). All this led him to the conclusion that the Aleuts were sea hunters from the beginning of the settlement of the islands. Implements for the hunting of sea mammals, needles for the sewing of clothing, and the remains of dwellings were also found.

Advancing his assumptions about the early history of the Aleuts, Iokhel'son concluded that the Aleuts came to the islands with a comparatively high culture which was not far from that found by the first Russians. He agreed with Dall that the geographic conditions did not allow the Aleuts to reach the Aleutian Islands from Asia. And Iokhel'son posed the question: did the Bering Land Bridge (which, according to Dall's supposition, was to the north of Bering Strait) reach the Aleutian chain? Could it be that the present Aleutian Islands represent remains of that ancient bridge? And did that bridge perhaps exist in the Pleistocene era, that is, at the time of the earliest possible migration of man from the Old World into the New? Iokhel'son wrote that if it were geologically proven that such a bridge existed at the location of the Aleutian Islands, then it would be possible to speak of the Aleuts coming from the west. The question of their origin should be, moreover, connected with the origin of the aboriginal population of America—the Eskimos and Indians. For Iokhel'son, the close kinship between the Aleuts and Eskimos was beyond doubt (language, culture, and somatic indicators). He explained the high cephalic index of the Aleuts, similar to the index of the northwestern Indians or Paleo-Asiatics, not by their mixture with their contemporary American or Asiatic neighbors, but either by their mixture in ancient times with the Athabaskans (per Hrdlička's hypothesis), or by gradual acquisition [of this trait] under the conditions of prolonged insular isolation. He proposed that early skeletal remains are absent because in caves or in burial huts they would have decayed in the course of such a prolonged period. He attributed the kitchen middens (shell heaps) to the contemporary geological era. He concluded that the Aleuts came to the islands in a very distant time, possibly even at the time of the earliest settlement of northwestern America. He attributed the "shell heap" culture to the Stone Age. The latest period of Aleut history he defined as one transitional to the Neolithic; the latter did not have time to develop because of the arrival of the Russians.

According to Iokhel'son, the character of the Aleut culture allows one to conclude that the cultural, spiritual, and physical features of the Aleuts basically indicate their close connection with the inhabitants of the American continent, and not with Asia.

In another work, Iokhel'son more definitely states that the area of the formation of Aleut (and Eskimo) culture lies in northwestern America, in the territory presently inhabited by the Tlingit (where Dall found traces of an ancient Eskimo presence) or somewhere in the western part of Canada.[53] This work contains an account of the history of Aleut studies, an ethnographic essay utilizing a number of old Russian sources and personal observations and information about the physical type of the Aleuts. Here Iokhel'son notes that, according to skin color, facial breadth, and the shape of the eyes, the Aleuts resemble more the Mongoloids than the Paleo-Asiatic type or the Indian one.

Iokhel'son's linguistic studies of the Aleut language and his publication of folklore materials are of great interest.[54]

The craniological material collected by Iokhel'son on the Aleutian Islands[f] was processed by T. Ia. Tokareva.[55] Iokhel'son dated this material to the pre-Russian period (to the middle of the eighteenth century). Tokareva concludes that analysis of the Aleut skulls by measurement and descriptive features indicates attribution to the Mongoloid race. When determining the place of the Aleutian type within the Mongoloid race she notes that, despite the cultural and linguistic commonality of the Aleuts and Eskimos, in physical type, the two groups have very little in common. Coupled with this, in her opinion, greater similarity can be observed with the skulls of the other neighbors of the Aleuts, the Tlingits of northwestern America. In comparing the skulls of the Aleuts with the skulls of the peoples of the Asian continent, Tokareva determined similarity with the inhabitants of Cisbaikalia [Lake Baikal region] (the Tungus in particular).

Tokareva believes that the insular life of the Aleuts was the determining factor in the development of their racial type in a particular way. The Aleutian type shows the greatest similarity to the Cisbaikal type. On the basis of the wide geographic distribution of the "Baikal" race and its

---

f. The physical anthropological work was done by Iokhel'son's wife—W. W.

great antiquity, Tokareva concludes that the initial stage in the racial development of the Aleuts was the racial type known in the Cisbaikal Neolithic as type "A." She proposes that the distribution of this type in some very distant early epoch encompassed a vast territory, including the Bering Sea basin and, possibly, northwestern America. The Aleutian Islands were also settled by the people of this racial type, but, under a condition of isolation on the islands, the given type changed in a definite direction, toward the brachycranic, while at the same time retaining the rest of the racial [Baikal type "A"] features. The mechanism of that process is explained by the rise of hereditary variability under conditions of isolation. Tokareva writes that Iokhel'son was also close to that conclusion.

The prehistoric epoch of the American continent was one of the principal themes of studies by the well-known American anthropologist A. Hrdlička.[56] From 1926 on, Hrdlička's interest was concentrated on the study of Alaska in connection with development of the theory of the settlement of the American continent from Asia, of which he was a consistent supporter. He carried out anthropological and archaeological investigations in the interior of Alaska and on the ancient communication routes between Asia and America (that is, on the Bering Sea littoral and the adjacent islands) and on the Aleutian Islands. Hrdlička devoted special attention to southern Alaska, which he viewed as the horizon [*areal*] of the initial migratory waves and as a "melting pot" for the formation of American man. He describes the ancient territory of Alaska as the site of the settling of newcomers from Asia who were of very mixed ethnic composition.

In the period 1936–1938, Hrdlička conducted archaeological and anthropological investigations on the Aleutian and Commander islands. By his own admission, it was the culmination of all of his anthropological investigations in Alaska. The object was to solve the problem of who the Aleuts were, how and when they appeared on the islands, whether there was anyone on the islands before them, and whether the Commander and Aleutian islands were a second route for Asiatic-American migrations. The expedition found ancient sites and burial caves on all the formerly inhabited islands. During the expedition of 1936 investigations were conducted on the islands of Amaknak, Atka, Kiska, Little Kiska, and Kagamil. In 1937, the southern part of the Alaska Peninsula, the islands of Unalaska, Umnak, Amaknak, the Commanders, Attu, Agattu, Tanaga, Ilak and Adak were investigated, and in 1938, Unalaska, Ship Rock, Umnak, Kagamil, Amlia, Kanaga, Ilak, Amchitka and the Commanders. New evidence was brought forward in support of the notion that the Commander Islands (prior to Russian voyages) were never inhabited.[g]

Hrdlička considered one of the principal results of investigations on the Aleutian Islands to be the conclusion that, at the outset, the entire archipelago was populated by "pre-Aleuts," and only later by "Aleuts." He believed that both were migrants from the Alaska Peninsula. He believed that on the islands to the west of Umnak, the remnants or even entire communities of "pre-Aleuts" lived as recently as, and right up to, the arrival of the Russians. This allowed Hrdlička to speak of the existence on the islands of representatives of a more ancient culture and of a later one, and of the intensive merging of the two.

A second important result of Hrdlička's excavations was his conclusion that physically, the "Aleuts" were not part of the Eskimo stock and that they were not even close relations of the Eskimos.

Hrdlička considered a third achievement of the expedition to be the acquisition of very rich collections on the culture of the "Aleuts" and the "pre-Aleuts." He hoped that a subsequent study of them would throw light on the early history of the entire region. In a work published in 1945, he presented only preliminary conclusions specially stressing several propositions.[57] On the basis of the fact that neither in the "pre-Aleut" nor in the "Aleut" period were there any noticeable traces of adaptation to new conditions, it was concluded that both the "Aleuts" and "pre-Aleuts" formerly lived under similar conditions and no fundamental changes occurred in their way of life with their migration to the islands. The "pre-Aleuts" were viewed as being the first inhabitants of the islands, although not very ancient ones (probably from the turn of our era or a little earlier). While basic cultural similarity was noted in the entire archipelago, cultural specialization by islands or groups of

---

g. Recent work by Russian archaeologists has provided evidence to the contrary. See V. D. Len'kov, G. L. Silant'ev, and A. K. Staniukovich, *The Komandorskii Camp of the Bering Expedition,* trans. K. L. Arndt, ed. O. W. Frost (Anchorage: Alaska Historical Society, 1992), p. 94—L. B.

islands was also noted (for example, the "Aleut" whale bone burials on the island of Amaknak, and "pre-Aleut" stone pots on the islands of Umnak, Amchitka and others). Hrdlička further concluded that the material culture was brought to the islands fully formed, agreeing in this with Iokhel'son, and not in a rudimentary state, as supposed by Dall.

Together with this, Hrdlička notes that although the "pre-Aleuts" and "Aleuts" were different anthropologically, in a cultural sense they were on the same level. Both the "pre-Aleut" and "Aleut" cultures stood closer to that of Kodiak, and in a number of features (in stone and bone artifacts) the "pre-Aleuts" as well as the "Aleuts" differed considerably from their neighbors, the southern Eskimos.

In Hrdlička's opinion, the "Aleuts" are very distant from the Eskimos anthropologically and are related more closely to the Mongoloids of Siberia and the Indians of the Northwest Coast. He accepted the possibility that one of the numerous Tungus tribes (which were variable according to physical features), spreading to the east, may have reached the Aleut-Kodiak region.

The skulls of "pre-Aleuts," in Hrdlička's opinion, are not like the Eskimo, either, but resemble more the skulls of some American tribes, particularly the Sioux Indians.

When comparing the "pre-Aleuts" and the "Aleuts" according to somatic features, Hrdlička wrote that there is an evident contrast. He considered the essential qualities indicating the similarities of these two groups to be the result of prolonged residence in similar conditions on the islands (functional similarity).

In the 1930s–1940s, in connection with the investigations of the problem of the routes of man's settlement of the New World, the articles of American and Danish archaeologists and ethnographers H. B. Collins,[58] F. de Laguna[59] and K. Birket-Smith[60] discussed the possibility of a cultural exchange between Asia and America through the Aleutian island chain. After the period of absolute denial that the routes of settlement of America went through the Aleutian Islands (on the basis of the arguments of Dall, Iokhel'son and in part Hrdlička), and the determination that the ancestral homeland of the Aleut culture was in America, the question was raised once again that the Aleutian Islands nevertheless served as the route of the penetration of the Asiatic cultures (and population) into America. But since direct archaeological evidence for these propositions was absent, great attention was devoted to determining cultural similarities in Asia and America according to ethnographic materials.

Collins and de Laguna presented evidence of a cultural exchange between Kamchatka and the Kuril Islands on the one hand, and the Aleutian Islands, Kodiak Island, and Cook Inlet on the other, which took place, in their opinions, through the Aleutian Islands: the roof entry into subterranean dwellings; oval stone lamps; hunting lamps with handles (or ears [lugs]); labrets; large bone points with blades, but without barbs; harpoon heads of Japanese form; toggle harpoon heads with closed socket and the same opening for a line and with a spur; and a number of other features. As a result, Collins concluded that indications of the cultural relationship between southern Alaska and the outlined territories along the eastern Asiatic coast were so clear that he anticipated evidence of settling of the Commander Islands in the past by local inhabitants.[61]

Birket-Smith and de Laguna presented a list of the cultural features characteristic of the circum-Pacific area: rectangular plank house; separate sleeping compartments in the house; a ladder in the form of a notched log; palisade [stockade] construction; raised structures for the storage of provisions; clothing [shirt] made of horizontally arranged strips of the skins of small fur-bearing animals; aprons; stone chipping [pecking] technique; stone mortar; weaving on vertical warps (twisted) [twined basketry]; boat-shaped containers; wooden quiver; hunting for sea mammals on the open sea; vegetable poison for arrows; slavery; transvestism; bride service custom; cremation; shaman's dolls; special treatment of dogs; sounding boards; Raven myths; legends about a girl and a dog. Under question were the following elements: nose ornaments; the notion of a girl changeling;[h] digging stick; wooden dugout boat; pits for the fermenting of fish; and others. The direction of the diffusion of these areal circum-Pacific cultural features was believed to be from Asia (apparently from the region of the Lower Amur) toward North America.[62]

---

h. Sic. Liapunova misread the term "weregild" used by Birket-Smith and de Laguna. It refers to compensation paid for the murder or disablement of a person—L. B.

American researcher R. F. Heizer also raised the question of cultural exchange between Asia and America through the Aleutian island chain in an article about the transfer of the aconite poison method of whale hunting from Asia to America through the mediation of the Aleuts.[63]

By different regions, Heizer describes whale hunting, which was one of the principal enterprises on the eastern Asiatic coast from Bering Strait to Japan, and on the American coast from Point Barrow to the Quinault River. But, as the author states, only in a part of this zone—on the island of Hokkaido, the Kuril and Aleutian islands, the southeast coast of the Alaska Peninsula, and Kodiak Island—was whale hunting practiced by a single method, by means of throwing a lance, the tip of which was smeared with aconite poison, which was different from whale hunting in other territories. Thus, Heizer proposes to add to the number of cultural elements and complexes coming to the New World from Asia through the Aleutian Islands, whale hunting by means of lance tips smeared with aconite poison.

The American investigator of the Aleuts G. I. Quimby considered the Aleuts to be a Pacific Eskimo group.[64] Moreover, he believed that Aleut culture was not only Eskimo in its character, but also Indian and Siberian. According to a number of features, he found it to be similar to the culture of Eskimos of Alaska, and according to other characteristics, similar to the culture of the northwestern Indians and, in some instances, to the culture of the tribes of Kamchatka.

He suggested the following hypothesis for the early history of the Aleuts. The Aleuts constituted an Eskimo-speaking group of hunting people who left Asia at the end of the Siberian Paleolithic era, about two thousand years ago or considerably earlier. Similarly, as had many other immigrants before them, the ancient Aleuts crossed into America through the region of Bering Strait; and like some of the other, earlier, immigrants who spoke Indian languages, the early Aleuts were carriers of a circumpolar and apparently circum-northern (subarctic) hunting culture originating in the Old World. The ancient Aleuts advanced to the southwest, until they were stopped by Indians with a similar culture who occupied the coastal and interior part of southern Alaska and British Columbia. The Aleuts proceeded to the Alaska Peninsula, and then to the Aleutian Islands. With the passage of time, new incoming Eskimo groups formed a wedge between the Aleuts and their Indian neighbors: the newcomers occupied a large part of the Alaska Peninsula and the coasts and islands to the north and south of it. Island existence turned the Aleuts into excellent sea hunters. In their skin boats they undertook voyages even to the shores of Kamchatka. Quimby writes that it is possible that changes in physical make-up of the Aleuts occurred in consequence of mixing with the population of Kamchatka. Trade relations linked the Aleuts not only with Kamchatka, but also with their neighbors, the southern Eskimos, by means of which Eskimo and Indian influences penetrated. In a later period the southern Eskimos and Aleuts came under the strong influence of the Northwest Coast Indians (whose culture developed from the ancient substratum of a hunting culture, the carriers of which blocked the southern movement of the ancient Aleuts). The geographic location of the Aleuts placed them in an intermediary position in the diffusion of Asiatic and American cultural features along the North Pacific shores of Asia and America. The Eskimos of Bering Strait, according to Quimby's proposition, played an analogous role, but independently of the Aleuts.

On the basis of study of the collections in the Chicago [Field] Museum of Natural History that were obtained from excavations of sites on the southwestern coast of Amaknak Island,[65] Quimby published a number of articles.

Based on material consisting of decorated artifacts from two excavated levels of a site, an earlier and a later one, Quimby concluded that two periods of "prehistoric" art on the Aleutian Islands are distinguishable.[66] In his opinion, decorative art was more highly developed in the earlier period and less so in the later; in character the art of the two periods differed greatly. Moreover, he maintained that one can hardly infer the development from the early form of art to the later one, although some motifs of the early style do appear on later artifacts. The early style is represented by straight, deeply incised lineal marks on the bone harpoon heads and spears; the later stage, by the ornamentation of bone artifacts with drilled dots, compass-engraved circles with dots in the center, rigid spurs, etc.

In Quimby's opinion, the early period of Aleut art is reminiscent of the art of the Dorset culture.[67] Besides that, there exists a similarity with some decorated artifacts of the Kachemak culture from all three periods of its development, especially the second and third.[68] Here Quimby cites the proposition of de Laguna that on the Aleutian Islands, just as in the rest of southwestern Alaska, there existed a pre-Punuk[69] stage of art which was similar to the Dorset one.[70] The later period of Aleut art, however, recalls to mind the developed Punuk and contemporary Eskimo art.

Thus, Quimby draws the conclusion that there is a relationship between the early Aleut and Dorset cultures, and also that there is a commonality between Dorset culture and the ancient cultures of southwestern Alaska.

In his article about toggle harpoon heads, Quimby shows that the collection from Amaknak Island illustrates two main styles of Aleut toggle harpoons, each of which characterizes a particular cultural period.[71] The heads of the early period have a bed for the blades, while the heads of the later period are slotted. Quimby indicates that the styles of Aleut toggle harpoon heads are very specific: as a whole, they can be included in the southern Alaskan type along with the toggle harpoon heads from Kodiak Island and the shores of Kachemak Bay. However, writes Quimby, the toggle-type harpoon head apparently was not fundamental to the Aleutian Islands where various types of long, barbed bone points had a wider distribution.

In an article about pottery on the Aleutian Islands, Quimby notes that, according to available historical information and evidence from previous archaeological excavations, the Aleuts had no pottery (except in cases when they built up the sides of their stone pans or griddles with clay).[72] However, according to material consisting of thirty shards collected on Amaknak Island, it is possible to speak of the existence of pottery among the Aleuts. The majority of the samples are so crudely and abundantly mixed with sand and stone particles that it is difficult to distinguish them from stone. For this reason, writes Quimby, and also by reason of their resemblance to stone vessels, the previous investigators did not distinguish the Aleut pottery articles from stone vessels. An analysis of the material and character of the vessels' surface (finger-like imprints were found) indicates that they are, after all, pottery.[i] Not a single sample is decorated. Quimby believes that the pottery from

---

i. But see the discussion of A. P. McCartney's work on this question, pp. 61–62, below. The question of the existence of pottery in the Aleutians is still debated—W. W. and L. B.

Amaknak Island is similar to that of Kachemak Bay,[73] but on the whole it has a unique style not related to the other well-known pottery styles of Alaska.[j] In the early period, in Quimby's opinion, there was no pottery; apparently, it appeared at the beginning of the late period and has as its prototype the stone pots or griddle-pans already mentioned.

Quimby dates the later period by stone lamps which were in use in Kamchatka and on the Aleutian Islands.[74] In this, he bases himself on the thesis that there were cultural ties between southern Alaska, the Aleutian Islands, Kamchatka and the Kuril Islands.[75] Quimby subscribes to Collins's hypothesis that the given form of lamps spread from the Aleutian Islands to Kamchatka. During his excavations on Kamchatka, Iokhel'son was finding such lamps in dwellings in association with twelfth-century Japanese coins. As those lamps in collections from Amaknak Island are found only in the later period, Quimby dates this period to the time after the twelfth century and up to 1721, and dates the early period to prior to the twelfth century.

Two articles on Aleut art by S. V. Ivanov are devoted to wooden hunting headgear and sculptural representations of man. These are based on study of the ethnographic collections of the museums of Moscow and Leningrad. The author came to a set of interesting conclusions about the place occupied by Aleut art among the artistic works of the Paleo-Asiatics and Indians.

In the article about Aleut hunting headgear, Ivanov speaks of the amazing similarity of the wooden hunting headgear of the Aleuts and western Eskimos with the zoomorphic masks of the Tlingits.[76] Aleut headgear, he notes, bears within itself the traces of very distant ties with the Indian zoomorphic prototypes; this could be explained by great territorial division and weakening of earlier close contacts between the Aleuts and the Indians. In addition, among the Aleuts and the Northwest Coast Indians, deep roots are found in the common tradition of marking the headgear of chiefs with a conical (and cylindrical) top. Common to many Indian tribes from Alaska to Peru is the "thunderbird" motif, an image of which, in the form of a large eagle holding in one claw some

---

j. Only two pottery shards were recovered by de Laguna at Kachemak Bay—W. W.

45

sort of animal and in the other a man, appeared on one Aleut hat. The polychromatic painting of Aleut headgear also brings it closer to Indian art.

An analysis of the decorations of the headgear, however, revealed features of an Eskimo character. Ivanov was inclined to attribute this to a much later cultural manifestation, and to connect it with the bone-carving art of the Paleo-Asiatics of the Pacific coast and with the geometric ornamentation of the Eskimos.

In an article about seated human figurines in the sculpture of the Aleuts, Ivanov notes that the squatting pose of a human appears rela-tively rarely in the sculpture of the Eskimos and the Paleo-Asiatics of Northeast Asia.[77] At the same time, it constitutes one of the character-istic features (having deep tradition) of the art of the northwest coast of North America. Ivanov explains the mixed character of Aleut art by the Aleut inheritance of their art forms from the more ancient inhabitants of the islands (these are the "pre-Aleuts" of the Hrdlička hypothesis). And, the author expresses the supposition that, in the character of the "pre-Aleut" population, both the most ancient features and the latest elements which appeared under the influence of the Indian culture of the north-west coast of North America were possibly preserved.

Ivanov's conclusions about the common features of the cultures of the Aleuts and Indians appear even more interesting in light of the data of the latest archaeological and anthropological investigations, accord-ing to which Hrdlička's "pre-Aleuts" and "Aleuts" are one and the same people.

The question of the origin of the Aleuts was also raised by L. S. Berg.[78] Analyzing the materials of early reports about the culture of the Aleuts and the existing hypotheses about their origin, he particularly focused on the Aleut ceremonial staff, represented on one of the manuscript charts by Waxell and described by Bering's companions. Such staffs, with the wings or the skin of a falcon on the top, were thrown to the Russians by the Aleuts during their first meeting on the sea (the Aleuts apparently took the Russians for spirits). Similar ceremonial staffs or calumets,[k] adorned with feathers, bird skins, or bird heads, were

---

k. A calumet was a special type of tobacco pipe used by Indians of the eastern woodlands and the Great Plains. The term is not used in northwestern North America—W. W.

characteristic of the Indians. Berg considered that if ceremonial staffs, resembling calumets, were proven to exist among the Aleuts and Eskimos, then the primordial residence of those peoples should be sought on the continent of America (in the region now occupied by Tlingit or somewhere in western Canada).

* * *

After the end of the Second World War, a stage of particularly intensive archaeological and anthropological study of the Aleuts by American scholars began. The main excavations on the Aleutian Islands were conducted by archaeological-anthropological expeditions headed by W. S. Laughlin, with incorporation of a great number of specialists.

At the same time, Soviet archaeologists and anthropologists carried on their investigations in the Far East, along the shores of the Sea of Okhotsk, Sakhalin Island, Kamchatka, Chukotka, and on the Kuril Islands. A whole series of works by Soviet archaeologists, anthropologists, and ethnographers, although not directly devoted to Aleuts, touched on questions of their ethnic history, contributing greatly to the study of this problem.

In 1953 A. Spaulding, characterizing the contemporary state of archaeological studies of the Aleuts, underlined the fact that the geographical location and the ecological conditions of the Aleutian Islands have special significance for solving the problem of the early history of the Eskimos.[79] He thought that the Aleutian Islands were populated by tribes from the Alaska Peninsula who had already formed a maritime way of life and who knew how to overcome considerable expanses of water, that is, people of Eskimo culture with all of its characteristic features: the technique of hunting sea mammals, skin boats, oil lamps, and probably sod-covered dwellings. According to Spaulding, the most ancient archaeological dates for the Aleutian Islands presuppose the existence of an even more ancient date for the Eskimo culture in Alaska. Assuming the settlement of the islands in the very distant past, Spaulding hoped that many features of the earliest Eskimoan coastal culture would be presented here in the least altered condition due to the limiting natural environment and few possibilities of contact with the mainland. But, ethnographic data give cause to assume the origin of some cultural elements directly from Asia, namely from Kamchatka and the Kuril Islands. However, writes Spaulding, this seems incredible for geographic reasons.

47

As to the history of the archaeological study of the Aleutian Islands, Spaulding values the works of Iokhel'son most highly, believing that his basic conclusions are not likely to be disproved. He places great hope in future archaeological investigations of the Aleutian Islands, noting the considerable success of work begun under the leadership of Laughlin.

Spaulding directed the group (which included W. R. Hart and H. A. Miller) conducting the archaeological investigation on Agattu Island in 1948–1961, part of the expedition to the Aleutian Islands sponsored by the University of Michigan.[80] The expedition excavated an ancient site on Krugloi Point on the southwest [*sic*; northeast] side of the island. By the radiocarbon method, the oldest date for the site was determined to be 615 B.C. Comparing this date with the age of the Chaluka site—1,000 B.C. determined in 1951 by Laughlin and Marsh—Spaulding assumes that it took approximately 500 years for the first inhabitants to reach the Near Islands from Umnak Island.

The author notes that comparative material from Agattu Island is scanty. There are only the materials of Hrdlička's excavations of the three sites near McDonald Cove to the southwest of Krugloi Point. Hrdlička noted the basic similarity between the artifacts from Agattu Island and from the Aleutian Islands in general, but noted distinctive features of stone implements and the scarcity of bone implements in the site.

Materials from the Krugloi Point site gave Spaulding the basis for the conclusion that there is a small array of artifact types there, especially those of bone. Especially characteristic was the absence of toggle harpoons, composite fishhooks, tanged stone knives, harpoon socket pieces, and polished stone lamps.

Taking into consideration Hrdlička's observations about the materials from McDonald Cove, Spaulding expresses the opinion that the specificity of the tool inventory from the Krugloi Point site appears to be the result of the settlement of Agattu Island by early Aleut groups from the Umnak region which is located at the opposite end of the chain. These groups brought with them simple archaic implements and preserved them, being in a comparatively isolated condition for more than a thousand years. The character of the Agattu Island industry supports the hypothesis that the main stream of diffusion went from the Alaska Peninsula to the west.

T. P. Bank II, a participant in the same University of Michigan expedition, conducted investigations on Unalaska and Amaknak, and also investigated the sites of ancient settlements on the islands of Tanaga, Adak, Atka and Umnak and burial caves of the islands of Kagamil, Kanaga and Tanaga.[81] Bank expresses the hypothesis that considerable cultural differences existed within the limits of the Aleut culture as a whole: certain islands or groups of islands apparently had local centers of cultural development which influenced each other little because of the considerable geographical isolation of the islands, especially those located at opposite ends of the chain. Bank does not consider it possible to speak of a second wave of the peopling of the islands, despite the apparent physical differences in the population ("pre-Aleuts" and "Aleuts" according to Hrdlička, "Paleo-Aleuts" and "Neo-Aleuts" according to Laughlin). He thinks that the Aleutian Islands were settled by a single population. Then, in the course of three thousand years or more of life on the islands, the Aleuts underwent physical, cultural, and linguistic differentiation. In addition, the complete isolation of the western part of the chain and the possibility of mixing with the mainland groups in the eastern part should be taken into consideration.

Concerning the origin of the Aleuts, Bank subscribes to the view that the Aleuts are the westernmost and southernmost Eskimos, and that it is possible that they also retain the culture of the very ancient Eskimos. But, he does not exclude the possibility of direct contact of the Aleuts with Kamchatka from the earliest times.[82]

Considerable merit in working out the problem of the early history of the Aleuts belongs to the contemporary American scholar, anthropologist, and archaeologist W. S. Laughlin. He began his study of the Aleuts while still a student, taking part in the expedition headed by Hrdlička. He continued the study of a range of problems pertaining to the early history of the Aleuts and Eskimos, the ancient routes of their migration to Alaska, and the ancient cultures of the northern part of the Pacific coast.

From 1948, Laughlin directed field investigations on the Aleutian Islands, carrying them out jointly with anthropologists, archaeologists, ethnographers, linguists, biologists, and geologists.

The excavations of the ancient settlement of Chaluka, discovered by Hrdlička in 1938 on the southwest end of Umnak Island, had special significance for the questions under investigation. Laughlin's and May's discovery and subsequent study of the Anangula site on the island of the same name had particular importance not only for the resolution of questions of the early history of the Aleuts, but also for the ethnic history of the entire North Pacific horizon and for resolution of the question of the settlement of America.

Laughlin did not immediately come to the final conclusions presented in his later works; in the course of many years he analyzed ever newer materials from the investigated area. In his works he also takes into account the achievements of the Soviet anthropological school (G. F. Debets, M. G. Levin). In the very first of his works, Laughlin already advances the thesis that Eskimos provide an excellent example of polymorphism, with major east-west gradations and with many local variants.[83] The basic Eskimo families [groupings] were isolated by Hrdlička, but he did not assign the Aleuts directly either to the Eskimos or to the Indians. Laughlin comes to the conclusion that it is possible to consider the Aleuts to be a morphological variant of the Eskimo. The polymorphism of the Eskimos, expressed primarily in head form, coexists with a basic similarity in blood groups. But the main morphological features, Laughlin thinks, also indicate a close relationship between the Aleuts and Eskimos. Brachycephaly and the low head height of the Aleuts, in his opinion, should not differ greatly from the indices of the neighboring group of Eskimos. The majority of the Eskimos living in the western part of Alaska are brachycephalic. Brachycephaly distinguishes them from the long-headed eastern Eskimo, who were earlier considered the classic type (and with whom the previous investigators compared the Aleuts). And indeed, a comparative anthropometric study of the Aleuts and Eskimos of Bristol Bay showed no significant differences between them. It was ascertained that series of indices of the Eskimo head form follow a gradient from the comparatively long-headed Eskimos of Greenland and the Arctic Ocean [coast] to the more round-headed Eskimos of the Bering Sea coast and the extremely round-headed Aleuts of the eastern islands of the Aleutian chain and the southern coast of Alaska. Laughlin and Marsh reject the presence of an Indian admixture among the Aleuts as a determinant for their round-headedness.[84]

Laughlin also questions the reason for the appearance of two groups of Aleuts, the eastern and the western. He critically evaluates Hrdlička's conclusion concerning two successive stages in the settlement of the Aleutian Islands by "pre-Aleuts" and "Aleuts," and does not consider them representatives of different peoples. He views the eastern and western Aleuts as two branches ("isolates") of one and the same people. Consequently, it was recognized as more advisable to call the "pre-Aleuts" of Hrdlička "Paleo-Aleuts," and the "Aleuts" "Neo-Aleuts."

Archaeological material from the Chaluka site, argues Laughlin, demonstrated that among the Aleuts a maritime culture existed from the beginning of the settlement of the islands (more than four thousand years ago).

In his 1952 publication, Laughlin notes that the significance of the problem of the [biological] anthropology of the Aleuts and the Eskimos of southern Alaska becomes all the more timely in connection with the hypothesis advanced in recent years that the southwestern part of Alaska was the homeland of the Eskimos.[85] One can also expect, Laughlin thinks, that some common features of the Eskimos and the Indians have their origin within the earliest and numerous Proto-Aleut-Eskimos.

Considering the antiquity and variability of the material culture of the Aleuts,[86] Laughlin points out that the great number of local variants of the Eskimos and Aleuts greatly hampered a determination whether the Aleuts were a people of Eskimo stock. Although as a whole the Aleut culture was considerably uniform through time, the excavations at Chaluka evidenced a large number of synchronous styles, while ethnographic material even illustrates individuality in the manufacturing of separate items. But, as already indicated, the excavations on Anangula Island had even greater significance than the investigation of Chaluka. Ancient implements were found on that island already in 1938, during Hrdlička's third expedition to the Aleutian Islands. A brief report about this was published by Laughlin in 1951.[87] In 1952, Laughlin returned to investigations on Anangula. Lamellar flakes, polyhedral cores, and chipped tools were collected there. In 1954, Laughlin and Marsh published these materials and their preliminary conclusions.[88] Since a large number of preforms were found at the site, the authors came to the conclusion that this was a workshop and not a place of settlement, but later they discarded this assumption. The true significance of Anangula was revealed only after its sensational dating (see below, p. 54).

In 1956, in his presentation at the Thirty-Second Congress of Americanists, Laughlin stressed that the "Aleutian Problem" contains within itself a number of important questions: the direction of population movement, population composition, the change and variability of the population and its culture, and the connections between separate groups of population ("isolates") and their culture.[89] Laughlin noted that changes occurring in the culture of the Aleuts since the settlement of the islands are reflected in consecutive levels of the Chaluka site. These include changes in manufacturing technique, in form or style, and in the relative quantity of different objects. But, all the main categories of implements, such as boats, lamps, toggle harpoon heads, etc., apparently were present at all times. Laughlin's conclusion that an increase in brachycephaly is a common tendency in many Eskimo groups that may readily be traced among western Alaskan populations, is important.

In 1961, Laughlin and Reeder published a paper in which they outlined the methodological principles used by them in their study of the problems of the early history of the population of southern Alaska and the Aleutian Islands.[90] In the course of their investigations they took into account evolutionary changes connected with development of the substantial physical differences that set apart the earliest populations of southern Alaska, the Paleo-Aleuts and Paleo-Koniags, from the later Neo-Aleuts and Neo-Koniags. Great attention was devoted to ecological investigations. Ancient archaeological sites with good stratigraphy make it possible to describe the relationships between the most important game animals, other food sources, and people within this subarctic ecosystem. [The authors note that] the combination of such sciences as [physical] anthropology, archaeology, botany, zoology, and geology is necessary for site analysis.

In a brief report about continued excavations at the Chaluka site, Laughlin stated in 1961 that among other interesting finds, the remains of a dwelling in the form of a stone circle were found.[91] By radiocarbon analysis, the age of the new finds was determined to be 2,000 B.C.

The new materials and the new dating allowed the formulation of a number of supplementary conclusions.[92] The long-headed Paleo-Aleuts, according to Laughlin, reveal some similarity with the Ipiutak people of Point Hope, described by G. F. Debets,[93] and with the Paleo-Koniags. But a series of skeletal finds from the lower levels of Chaluka represents the most ancient unquestionable Mongoloids, not counting the Chinese finds. Consequently, in order to arrive at definite conclusions, knowledge of the laws of evolution in the development of anthropological types and the antiquity of the Mongoloid type is necessary. The authors now pose the question: were the early Aleuts (Paleo-Aleuts) pushed out by the Neo-Aleuts, or did the Paleo-Aleuts develop into the Neo-Aleuts as a result of evolution? A sufficiently long period of time, they feel, is an indicator of the possibility of evolution.

Examining the origin of the Eskimo-Aleut stock, Laughlin takes into consideration much data pertaining to this question (from L. H. Morgan and F. Boas to G. F. Debets, I. V. Jorgenson, B. Chown, M. G. Levin and others).[94] He closely connects the Eskimo-Aleut problem with the settlement of America, with the Indians, and with the process of race formation.

Laughlin points out the great significance of ecological conditions, and of certain cultural achievements that determine economics, for the evolution and dispersal of the Eskimos. Simultaneously, he raises a very interesting question about the relationship of the Indians and the Es- kimo-Aleuts.[95] He emphasizes the fact that the Eskimos and Aleuts have closer racial kinship with Asiatic Mongoloids than with Indians. The difference between the Eskimos and the Indians is so great that it allows assumption of the very great antiquity of their divergence. But that distinction could not be earlier than 4,000 to 6,000 years ago, and besides that, it is possible that formerly the Proto-Eskimo-Aleuts were, at some time, in contact with the Proto-Wakashan peoples.

Defining the skeletal characteristics of the early Aleuts (Paleo- Aleuts), Laughlin notes their great difference from the central and eastern Eskimo types, but some commonality with Ipiutak peoples and Paleo-Koniags.[96] The relationship to the Alaska Indians is still unclear because of the scarcity of finds of skeletal remains of the Tlingits and Athabaskans. It is possible, writes Laughlin, that very early Aleuts and Koniags, as well as other early southern and western Eskimos, will reveal more similarities with the early Indians than later inhabitants of these territories (if the early Aleuts and Koniags really reflect the beginning or partial differentiation between the Mongoloid Eskimo- Aleut branch and the Indians). In other words, it is likely that the existing difference has increased with time, but this question requires further investigation.

Laughlin dwells on the question that the Eskimos and Aleuts present us with the only opportunity for the study of microevolution in population history from the point of view of genetics and biological and cultural adaptation.[97] The conditions for this are the antiquity of the population, the presence of evolutionary changes in the successive groups, and the presence of variations conditioned by the distribution of this population along the long coastline. Such a study is possible thanks to the availability of a stratified site such as Chaluka, rich in manufactured articles and faunal and human skeletal remains. Besides that, blood-group studies of contemporary individuals secured the conclusion concerning the basic similarity of the whole Eskimo-Aleut stock and its difference from the Indian one (although such an indicator as the commonality of the rare blood group N unites both the Eskimo-Aleuts and the Indians). Linguistic diversity and, at the same time, the internal unity of the Eskimo-Aleut stock also provide valuable data on which conclusions may be based.

However, the most important event in the history of the study of the "Aleutian Problem" and the entire early history of the peoples of the North Pacific basin was the determination of the age of the Anangula site, which, on the basis of stratigraphic investigation, proved to be not a workshop, but the location of a settlement of ancient man. Three dates indicating the ancient age of this site were obtained as a result of radiocarbon analysis of materials from the excavation of 1962: 8,425 ±275, 7,990 ±230, and 7,660 ±300 years B.P.[1] The presence of a large number of stone tools at the site illustrates the richness of the stone industry and provides valuable comparative material (although skeletons and fauna are absent here). A new picture of the ethnic history of Alaska and its adjacent territories and the history of the settling of America, Laughlin explains, arises in connection with such a dating of the Anangula site and the results of the latest geological investigations, which establish the existence in ancient times (in the Pleistocene period) of a land bridge from Asia to America—the Bering Sea platform—in part of the present Bering Sea. The investigations of R. F. Black, who is engaged in the geological study of this area, determined that 8,000 years ago Anangula Island and Umnak Island formed a single territory, and that 12,000 years ago Umnak Island was part of the American continent and represented the edge of the Alaska Peninsula and the southern corner of ancient Beringia connecting Asia with America.

_l._ See note _f._ in Introduction—L. B.

Laughlin thinks that the early migrants from Asia passed along the southern edge of the platform and reached the rich hunting territories without losing contact with the sea which provided them with food resources. The islands of St. Lawrence, Nunivak, and the Pribilofs, like Umnak and Anangula, are, according to this new hypothesis, the remains of high hills on this now flooded platform.

Simultaneously, a comparison of finds from Anangula and Chaluka permitted Laughlin to conclude that the artifacts from the lower levels of Chaluka are approximately of the same kind as those of Anangula, that is, continuity [succession] exists between them. It follows that the Anangula inventory represents the technology of a people of a maritime culture similar to that of the Paleo-Aleuts of 4,000 years ago—the long-headed Mongoloid group.

The Anangula industry, in the opinions of Laughlin and Japanese archaeologist M. Yoshizaki (with whom he investigated the settlement in 1962–1963), resembles the stone industry of Japan and Siberia in the eleventh to seventh millennia B.C., namely, the microlithic industry of Sakkotsu on the island of Hokkaido, the implements of the Araya site on the island of Honshu, and the Budun site in Siberia. The Anangula industry is defined as more Asiatic in appearance than implements of the so-called microlithic Arctic tradition [Arctic Small Tool tradition] of which an early representative is the Denbigh Flint complex.

The Chaluka site represents Aleut habitation of 4,000 years' duration. Here well-stratified human skeletons, hunting implements, remains of dwellings, fauna, etc., were well preserved. By a comparison of the various levels of Chaluka, it became clear that change occurred in the styles of implements and other articles of everyday use and that these levels were associated with the skeletal remains first of the Paleo-Aleuts and then of the Neo-Aleuts. Just the same, the character of the site as a whole in the course of those 4,000 years shows amazing stability: there is no indication of noticeable changes in the way of life of its inhabitants or in the character of utilization of the natural environment. This allowed Laughlin to conclude that, apparently, there were no new migrations (of Neo-Aleuts), but only internal changes which took place in both the cultural sphere and in the physical type of the inhabitants.

In this way, contrary to Hrdlička's hypothesis of two successive waves of diverse populations, Laughlin and Marsh advance the theory of the evolution of the Paleo-Aleuts (Hrdlička's "pre-Aleuts") into the Neo-Aleuts (Hrdlička's "Aleuts").

Based on the materials from the Anangula site, Laughlin draws a picture of the direct (not through Alaska) settling of the New World from Asia by the Eskimos and Aleuts. The Bering Sea platform was inhabited by contiguous "isolates," stretching from the island of Hokkaido to the location of the present island of Umnak, probably from 10,000 to 15,000 years ago. On the Bering Sea platform in the region of Umnak Island there were very favorable conditions for the flourishing of the maritime cultures of the early Mongoloid groups thanks to the abundance of marine fauna. Since deglaciation proceeded from west to east, the population spread in two directions: following the receding ice eastward and proceeding in boats to the western Aleutian Islands. Laughlin believes that, after establishment of the contemporary coastlines, the principal migrations ended.

The age of the earliest known Aleutian skeletons is about 4,000 years. The early skeletons from Kodiak are a little younger and are easily distinguished from the Aleutian ones. The populations of these regions do not become more similar, but undergo some parallel changes.

Laughlin thinks that the Mongoloids are the result of comparably recent evolutionary development which took place during the last 15,000 years, and that the sources of their evolution were connected with the mid-Pleistocene Sinanthropus species.

In 1964, Laughlin and Black, on the basis of geological evidence, moved the dates of the Anangula site from 8,000 back to 12,000 years.[m] The authors write that the stone industry of Anangula (lamellar flake industry) survived to our day thanks to a unique combination of geological factors which preserved this site.[98] It is possible that ancient sites belonging to the inhabitants of the Bering Sea platform edge—peoples with a maritime culture orientation—are now under many meters of water. That these were people with a culture oriented to the sea is witnessed by the site on the island of Anangula. This is the most ancient site on the Alaskan Bering Sea coast. Its Asiatic origin is not subject to challenge. The possibility of finding cultures older than Anangula in

m. The 12,000-year date for Anangula was an error. A date of 8,000 years is now generally accepted—W. W.

that region is unlikely. Rising sea level flooded the majority of the earlier sites and the erosion of seashores caused further devastation. The last glacial advance in Alaska erased the traces of ancient man here. The only area on the Alaskan Bering Sea coast where a site older than Anangula may be found is the eastern Aleutian Islands.

An entire issue of *Arctic Anthropology*, edited by W. S. Laughlin and W. G. Reeder, was devoted to the results of the study of the early history of the Aleuts, and also of the Koniags ("Aleutian-Kodiak Prehistory").[99]

On the basis of the latest data, the first article in this issue summarized the geological history of the Bering Sea coast of Alaska in the epoch of the settling of America by man.[100]

In the section "Aleutian Studies," articles were presented which thoroughly analyzed materials from the excavations of the Anangula, Chaluka and Port Moller sites.

In the article by A. P. McCartney and C. G. Turner II, an analysis of Anangula is presented: its location, the results of the excavations of the years 1952, 1962, and 1963, the succession of layers of deposited volcanic ash, the results of radiocarbon analysis, and the basis of the economy of its inhabitants.[101] The authors conclude that the age of the site exceeds 8,000 years. The thin cultural zone and the uniformity of implements are evidence that people lived on that cape for a comparatively short time. They [the authors] see on Anangula the remains of early groups of hunters and gatherers inhabiting the Bering Sea platform who do not display a similarity with the cultural complexes and traditions of Alaska and the New World.

In the article by W. S. Laughlin and J. S. Aigner, an analysis is given of the stone industry of Anangula.[102]

The materials from the Chaluka site are examined in three articles. In J. S. Aigner's article, the bone implements obtained during the excavation of 1962 ("trench A") are analyzed and the decorative motifs found at Chaluka are investigated.[103] The bone implements, represented in the materials from the excavations by hunting equipment (compound fishhooks, spearheads, harpoon socket pieces, harpoon heads) and by work implements (awls and needles, wedges for splitting wood and bone, ocher grinders, etc.) are presented in accordance with the four stratigraphic units of the site and classified by type. The items of personal adornment (labrets and pendants) are also listed with an indication of the site stratigraphic units and by type. These materials allowed [Aigner] to trace changes in the economics of the Aleuts and in artistic styles through four stratigraphic units of the site dated 1,700–1,300 B.C. (unit IV), 1,200–1,100 B.C. (unit III), 1,100–700 B.C. (unit II), and 700 B.C. to A.D. 500 (unit I). It is noted that the styles of Chaluka's artifacts, even those from the earliest periods, basically differ from the styles of artifacts from Kodiak Island and the Alaska Peninsula.

G. B. Denniston's article about the cultural changes at Chaluka are also based on the materials from the excavations of 1962 ("trench A").[104] The author isolates seven levels and three cultural strata in the site— Lower Chaluka (levels VII–V), Middle Chaluka (levels IV–III) and Upper Chaluka (levels II–I). Based on an analysis of excavated dwellings and stone tools, she concludes that the most abrupt cultural change at Chaluka falls in the interval between levels III and II (between Middle and Upper Chaluka), while the other levels show a more stable development of the fundamental stone industry tradition.

An article by L. K. Lippold is devoted to the economic structure of the ancient Aleuts as it appears according to the excavations at Chaluka.[105] In it the author notes that Chaluka represents the stable coastal adaptation of hunter and gatherer groups.

W. B. Workman's article about excavation of the Port Moller site (on the southwest part of the Alaska Peninsula)[n] opens up an interesting question about the place of this site in the early history of southwestern Alaska.[106] Contrary to opinions that it belongs to the ancestors of Eskimo-Aglegmiuts or to a variant of the ancient culture of Cook Inlet (Kachemak III), the author, based on a large amount of material from recent excavations, is inclined to define the culture of this site as Aleut.[o] In that way the extent of the ancient settling of Aleuts on the Alaska Peninsula up to Port Moller is established. The age of the site—2,500–

---

n. There have been a number of Japanese excavations at Port Moller since Workman's paper of 1966. They are published in a series of preliminary reports by H. and Atsuko Okada and others—W. W.

o. A. P. McCartney disagrees with Workman's position that Port Moller was Aleut. See his paper "Prehistoric Aleut influences at Port Moller," *Anthropological Papers of the University of Alaska* 14, no. 2 (1969), pp. 1–16—W. W.

3,000 B.C.—allows one to consider it in line with the ancient cultures of southwestern Alaska and the Aleutian Islands.

Laughlin's article, in which he determines two skulls from Port Moller to be Paleo-Aleut, is a confirmation of Workman's position, that is, characterization of the Port Moller site as being Aleut.[107]

Laughlin's article about the ancient migrations of man and the settling of the Bering Sea area was published in 1967 in the collection *The Bering Land Bridge*, devoted on the whole to the geological substantiation of the existence of the Bering Land Bridge in the Pleistocene.[108]

Acknowledgment of the circumstance, writes Laughlin, that the eastern Aleutian Islands were formerly a part of the Bering Land Bridge and that the Aleuts living there are the descendants of the first inhabitants of that strip of dry land, presents valuable information for the understanding of the origin of the Mongoloids of the Bering Sea and of the American Indians. The Bering Land Bridge was a huge territory, stretching from south to north for 1,500 kilometers. The southern coastal region was quite unlike the inland regions ecologically, and on this basis the difference arose between the coastal tribes and the tribes of hunters of the inland territories.

According to Laughlin, the ancestors of the Aleuts and Eskimos as well as, possibly, the ancestors of the Chukchi, Koriak, and Kamchadal, were permanent settlers of the coastal edge of the bridge, and the ancient Indians inhabited its interior. The closer connection of the Aleuts and Eskimos with the Asiatic Bering Sea Mongoloids (the Chukchi, Koriak, and Kamchadal) than with American Indians, Laughlin explains by their coastal (ancestors of the Aleuts and Eskimos) and inland (ancestors of the Indians) adaptations on the Bering Sea platform. Thus, the difference between the Aleuts and Eskimos on the one hand, and the Indians on the other, Laughlin is inclined to explain by their ecological differentiation and not by different times of migrations. In discussing the conditions of life in the interior of the bridge and along its southern coast, Laughlin notes more favorable conditions in the coastal zone thanks to the broad opportunities of food gathering on the seashore, apart from hunting and fishing. Laughlin explains the long duration of the occupancy of that region (over 8,000 years) by the special position of the given territory which was an "ecological magnet" for sea mammals and for people as well.

59

The Anangula site, being more similar to ancient Asiatic cultures than to the cultures of Alaska, points directly to coastal migrations from Asia. And, there is evidence of succession between Anangula and Chaluka: the similarity of the stone industry, the proximity of those two territories (prior to their separation by the strait, a short land route [lay between them]), and the lack of possibilities of invasion from the outside (the contiguous Kodiak area, according to existing data, was settled not earlier than 5,000 years ago).[p]

The Chaluka site begins with a considerably developed coastal culture, which presupposes a long previous period of adaptation in that area. Its subsequent levels demonstrate a change in styles, but preservation of the fundamental way of life. The upper level of Chaluka illustrates the transition to the culture of the present-day Aleuts, and to this day the Aleuts, inhabitants of the Nikolski settlement, occupy part of the Chaluka mound. And thus, Laughlin considers the contemporary Aleuts to be the descendants of the peoples of the ancient Bering Land Bridge. The ancestors of the Eskimos, on the other hand, were compelled to migrate into the more severe regions of the Arctic, and the ancestors of the Indians settled the entire American continent. Laughlin emphasizes that this hypothesis still requires a considerable amount of additional evidence, which could be provided by new early sites and skeletal materials.

The works of D. E. Dumond, dedicated to the early history of the inhabitants of Alaska, and especially to the archaeological study of the northeastern part of the Alaska Peninsula, throw light on questions of the origin of the Aleuts.

In one of his articles, Dumond examines the classification of Eskaleut [Eskimo-Aleut] peoples on the basis of linguistic principle, using the data of lexicostatistical analysis for determining the time of divergence of the separate languages.[109] He compares that classification with archaeological data.[q]

---

p. Ocean Bay I on Kodiak is at least 6,000 years old. There is one date, as yet unpublished, of over 7,000 years—W. W.

q. See the second edition of Dumond's *Eskimos and Aleuts* (New York: Thames and Hudson, 1987) for his more recent thinking on language relationships—W. W.

In his opinion, the region where it is possible to search for the common linguistic ancestors of the Aleuts and Eskimos is restricted to the Aleutian Islands and southern Alaska. And this, apparently, was the time between 6,000 and 4,000 B.C.

Further, Dumond proposes the following hypothesis. Peoples who spoke the Proto-Eskimo-Aleut language lived before 4,000 B.C. and were related to the peoples whose cultural remains are found on Anangula Island. On one side, they were ancestors of the bearers of the Arctic Small Tool tradition, and on the other, ancestors of the Chaluka people and the contemporary Aleuts. The Arctic Small Tool tradition appeared after the separation of the Eskimo-Aleuts into the Eskimos and the Aleuts. And the industry of Anangula, according to him, could be in some measure the ancestor of the Arctic Small Tool tradition. The bearers of the latter were the first clearly identifiable Eskimos, both linguistically and by adaptation to the cold sea coasts.

Investigations of the ancient sites in the Naknek and Brooks river system and on the shore of Kukak Bay, on the Pacific Ocean, resulted in material which allowed definition of the limit of the spread of Paleo-Aleut culture to the Alaska Peninsula and its mutual ties with neighboring cultures.[110] In particular, on the basis of the comparison of two collections—the Takli Alder site on Takli Island on the Pacific coast of the Alaska Peninsula, dated to 4,000–3,000 B.C., and the Krugloi Point site on Agattu Island (in the Near Island group [of the Aleutian archipelago]), dated to 600 B.C.—Dumond arrives at a number of conclusions. He establishes the similarity of the stone inventory of these two sites on the basis of many diagnostic features: [relative] proportions of the main classes of implements and the specific similarity of the knives, projectile blades and spear blade tangs. The Krugloi Point site is considered by him (following Spaulding) to be the most peripheral of the Paleo-Aleut cultures and the most archaic. Because of the temporal break, those sites cannot be considered as having a single ancestor. But based on material from excavations on the Pacific coast of Alaska, Dumond comes to the conclusion that about 4,000 B.C., the territories along the Pacific coast of the Alaska Peninsula to Kukak Bay were settled by the ancestors of the Aleuts. He writes that it still is not known whether this people originated from Anangula.

In his 1970 article, A. P. McCartney again (after Quimby) turns to the question of whether pottery existed on the Aleutian Islands.[111] For that he turns (as did Quimby) to the collections of A. R. Cahn from Amaknak Island. This second study (enlisting the service of specialist geologists) of the collections' fragments of vessels for the preparing and preserving of food determined that they were carved from a tufa-like volcanic substance, and not fashioned from clay. Thus, the assumptions of Dall and Iokhel'son about the absence of pottery among the Aleuts received another corroboration, and the Aleutian archipelago again was recognized as an area of aceramic culture, while pottery existed among the contemporary neighboring Eskimo groups (of southern and southwestern Alaska).[r] The Port Moller site (the last [easternmost] of the known Aleutian sites on the Alaska Peninsula), which had no articles of pottery, defines the limit of the distribution of pottery on the Alaska Peninsula. The tradition of the production of stone vessels on the Aleutian Islands is traced from the Anangula site as shown by the finds, in 1963, of fragments of stone vessels dated to the sixth and seventh millennia B.C.

The question of the relationship of the archaeological cultures of the eastern and western Aleutian Islands is again raised by McCartney on the basis of more extensive archaeological materials.[112] On the basis of materials from the Near Islands (Attu, Agattu, etc.) excavated by Iokhel'son, Hrdlička, and Spaulding, and surface finds from World War II, he lays the foundation for the view that there is evident in these islands a separate [specific] cultural phase, distinct from the cultures of the central and eastern island groups of the [Aleutian] chain. The author connects the origin (as a result of population movement from the central islands of the chain) and the existence of this phase, which lasted, possibly, from 1000 B.C. to A.D. 1000 or much later, with the specific geographic isolation of the [Near] islands: their extreme western position in the chain and, in addition, their distance (the greatest in the archipelago) from the nearest island group (the Rat Islands) [to the east]. Contrary to Spaulding and Dumond, McCartney does not define the character of the implements of the Near Islands as having become

---

r. There is pottery allegedly from Shemya at the University of Pennsylvania Museum, but this material has not been examined by McCartney—L. B. Pottery has since been found by McCartney at Izembek Lagoon. See M. Yarborough, "Analysis of pottery from the western Alaska Peninsula," *Anthropological Papers of the University of Alaska* 16, no. 1 (1974), pp. 85–89— W. W.

simplified and regressive in comparison with the character of the collections from the central and eastern islands. He notes the excellent workmanship manifest in the articles and their distinctive style. McCartney expresses doubt about the validity of Dumond's assumption concerning the similarity of the material from the Takli Alder site with the material from the Krugloi Point site on the Near Islands, and the assertion that the material from Takli Island is ancestral in relation to the material from Krugloi Point. The distinctiveness of the characteristic features of the Near Islands phase McCartney considers to be the result of geographic isolation, and the stylistic drift which resulted from it.

The question of the origin of the Aleuts has been studied in the last several decades by Soviet investigators, primarily not as an independent problem, but as a component part either of the problem of the origin of the northeastern Paleo-Asiatics, or in the context of the Eskimo problem.

G. F. Debets, who distinguished local subgroups within the arctic [biological] race, names Aleut as one of the five defined types.[113] He notes that the problem of the systematization of the Aleut type is very complicated. The similarity of Aleut skulls to those of the Evenk of the Baikal region [Cisbaikalia] and not to the Eskimo skulls, as established by T. Ia. Tokareva, does indeed exist, and Hrdlička "accepted Tokoreva's hypothesis but presented it in a rudimentary [simplistic] metaphysical form." But, Debets does not consider it possible [valid] to take the cranial index as the basis of a classification because [such a practice] would lead to a break with the genetic descent principle. As demonstrated by Debets, the types defined solely on the basis of [cranial] height sometimes form separate "islets" which do not differ from the rest of the types of the given region according to any other important parameter. Such is the Aleut "islet" among the Chukchi and Eskimos. According to the complex of features crucial for the genetic classification of the Mongoloids of northern Asia and the adjacent regions of America, the Aleuts should be, according to Debets, considered members of the arctic race.

Hrdlička's separation of the Aleut skulls into "Aleut" and "pre-Aleut," and the assertion in connection with this that the contemporary Aleuts are not descendants of the ancient inhabitants of the islands, met with a decisive objection from Debets. Changes in cranial indices over time, he writes, are now recorded in all parts of the world without any possibility of considering them the result of migrations. Debets cites M. G. Levin, who, on the basis of the same materials used by Hrdlička, convincingly substantiates the presence of the process of brachycephalization in the northern portion of the Pacific basin as well. Hrdlička's archaeological data indicate complete cultural continuity between the "pre-Aleuts" and the "Aleuts," and, most important, the late age of "pre-Aleut" burials. Hrdlička's postulated migration of the Aleuts from Asia and the ousting of the "pre-Aleuts" would fall about two to three centuries prior to the discovery of the islands by the Russians, in which case it should indubitably be reflected in ethnographic and linguistic data.

Thus, according to Debets, the round form of the cranial vault is not an indication of the ancient separation of the Aleuts from the Eskimos. Instead, it was the result of their insular isolation, as originally proposed by Tokareva.

However, the Aleuts differ from the Eskimos not only in cranial index, but also according to a number of diagnostic cranial features (height of cranial vault, breadth of nose, and facial height). Debets contends that according to these features the "pre-Aleuts" occupy in general an intermediate position between the Eskimos and the Aleuts; as a group, they are transitional from the Eskimo type to the Aleut type. In conditions of isolation, certain features lost their specific "Eskimoid" peculiarities and others, on the contrary, became more pronounced. Such a conception, in Debets's opinion, is in better agreement with ethnographic and linguistic facts than the one proposed by Tokareva and Hrdlička.

Consequently, Debets considers the Aleuts to be a local form [variant, subtype] of the Arctic race, albeit the most divergent one.

Levin's treatment of the problem of the origin of the Eskimos serves as a starting point for the formation of conceptions about the early history of the Aleuts. It is, first, a detailed criticism of hypotheses concerning the origin of the Eskimos as a result of migrations that brought into the Bering Sea region an economic and cultural complex which was formed somewhere else, and the basis for the theory of the formation of the Eskimos and their culture and language as a result of lengthy and complicated processes in the regions adjacent to the Bering Sea. Then [second], it is a definition of the Aleuts as a people anthropologically [biologically] close to the Eskimos. Levin demonstrated the lack of validity of the theories of the "Eskimo wedge" (the tip of which, according to some, is the Aleuts). [These theorists] considered the Eskimos to be migrants either from the forest regions of Canada (Boas, Iokhel'son), or from the islands of southeastern Asia (Rudenko) or from northwestern Siberia (Larsen and Rainey).[114]

A number of theoretical positions worked out by Levin have great significance for the anthropological [biological] study of Aleuts. The [physical] differences in the anthropological types of the Eskimos and Aleuts, established by earlier researchers, contradict their cultural and linguistic closeness. This was the basis for a number of hypotheses about the diverse origins of the Aleuts and Eskimos. Already in 1947, Levin expressed the thought that the shift from the dolichocephalic type to the mesocephalic one was the result of epochal change—a consequence of the process of brachycephalization.[115] This was confirmed by Debets. In assessing the type differences between the individual local Eskimo groups, writes Levin, it is also necessary to take into account that these groups, as a result of their great dissociation, could not escape the effects of prolonged isolation. In the conditions of isolation and very small population numbers that are characteristic of individual Eskimo groups, the processes of intra-group variability work themselves out with particular intensity. Levin noted that Laughlin (1951) came to the same conclusion when he argued the racial unity of the Eskimos, within the limits of which the Aleuts were defined as a group [subgroup] related to the Eskimos.

R. S. Vasil'evskii's investigations of the Old Koriak culture on the basis of the archaeological excavations of 1930–1932 (by M. G. Levin and V. I. Levin), of 1946 (under the supervision of A. P. Okladnikov), of 1955–1956 (Magadan Regional Museum), and of 1958–1961 and 1964 (by Vasil'evskii himself) in the northern part of the Okhotsk seaboard, throw light upon the question of the formation of the cultures of the marine mammal hunters in the northern sector of the Pacific Ocean.[116]

The parallels established by Vasil'evskii between the Old Koriak culture and the Paleo-Aleut culture in a number of categories of implements, and particularly in the bone artifact complex, are of great interest; parallels were also revealed in stone tools. Also, in his opinion, the Old Koriak harpoons (type A) are similar to the Dorset (type II), and the Old Koriak points (type 2) are similar to the points of the Kachemak

I culture. At the same time, Vasil'evskii notes the difference, in many diagnostic specific features, of the Old Koriak culture from the main Eskimo cultures. He concludes that the Old Koriak, Okhotsk Sea, and Paleo-Aleut cultures differ considerably in their basic features from the Eskimo cultures of northeastern Asia, and of northern and northwestern Alaska. On this basis, he defines the North Pacific sphere [horizon] of maritime hunting cultures which encompasses the northern part of Hokkaido, Sakhalin, the Kuril Islands, the Okhotsk seaboard, Kamchatka, the Aleutian Islands, Kodiak Island, and a portion of the coast of southwestern Alaska. The Eskimo cultures of northeastern Asia, northern and northwestern Alaska, he defines as constituting a second sphere of maritime hunting cultures, with the center in the southwestern Alaska area, independent of the first [sphere].

The archaeological excavations carried on in southern Sakhalin in 1953–1955 provided the basis for R. V. Kozyreva (Chubarova) to speak of the similarity of the stone and bone inventory of the ancient cultures of Sakhalin (first millennium B.C.) with the cultures of the Kuril and Aleutian islands and the ancient Eskimo cultures (especially with the Dorset culture). Examining the question of the ethnic identity of the bearers of the ancient cultures of Sakhalin, Kozyreva advanced the hypothesis of a pre-Ainu population, the Tonchi, supposedly ousted by the Ainu to the Aleutian Islands. She characterizes the culture of the Tonchi as coastal and considers it as linking up with the northern Eskimo culture sphere.[117]

Investigations by N. N. Dikov on Kamchatka uncovered multi-layered sites near Ushki Lake—Ushki I, II, and IV—with lower, Pale-olithic layers, the age of which, according to carbon 14, is 14,000 to 15,000 years (at Ushki I, layer VII is the Early Ushki Upper Paleolithic culture) and 11,000 to 13,000 years (Ushki I, II, and IV, where layers V and VI represent Late Ushki Upper Paleolithic culture). The discovery of the Paleolithic on Kamchatka allowed the addition of new essential data to the hypothesis about the routes of the initial settling of America from Asia.[118] Prior to these finds, there was no direct archaeological evidence indicating the territories through which ancient migrations passed from Asia into America.

Dikov points to the similarity of the Paleolithic of Kamchatka with the southern Siberian Late Paleolithic (Afontova Gora II, Krasnyi Iar, Fediaevskaia, Verkholenskaia Gora), and with the Paleolithic of

Mongolia. Further, Dikov perceives in the stone industry of Kamchatka a closeness to the ancient pre-ceramic cultures of Japan. And finally, he notes the considerable technological similarity with some Late Paleolithic and Early Mesolithic complexes in Alaska (Onion Portage, Healy Lake, Anangula, and others). He even speaks of close similarities between lanceolate pressure-flaked and retouched stone points from the upper layers of the Ushki sites, and the American Early Mesolithic points of the Cordilleran sites. The Ushki stemmed points from the lowest layer, in his opinion, are presumably the relics of the most ancient Proto-Indian culture.

From the paleogeographic conditions of that time (Gremaldian regression of the world ocean at the height of the last ice age) Dikov deduces the probable migration route of the cultures ancestral to those of America [to be] from the regions southwest of the Sea of Okhotsk toward the northeast, to Kamchatka and farther via the Bering Land Bridge to America. He does not exclude the possibility of contemporaneous population movement by the northern route.

Dikov sees the sources of Eskimo culture formed already in America, first in the spreading of separate cultural elements from the south, from the direction of Kamchatka, via the Aleutian Islands (second to first millennium B.C.). A later spread of elements of the Eskimo culture, in Dikov's opinion, occurred from the Bering Strait coast (in the middle of the first millennium B.C.) and then, beginning with the second millennium A.D., from Alaska and Canada to the west in the direction of Kolyma.

Dikov sees great significance in the finds on Kamchatka of labrets, which are characteristic of the Aleuts, Eskimos, and Indians of the northwest coast of North America. He cites evidence for the southern origin of these adornments and the transference of the custom of their use to the Aleuts and then to the Eskimos.

Study of the social structure of the Aleuts and of the Eskimos was undertaken by L. A. Fainberg.[119] On the basis of extensive archaeological material concerning the stages of cultural development among the Eskimos and Aleuts, Fainberg concludes that the culture of the Aleuts in the state in which it was found by the Russians, to a larger extent than the culture of the Eskimos of the same time, preserved features of an ancient social organization. Noting among the Aleuts the presence of matrilineal clan [lineage] structure which was, however, in a state of decay, Fainberg concludes that matriliny also existed among the Eskimos in the past. In such a way, Fainberg manages to show that the typical "non-lineal" society of the Eskimos, as it is considered by a majority of bourgeois scholars, opponents of the concept of the unity of the historical process, in reality passed in antiquity through a stage of matrilineal clan structure as did all other peoples of the earth.[s]

I. S. Vdovin raised the problem of the historical-cultural connections of the northeastern Paleo-Asiatics (particularly, the Itel'men and Koriak of the eastern coast of Kamchatka) with the Eskimos and Aleuts. He brings into the discussion a broad spectrum of archaeological and historical evidence, extensive ethnographic material, and linguistic data illustrating the common elements in the culture of the Koriak and Itel'men and [the culture of] the Aleuts. This [cultural] commonality the author considers most likely to be a result of the prolonged direct linkages [contact] between the above-named peoples, which existed on the Pacific coast of Kamchatka. Basing himself on the data from archaeological investigations carried out in the last two decades on the shores of the Sea of Okhotsk, Kamchatka, Sakhalin, and Hokkaido, the author concludes that the ancestors of the Aleuts inhabited the western shores of Hokkaido, the Kuril Islands and undoubtedly the east coast of Kamchatka in the past.[120]

Questions of Eskimo-Aleut linguistic community [commonality] and its relation to other languages were studied by G. A. Menovshchikov.[121] He notes that the history of the settling and mastering of the northeastern border regions of Siberia and the subarctic zone of North America by man is linked to the history (as of yet not completely clear) of the formation and separation of the Eskimo-Aleut linguistic community. The question of the genetic relationship of the Eskimo-Aleut languages with other languages also remains open.

Menovshchikov reconfirms that the origin of the Aleut and Eskimo languages from a common base is not open to doubt. But, a cardinal difference in the vocabulary of those languages pertaining to the marine mammal nomenclature and the items [characteristic of] the coastal

---

s. Fainberg actually shows that Aleuts were patrilineal, but he, and Liapunova at the time she wrote this book, were constrained by the obligatory formula propounded by Engels in his *Origin of the Family, Private Property, and the State*—L. B.

68

culture, provides a basis for the conclusion that the separation of the Proto-Eskimo-Aleuts could have taken place either at the time of their arrival on the sea coast or in earlier ecological conditions of primitive continental culture. It may be assumed, says Menovshchikov, that the common Proto-Eskimo-Aleut language had, at the time of the separation of its bearers, a fully developed grammatical structure and was in concordance with that primitive Paleolithic culture which the Proto-Eskimo-Aleuts brought with them to the new lands many thousands of years ago. Moreover, the high level of the island culture of the Aleuts was achieved as a result of thousands of years of separate development on the Aleutian Islands. The Aleut society itself, being scattered on distant islands, developed unevenly in linguistic aspects, and that had a considerable influence on the formation of several Aleut dialects.

Menovshchikov concludes that a genetic relationship of the Eskimo-Aleut languages to the Ural-Altaic or the Indo-European is not convincingly confirmed on the basis of existing facts of typological similarity of their separate structural elements. As to contact links established by comparison of the linguistic data, they are found to be greatest between the Eskimo-Aleut and the Paleo-Asiatic languages of Chukotka and Kamchatka, and least with the other languages of the Far East, Siberia, and North America.

Problems of Aleut [biological] anthropology were investigated in recent years by members of the Department of Anthropology of Moscow State University under the leadership of Iu. G. Rychkov.[122] This study was undertaken in connection with investigation of problems of the aboriginal population of the northern part of the Pacific basin, and also problems of the adaptation of the inhabitants of ancient Beringia.

First of all it is necessary to cite the conclusion of the investigators that the Aleuts of the Commander Islands are, indeed, Aleuts, despite the existing opinion about their heterogeneity. The population of the Commander Islands, in the investigators' opinion, differs from other Aleut populations no more than these latter [populations] differ among themselves.

The population-genetics data obtained, support the conclusion that the Aleuts of the Commander Islands (and, consequently, the Aleuts in general) are no less close to the population of northeastern Asia as a whole than to the people of the western hemisphere (i.e. Indians).

The authors' conclusion that the Aleuts of the islands of the Unalaska district (the eastern Aleuts) left the largest trace in the genetic structure of the contemporary generation of the Aleuts of the Commander Islands is very interesting. This explains the greatest divergence between the Commander Aleuts and the group of Attu-Atka on the one hand, and, on the other hand, confirms the genetic deviation of the Attu-Atka group, the westernmost and most distant in the chain, from the Aleuts of Unalaska Island (the eastern group). As a corollary, there follows the assumption that on the westernmost islands (the Near and Rat) was preserved the most isolated Aleut group, untouched by the influences from the American continent (which are established for the eastern Aleuts). This assigns to the investigations of the western Aleuts a decisive significance in solving the problem of the ancient settlement of the southern rim of Beringia and in resolving the still vague question of the development of the Paleo-Aleuts into the Neo-Aleuts.

Further, it is of interest that the comparative study of features that have genetic markers, such as certain cranial anomalies, confirmed the suggestions made by T. Ia. Tokareva and A. Hrdlička that there is a similarity between the Aleuts and the Neolithic population of Cisbaikalia. This is regarded by the authors as an additional example of the reproduction of the features of the ancestral group, which they consider to be one of the principal characteristics of the population system of the contemporary population.

The authors also sketch the probable development of the Commander population: from the "Mongoloids of northern Asia and America" through "the peoples of northern Asia" to "the Paleo-Asiatics of northern Asia," "the Chukchi and Eskimos," then to "the Asiatic Eskimos." And then the Commander Aleuts are placed next to the latter.

* * *

One can see from this survey of the history of the "Aleutian Problem" that the majority of scholars, in one degree or another, were addressing the questions of when and whence the Aleuts came, by which route the islands were settled and whether the Aleuts were the first inhabitants of the islands.

It is necessary to note that until recently, the principal question— whence and when did the ancestors of the Aleuts come—was resolved in the context of migration, 3,000 years ago and later, either from the northeastern Asiatic coast (Steller, Veniaminov, Quimby, Collins, de

Laguna, Heizer, and Kozyreva) or from Alaska (Dall, Iokhel'son, Hrdlička, Spaulding, and Bank). Only the studies of Debets, Levin, Dikov, Vasil'evskii, and Laughlin allow the view that the formation of the Aleuts, with all the features of their physical type, language and culture, occurred in the same territory where they were found by the first Europeans, that is, on the Aleutian Islands (and part of the Alaska Peninsula).

The second important question, raised in the process of solving the problem of the origin of the Aleuts, was the route by which the Aleutian Islands were settled. The discussion of this question unavoidably led the majority of the authors to the problem of the settling of America in general, and of the ancient routes of migration of man from Asia to America. Here two points of view are to be noted: settlement from the west, through Kamchatka and the Commander Islands, and settlement from the east through Alaska. But the geographic situation of the Aleutian Islands gave little possibility for assumptions about a western route, and at a relatively early time, there already appeared an assumption about the existence of a land bridge between Asia and America (Dall and Iokhel'son). Nevertheless, a number of contemporary authors (Quimby, Spaulding, Bank) adhere to the opinion that the islands were settled from the east, through Bering Strait and Alaska. Laughlin's substantiation, on the basis of the data of contemporary geological studies, of the Aleuts' ancestors' route along the Bering Sea platform, supported by the material from the Anangula site (indicating a time corresponding to the existence of this [land] bridge), provides the most convincing solution of this problem.

The question of whether the Aleuts were the first inhabitants of the islands was discussed from the beginning of archaeological investigations of them. Here the view that there were two waves of settlement of the islands (Hrdlička, Quimby, and Laughlin in the first stage of investigation) or even three (Dall), is opposed by the view of a single period of settlement (Iokhel'son, Spaulding, Bank, and Laughlin). The archaeological investigations of later years, headed by Laughlin, provided evidence supporting the idea that the islands were settled at a single time.

The question of the correlation of the Eskimos and the Aleuts also stands before the investigators. Here, too, we are confronted by various points of view: the full acknowledgment of the Aleuts being a southern

Eskimo group (Quimby, Bank), the separation of the Aleuts in a greater or lesser degree from the Eskimos (Dall, Iokhel'son, Tokareva, Hrdlička), and finally, the determination of such a remote time of their separation that it caused the independent ethnic formation of the Aleuts (Menovshchikov, Laughlin, Dikov, Vasil'evskii).

CITATIONS AND NOTES

1. L. S. Berg, *Otkrytie Kamchatki i ekspeditsii Beringa 1725–1742 gg*. [Discovery of Kamchatka and the Bering expeditions 1725–1742], 3rd ed. (Moscow and Leningrad, 1946).

2. G. F. Müller, "Instruction G. F. Müllers für den Akademiker-Adjunkt J. E. Fischer," *Sbornik Muzeia antropologii i etnografii im. Petra I*, t. 1 (1900).

3. G. W. Steller, *Reise von Kamtschatka nach Amerika mit dem Commandeur-Capitän Bering* (St. Petersburg, 1793), p. 73; idem, *Beschreibung von dem Lande Kamtschatka* (Frankfurt and Leipzig, 1774), pp. 239–252, 297–303.

4. Sven Waxell [Vaksel'], *Vtoraia Kamchatskaia ekspeditsiia Vitusa Beringa* [The Second Kamchatka Expedition of Vitus Bering] (Leningrad and Moscow, 1940).

5. *Russkie otkrytiia v Tikhom okeane i Severnoi Amerike v XVIII v.* [Russian discoveries in the Pacific Ocean and North America in the eighteenth century], ed. A. I. Andreev (Moscow, 1948), pp. 106–110.

6. G. W. Steller, *Reise von Kamtschatka...*, p. 73.

7. G. W. Steller, *Beschreibung...*, pp. 297–303.

8. The history of the investigation of the Aleutian Islands is elucidated in the following works: A. V. Efimov, *Iz istorii velikikh russkikh geograficheskikh otkrytii* [From the history of the great Russian geographical discoveries] (Moscow, 1949); L. S. Berg, *Otkrytie Kamchatki...*, part 3, chpt. 19; S. B. Okun, *Rossiisko-Amerikanskaia kompaniia* [The Russian-American Company] (Moscow and Leningrad, 1939); Z. N. Zubkova, *Aleutskie ostrova* [The Aleutian Islands] (Moscow, 1948); R. V. Makarova, *Russkie na Tikhom okeane vo vtoroi polovine XVIII v.* [Russians on the Pacific Ocean in the second half of the 18th century] (Moscow, 1968); V. A. Divin, *Russkie moreplavaniia na Tikhom okeane v XVIII v.* [Russian voyages in the Pacific Ocean in the 18th century] (Moscow, 1971).

9. The peredovshchik was the organizer of the ship's economy and fur trade and was also responsible for carrying out the instructions of the administration of the port from which the ship departed.

10. L. S. Berg, "Iz istorii otkrytiia Aleutskikh ostrovov" [From the history of the discovery of the Aleutian Islands], *Zemlevedenie*, t. 26, v. 1–2 (1924), pp. 114–132.

11. *Russkie otkrytiia v Tikhom okeane i Severnoi Amerike v XVIII– XIX vv.* [Russian discoveries in the Pacific Ocean and North America in the 18th and 19th centuries], ed. A. I. Andreev (Moscow and Leningrad, 1944).

12. *Russkie otkrytiia…*, 1948.

13. A. S. Polonskii, "Perechen' puteshestvii russkikh promyshlennykh liudei v Vostochnom okeane s 1743 po 1800 god" [An enumeration of the voyages of Russian promyshlenniki in the Eastern Ocean from 1743 to 1800], AGO, r. 60, op. 1, no. 2; idem, "Promyshlenniki na Aleutskikh ostrovakh (1743–1800 gg.)" [Promyshlenniki on the Aleutian Islands (1743–1800)], ibid., no. 3.

14. All trading companies were required (up to 1774) to pay one-tenth of all furs obtained to the treasury. Besides that, the promyshlenniki were required to make the inhabitants of the newly discovered lands Russian subjects and to collect iasak from them for the treasury.

15. A. P. Sokolov, "Ekspeditsiia k Aleutskim ostrovam kapitanov Krenitsyna i Levashova, 1764–1769 gg." [Expedition by captains Krenitsyn and Levashov to the Aleutian Islands, 1764–1769], *Zapiski Gidrograficheskogo departamenta Morskogo ministerstva*, part 10 (1852).

16. R. G. Liapunova, "Etnograficheskoe znachenie ekspeditsii kapitanov P. K. Krenitsyna i M. D. Levashova na Aleutskie ostrova (1764–1769 gg.)" [Ethnographic significance of the expedition of captains P. K. Krenitsyn and M. D. Levashov to the Aleutian Islands (1764–1769)], *Sovetskaia etnografiia*, 1971, no. 6.

17. *Neue Nordische Beitrage* (St. Petersburg and Leipzig), Bd. I–IV, 1781–1788; Bd. V–VII, 1793–1796.

18. W. Coxe, *Account of the Russian Discoveries Between Asia and America* (London, 1780).

19. Intending to write a history of voyages to America, G. Müller collected a great number of valuable materials from the archives of the Siberian chancelleries, and also the Moscow and St. Petersburg chancelleries, but he died in 1783 and did not complete his work.

20. James Cook, *A Voyage to the Pacific Ocean*, vol. 3 (London, 1785).

21. G. A. Sarychev, *Puteshestvie po severo-vostochnoi chasti Sibiri, Ledovitomu moriu i Vostochnomu okeanu* [Voyage to the northeastern part of Siberia, the Arctic Sea and the Eastern Ocean] (Moscow, 1952).

22. M. Sauer, *An Account of a Geographical and Astronomical Expedition to the Northern Part of Russia, Performed by Commander Joseph Billings in the Year 1785 to 1794* (London, 1802).

23. *Russkie otkrytiia...*, 1948, pp. 69–70.

24. A. Jacobi, "Carl Heinrich Mercks ethnographische Beobachtungen über die Völker des Beringsmeers, 1789–1791," *Baessler-Archiv*, 1937, Bd. 20, Hf. 3–4, pp. 114–137.

25. I. F. Kruzenshtern, *Puteshestvie vokrug sveta v 1803–1806 gg. na korabliakh Nadezhda i Neva* [A voyage round the world in 1803–1806 on the ships *Nadezhda* and *Neva*] (Moscow, 1950); Iu. F. Lisianskii, *Puteshestvie vokrug sveta na korable Neva v 1803–1806 gg.* [A voyage round the world on the ship *Neva* in 1803–1806] (Moscow, 1947).

26. T. V. Staniukovich, *Kunstkamera Peterburgskoi Akademii nauk* [The Kunstkamera of the St. Petersburg Academy of Sciences] (Moscow and Leningrad, 1953), pp. 178–183.

27. G. H. Langsdorff, *Voyages and Travels in Various Parts of the World during the Years 1803–1807,* vol. 2 (London, 1814).

28. V. M. Golovnin, *Puteshestvie vokrug sveta, sovershennoe na voennom shliupe* Kamchatka [A voyage round the world, undertaken on the sloop *Kamchatka*] (Moscow, 1965).

29. F. P. Litke, *Puteshestvie vokrug sveta na voennom shliupe* Seniavin *v 1826–1829 godakh* [A voyage round the world on the sloop S*eniavin* in 1826–1829] (Moscow, 1948).

30. T. V. Staniukovich, *Kunstkamera...*, pp. 185–187.

31. The most interesting, rare and, finally, earliest published drawings of the inhabitants of the Aleutian Islands, articles of their culture, and way of life are presented in the present work.

32. R. G. Liapunova, "Rukopis' K. T. Khlebnikova 'Zapiski o koloniiakh v Amerike' kak istochnik po etnografii i istorii Aliaski i Aleutskikh ostrovov" [The manuscript of K. T. Khlebnikov's 'Notes on the colonies in America' as a source on the ethnography and history of Alaska and the Aleutian Islands], in *Ot Aliaski do Ognennoi Zemli* [From Alaska to Tierra del Fuego] (Moscow, 1967), pp. 136–141. [Khlebnikov's notes have since been published as *Russkaia Amerika v neopublikovannykh zapiskakh K. T. Khlebnikova* [Russian America in the unpublished notes of K. T. Khlebnikov], comp. and ed. R. G. Liapunova and S. G. Fedorova (Leningrad: Nauka, 1979)—L. B.]

33. M. V. Stepanova, "I. Veniaminov kak etnograf" [I. Veniaminov as ethnographer], *Trudy Instituta etnografii*, n.s., t. 2 (1947), pp. 294–314.

34. I. Veniaminov, *Zapiski ob ostrovakh Unalashkinskogo otdela* [Notes on the islands of the Unalaska district], vols. 1–3 (St. Petersburg, 1840).

35. Ibid., vol.1, p. 1.

36. Ibid., p. 113.

37. I. Veniaminov, *Opyt grammatiki aleutsko-lis'evskogo iazyka* [Tentative grammar of the Aleut-Fox language] (St. Petersburg, 1846).

38. K. K. Gil'zen, "Il'ia Gavrilovich Voznesenskii. K stoletiiu so dnia ego rozhdeniia (1816–1871)" [I. G. Voznesenskii. In commemoration of the 100th anniversary of his birth (1816–1871)], *Sbornik Muzeiia antropologii i etnografii im. Petra I*, t. 3 (1916), pp. 1–14; M. V. Stepanova, "I. G. Voznesenskii i etnograficheskoe izuchenie severo-zapada Ameriki. K stoletiiu ego ekspeditsii" [I. G. Voznesenskii and the ethnographic study of northwestern America. Commemorating the 100th anniversary of his expedition], *Izvestiia Vsesoiuznogo geograficheskogo obshchestva*, t. 76, v. 5 (1944), pp. 277–279; B. A. Lipshits, "Etnograficheskie materialy po Severo-Zapadnoi Amerike v arkhive I. G. Voznesenskogo" [Ethnographic materials on northwestern America in the archives of I. G. Voznesenskii], *Izvestiia Vsesoiuznogo geograficheskogo obshchestva*, t. 82, v. 4 (1950), pp. 415–420; E. E. Blomkvist, "Risunki I. G. Voznesenskogo (ekspeditsiia 1839–1849 godov)" [The drawings by I. G. Voznesenskii (the expedition of 1839–1849)], *Sbornik Muzeia antropologii i etnografii im. Petra I*, t. 13 (1951), pp. 230–303; R. G. Liapunova, "Ekspeditsiia I. G. Voznesenskogo i ee znachenie dlia etnografii Russkoi Ameriki" [The expedition of I. G. Voznesenskii and its significance for the ethnography of Russian America], *Sbornik Muzeia antropologii i etnografii im. Petra I*, t. 24 (1967), pp. 5–33.

39. L. Shrenk, *Ob inorodtsakh Amurskogo kraia* [About the inorodtsy of the Amur region], vol.1 (St. Petersburg, 1883), p. 11. [In Tsarist Russia an inorodets was a native of the eastern, for the most part, outlying districts of Russia, belonging to one of the national minorities—Trans.]

40. S. Patkanov, *Statisticheskie dannye, pokazyvaiushchie plemennoi sostav naseleniia Sibiri, iazyk i rody inorodtsev* [Statistical data illustrating the tribal composition of the population of Siberia and the language and families of inorodtsy], vol. 1 (St. Petersburg, 1912), pp. 105–129.

41. E. A. Herron, "William Healey Dall, Alaska pioneer," *Natural History* 57, no. 4 (1948), pp. 176, 179.

42. W. H. Dall, "On the distribution of the native tribes of Alaska," *Proceedings of the American Association for the Advancement of Science* 18 (1869), pp. 267–273; idem, "On the distribution and nomenclature of the native tribes of Alaska," *Contributions to North American Ethnology*, vol. 1 (Washington: Government Printing Office, 1877), pp. 7–40.

43. At approximately the same time the French ethnologist A. Pinart visited the Aleutian Islands. In 1871 on Unga (Shumagin Islands) in a burial cave at Delarof Harbor he found the remains of four skeletons, human figurines carved from bone, fragments of painted wooden masks, and other painted wooden articles. Later the lower level of that cave was excavated by Dall. Pinart also investigated the cave on Amaknak Island (near Unalaska), where skeletons and cultural remains were also discovered. A. L. Pinart, *La Caverne d'Aknanh, Île d'Ounga* (Paris, 1875), pp. 1–11, pl. I–VIII; idem, *Catalogue des collections rapportées de l'Amérique Russe, par A. Pinart, exposées dans le Musee d'Histoire Naturelle de Paris* (Paris, 1872).

44. W. H. Dall, "Alaskan mummies," *American Naturalist* 9, no. 8 (1875), pp. 433–440; idem, "On the remains of later prehistoric man obtained from caves in the Catherina archipelago, Alaska Territory, and especially from caves of the Aleutian Islands," Smithsonian Publication 318, *Contributions to Knowledge* 22 (Washington, 1878).

45. W. H. Dall, "On succession in the shell-heaps of the Aleutian Islands," *Contributions to North American Ethnology*, vol. 1 (Washington: Government Printing Office, 1877), pp. 41–91.

46. The same assumptions were also expressed by Dall in two of his earlier notes about the archaeological finds on the Aleutian Islands. W. H. Dall, "Notes on the pre–historic remains in the Aleutian Islands," *Proceedings of the California Academy of Science* 4 (1868–1872), pp. 283–287; idem, "On further examinations of the Amaknak cave, Captain's Bay, Unalaska," *Proceedings of the California Academy of Science* 5, (1873–1874), pp. 196–200.

47. W. H. Dall, "Remarks on the origin of the Innuit," *Contributions to North American Ethnology*, vol. 1 (Washington: Government Printing Office, 1877), pp. 93–106.

48. W. H. Dall, "Masks, labrets and certain aboriginal customs," *Third Annual Report of the Bureau of American Ethnology for the years 1881–1882* (Washington, 1884), pp. 73–151.

49. W. H. Dall, "On geological aspects of the possible human immigration between Asia and America," *American Anthropologist*, n.s. 14, no. 1 (1912), pp.12–18.

50. W. I. Jochelson, "The Koryak," *The Jesup North Pacific Expedition* vol. 6, *Memoirs of the American Museum of Natural History* (1905–1908), pp. 1–2; idem,"The Yukaghir and Yukaghirized Tungus," ibid. vol. 9, *Memoirs of the American Museum of Natural History* (1920–1924), pp. 1–3; idem, "The ethnological problems of the Bering Sea," *Natural History* 26, no. 1 (1926), pp. 90–95; idem, "The ancient and present Kamchadal and the similarity of their culture to that of the northwestern American Indians," *Proceedings of the International Congress of Americanists* 23 (New York, 1928), pp. 451–454.

51. For a critique of the theory of "the Eskimo wedge" see M. G. Levin, *Etnicheskaia antropologiia i problemy etnogeneza narodov Dal'nego Vostoka* [Ethnic anthropology and problems of the ethnogenesis of the peoples of the Far East] (Moscow, 1958), pp. 212–218.

52. W. I. Jochelson, *Archaeological Investigations in the Aleutian Islands, Carnegie Institution of Washington Publication* 367 (Washington, 1925).

53. W. I. Jochelson, *History, Ethnology and Anthropology of the Aleut, Carnegie Institution of Washington Publication* 432 (Washington, 1933).

54. See, for example, W. I. Jochelson, "The Aleut language and its relation to the Eskimo dialect," *Proceedings of the International Congress of Americanists* 18 (London, 1912), pp. 96–104; V. I. Iokhel'son, *Materialy po izucheniiu Aleutskogo iazyka i fol'klora* [Materials on the study of the Aleut language and folklore] (Petrograd, 1928).

55. T. Ia. Tokareva, "Materialy po kraniologii aleutov" [Materials on the craniology of the Aleuts], *Antropologicheskii zhurnal*, 1937, no. 1, pp. 57–71.

56. The principal published works of Hrdlička connected with this theme are: *Skeletal remains suggesting or attributed to early man in North America, Bulletin of the Bureau of American Ethnology* 33 (1907); *Old Americans* (Baltimore, 1925); *Anthropological Survey in Alaska, Annual Report of the Bureau of American Ethnology* 35 (1931); "Lower jaw," *American Journal of Physical Anthropology* 27, no. 2–3 (1940).

57. A. Hrdlička, *The Aleutian and Commander Islands and Their Inhabitants* (Philadelphia: Wistar Institute of Anatomy and Biology, 1945).

58. H. B. Collins, *Archeology of St. Lawrence Island, Alaska, Smithsonian Miscellaneous Collections* 96, no. 1 (1937); idem, "Culture migrations and contacts in the Bering Sea region," *American Anthropologist* 39, no. 3 (1937), pp. 375–384; idem, "Outline of Eskimo prehistory," *Smithsonian Miscellaneous Collections* 100 (1940), 533–592.

59. F. de Laguna, *The Archaeology of Cook Inlet, Alaska* (Philadelphia, 1934).

60. K. Birket-Smith and F. de Laguna, *The Eyak Indians of the Copper River Delta, Alaska* (Copenhagen, 1938).

61. H. B. Collins, *Archeology of St. Lawrence Island...*, p. 377.

62. K. Birket-Smith and F. de Laguna, *The Eyak...*, pp. 519–520.

63. R. F. Heizer, "Aconite poison whaling in Asia and America: an Aleutian transfer to the New World," *Bulletin of the Bureau of American Ethnology* 133 (1943), pp. 415–468.

64. G. I. Quimby, *Aleutian Islanders* (Chicago, 1944).

65. Collections donated to the Chicago Museum by A. R. Cahn, who excavated site "D" on the same island where Iokhel'son carried out his excavations. Iokhel'son did not notice this site.

66. G. I. Quimby, "Periods of prehistoric art in the Aleutian Islands," *American Antiquity* 11, no. 2 (1945), pp. 76–79.

67. The culture existing in Canada and Greenland for a period of more than 1,500 years, approximately from the middle of the first millennium B.C. to the eighteenth and nineteenth centuries A.D. [Few would bring the Dorset culture down to this late a period. It was mostly gone by or before A.D. 1400—W. W.]

68. Kachemak I, II, and III are the ancient Eskimo cultures of southwestern Alaska. They existed from the eighth century B.C. (Kachemak I) to the sixteenth century A.D. (Kachemak III). The latter changed directly into the culture of the Chugach Eskimos and Kodiak Islanders. Kachemak I and II are attributed to the Paleo-Eskimo cultures, and Kachemak III to the Neo-Eskimo. [The date cited here for the end of Kachemak III (sixteenth century A.D.) is de Laguna's original estimate before radiocarbon dating. In Kachemak Bay, Kachemak III was probably gone by A.D. 500 to 600 and the related Three Saints Bay phase on Kodiak was gone by ca. A.D. 1000 to 1100. Strong continuity, but not perfectly smooth development, is noted on Kodiak from the Three Saints Bay phase to the prehistoric Koniag. Derivation of the Chugach from a Kachemak base is much more debatable—W. W.]

69. Punuk is one of the Neo-Eskimo cultures of the Bering Sea, existing approximately from the last centuries B.C. and already succeeded by the Eskimo cultures in the fifteenth and to nineteenth centuries. [Punuk is now generally dated between ca. A.D. 600 and 1000. See R. E. Ackerman, "Prehistory of the Asian Eskimo zone," *Handbook of North American Indians,* vol. 5, *The Arctic*, ed. D. Damas (Washington: Smithsonian Institution, 1984), p. 110—W. W.]

70. F. de Laguna, *The Archaeology of Cook Inlet...*, p. 209.

71. G. I. Quimby, "Toggle harpoon heads from the Aleutian Islands," *Fieldiana: Anthropology* 36, no. 2 (1946), pp. 15–23.

72. G. I. Quimby, "Pottery from the Aleutian Islands," *Fieldiana: Anthropology* 36, no. 1 (1945), pp. 1–13.

73. F. de Laguna, *The Archaeology of Cook Inlet...*, p. 68.

74. G. I. Quimby, "The sadiron lamp of Kamchatka as clue to the chronology of the Aleut," *American Antiquity* 11, no. 3 (1946), pp. 202–203.

75. H. B. Collins, *Archeology...*, p. 40; F. de Laguna, *The Archaeology of Cook Inlet...*, p. 410; R. F. Heizer, "Aconite poison...."

76. S. V. Ivanov, "Aleut hunting headgear and its ornamentation," *Proceedings of the International Congress of Americanists* 23 (1928), (New York, 1930), pp. 477–504. See also: S. V. Ivanov, "Materialy po izobrazitel'nomu iskusstvu narodov Sibiri XIX-nachala XX v." [Materials on the depictive art of the peoples of Siberia in the nineteenth and early twentieth century], *Trudy Instituta etnografii*, n.s., 22 (Moscow and Leningrad, 1954), pp. 483–504; idem, "Ornament narodov Sibiri kak istoricheskii istochnik" [Ornamentation of the peoples of Siberia as a historical source], *Trudy Instituta etnografii*, n.s., 81 (Moscow and Leningrad, 1963), pp. 163–248.

77. S. V. Ivanov, "Sidiachie chelovecheskie figurki v skul'pture aleutov" [Seated human figures in Aleut sculpture], *Sbornik Muzeia antropologii i etnografii im. Petra I*, t. 12 (Leningrad, 1949).

78. L. S. Berg, *Otkrytie Kamchatki...*, pp. 226–232; idem, "On the origin of the Aleuts," *Proceedings of the Fifth Pacific Science Congress* (Toronto, 1934), pp. 2773–2775.

79. A. C. Spaulding, "The current status of Aleutian archaeology," *Memoirs of the Society for American Archaeology* 9 (1953), pp. 29–31.

80. A. C. Spaulding, "Archaeological investigations on Agattu, Aleutian Islands," *Anthropological Papers of Museum of Anthropology, University of Michigan* 18 (1962).

81. T. P. Bank II, "Cultural succession in the Aleutians," *American Antiquity* 19, no. 1 (1953), pp. 40–49.

82. T. Bank II, *Birthplace of the Winds* (New York, 1956); idem, *Kolybel' vetrov* [Cradle of the winds] (Moscow, 1960).

83. W. S. Laughlin, "The Alaska gateway viewed from the Aleutian Islands," in *Papers on the Physical Anthropology of the American Indian,* ed. W. S.

Laughlin (New York: Viking Fund, 1951); idem, "Blood groups, morphology and population size of the Eskimo," in *Cold Spring Harbor Symposia on Quantitative Biology,* vol. 15 (Cold Spring Harbor, N.Y., 1950).

84. W. S. Laughlin and G. H. Marsh, "A new view of the history of the Aleutians," *Arctic* 4, no. 2 (1951), pp. 75–88.

85. W. S. Laughlin, "Contemporary problems in the anthropology of southern Alaska," in *Science in Alaska* (Washington, 1952), pp. 66–84.

86. W. S. Laughlin, "The Aleut-Eskimo community," *Anthropological Papers of the University of Alaska* 1, no. 1 (1952), pp. 25–46.

87. W. S. Laughlin, "Notes on an Aleutian core and blade industry," *American Antiquity* 17, no. 1 (1951), pp. 52–55.

88. W. S. Laughlin and G. H. Marsh, "The lamellar flake manufacturing site on Anangula Island in the Aleutians," *American Antiquity* 20, no. 1 (1954), pp. 27–39.

89. W. S. Laughlin, "Neo-Aleut and Paleo-Aleut prehistory," *Proceedings of the International Congress of Americanists* 32 (Copenhagen, 1956), pp. 516–530.

90. W. S. Laughlin and W. G. Reeder, "Rationale for the collaborative investigation of Aleut-Konyag prehistory and ecology," *Arctic Anthropology* 1, no. 1 (1962), pp. 104–107.

91. W. S. Laughlin, "Archaeological investigations on Umnak Island, Aleutians," *Arctic Anthropology* 1, no. 1 (1962), pp. 108–110.

92. W. S. Laughlin and W. G. Reeder, "Revision of Aleutian prehistory," *Science* 137, no. 3533 (1962), pp. 856–857.

93. G. F. Debetz [Debets], "The skeletal remains of the Ipiutak cemetery," *Proceedings of the International Congress of Americanists* 33, vol. 2 (San Jose, Costa Rica, 1958), pp. 57–64.

94. W. S. Laughlin, "Generic problems and new evidence in the anthropology of the Eskimo-Aleut stock," in *Prehistoric Cultural Relations Between the Arctic and Temperate Zones of North America,* ed. J. M. Campell, Arctic Institute of North America Technical Papers, no. 11 (Montreal, 1962), pp. 100–112.

95. W. S. Laughlin, "Bering Strait to Puget Sound: Dichotomy and affinity between Eskimo-Aleuts and American Indians," ibid., pp. 113–125.

96. W. S. Laughlin, "The earliest Aleuts," *Anthropological Papers of the University of Alaska* 10, no. 2 (1963), pp. 73–92.

97. W. S. Laughlin, "Eskimos and Aleuts: Their origins and evolution," *Science* 142, no. 3593 (1963), pp. 633–645.

98. R. F. Black and W. S. Laughlin, "Anangula: A geologic interpretation of the oldest archeologic site in the Aleutians," *Science* 143, no. 3612 (1964), pp. 1321–1322.

99. "Studies in Aleutian-Kodiak prehistory, ecology and anthropology," ed. W. S. Laughlin and W. G. Reeder, *Arctic Anthropology* 3, no. 2 (1966). The volume is dedicated to the memory of A. Hrdlička.

100. R. F. Black, "Late Pleistocene to recent history of Bering Sea-Alaska coast and man," *Arctic Anthropology* 3, no. 2, (1966), pp. 7–22.

101. A. P. McCartney, and C. G. Turner II, "Stratigraphy of the Anangula unifacial core and blade site," ibid., pp. 28–40.

102. W. S. Laughlin and J. S. Aigner, "Preliminary analysis of the Anangula unifacial core and blade industry," ibid., pp. 41–56.

103. J. S. Aigner, "Bone tools and decorative motifs from Chaluka, Umnak Island," ibid., pp. 57–83. Aigner singled out four units in the Chaluka site (not seven as did Denniston). They are correlated in the following manner: levels I and II of Denniston correspond to unit I of Aigner; Denniston's III and IV correspond to Aigner's II; Denniston's V and VI correspond to Aigner's III, and Denniston's VII corresponds to Aigner's unit IV.

104. G. B. Denniston, "Cultural change at Chaluka, Umnak Island: Stone artifacts and features," ibid., pp. 84–124.

105. L. K. Lippold, "Chaluka: the economic base," ibid., pp. 125–131.

106. W. B. Workman, "Prehistory at Port Moller, Alaska Peninsula, in light of fieldwork in 1960," ibid., pp. 132–153.

107. W. S. Laughlin, "Paleo-Aleut crania from Port Moller, Alaska Peninsula," ibid., p. 154.

108. W. S. Laughlin, "Human migration and permanent occupation in the Bering Sea area," in *The Bering Land Bridge*, ed. D. M. Hopkins (Stanford: Stanford University Press, 1967), pp. 409–450.

109. D. E. Dumond, "On Eskaleutian linguistics, archaeology and prehistory," *American Anthropologist* 67, no. 5 (1965), pp. 1231–1257.

110. D. E. Dumond, "Two early phases from the Naknek drainage," *Arctic Anthropology* 1, no. 2 (1963), pp. 93–104; idem, "Eskimos and Aleuts," in *Proceedings of the 8th International Congress of Anthropological and Ethnological Sciences,* vol. 3 (Tokyo, 1970), pp. 102–107.

111. A. P. McCartney, "'Pottery' in the Aleutian Islands," *American Antiquity* 35, no. 1 (1970), pp. 105–108.

112. A. P. McCartney, "A proposed western Aleutian phase in the Near Islands, Alaska," *Arctic Anthropology* 8, no. 2 (1971), pp. 92–142.

113. G. F. Debets, "Antropologicheskie issledovaniia Kamchatskoi oblasti" [Anthropological investigations in the Kamchatka district], *Trudy Instituta etnografii,* n.s., t. 17 (1951), pp. 73–75.

114. M. G. Levin, *Etnicheskaia antropologiia i problemy etnogeneza narodov Dal'nego Vostoka* [Ethnic anthropology and problems of the ethnogenesis of the peoples of the Far East] (Moscow, 1958), pp. 212–218, 238–248; idem, [Review of:] S. I. Rudenko, *Drevniaia kul'tura Beringova moria i eskimosskaia problema* [The ancient culture of the Bering Sea and the Eskimo problem], *Sovetskaia etnografiia,* 1949, no. 1.

115. M. G. Levin, "K antropologii eskimosov" [Toward the anthropology of the Eskimos], *Sovetskaia etnografiia; Sbornik statei* t. 6–7 (1947), pp. 216–223.

116. R. S. Vasil'evskii, "O pervonachal'nom formirovanii drevnekoriakskoi kul'tury v severnoi chasti Okhotskogo poberezhia" [On the initial formation of the Old Koriak culture on the northern part of the Okhotsk coast], in *Voprosy istorii sots.-ekon. zhizni Sibiri i Dal'nego Vostoka* [Questions of the history of the socio-economic life of Siberia and the Far East], vol. 1 (Novosibirsk, 1968), pp. 312–320; idem, *Proiskhozhdenie i drevniaia kul'tura koriakov* [Origin and ancient culture of the Koriak] (Novosibirsk, 1971).

117. R. V. Chubarova, "K istorii drevneishego naseleniia Sakhalina" [Toward a history of the most ancient population of Sakhalin], *Sovetskaia etnografiia,* 1957, no. 4; R. V. Kozyreva, *Drevnii Sakhalin* [Ancient Sakhalin] (Leningrad, 1967).

118. N. N. Dikov, "Otkrytie paleolita na Kamchatke i problema pervonachal'nogo zaseleniia Ameriki" [Discovery of the Paleolithic in Kamchatka and the problem of the initial peopling of America], in *Istoriia i kul'tura narodov severa Dal'nego Vostoka* [History and culture of the peoples of the north of the Far East] (Moscow, 1967), pp. 16–31; idem, *Drevnie kostry Kamchatki i Chukotki* [Ancient hearths of Kamchatka and Chukotka] (Magadan,

1969), pp. 102–119, 155–158, 206–213; idem, *Drevnie kul'tury Kamchatki i Chukotki* [Ancient cultures of Kamchatka and Chukotka], Synopsis of doctoral dissertation (Novosibirsk, 1971).

119. L. A. Fainberg, "K voprosu o rodovom stroe u aleutov" [Toward the question of clan structure among the Aleuts], *Kratkie soobshcheniia Instituta etnografii*, t. 23 (1955); idem, *Obshchestvennyi stroi eskimosov i aleutov* [Social structure of the Eskimos and Aleuts] (Moscow, 1964).

120. I. S. Vdovin, "The traces of an Aleut-Eskimo culture on the Kamchatka Pacific shore," *Proceedings of the Ninth Pacific Science Congress*, Tokyo, 1966 (Moscow, 1966); idem, "Sledy aleutsko-eskimosskoi kul'tury na Tikho-okeanskom poberezh'e Kamchatki" [Traces of Aleut-Eskimo culture on the Pacific shore of Kamchatka], in *Strany i narody Vostoka* [Lands and peoples of the East], vol. 13 (Moscow, 1972), pp. 41–51.

121. G. A. Menovshchikov, "Eskimossko-aleutskie paralleli" [Eskimo-Aleut parallels], in *Uchenye zapiski Leningradskogo gosudarstvennogo pedagogicheskogo instituta im. A. I. Gertsena*, t. 167 (Leningrad, 1960), pp. 171–192; idem, Eskimossko-aleutskaia iazykovaia obshchnost' i ee otnoshenie k drugim iazykam" [The Eskimo-Aleut linguistic community and its relation to other languages], in *Proiskhozhdenie aborigenov Sibiri i ikh iazykov* [Origin of the aborigines of Siberia and their languages], Mat. Vsesoiuzn. konf. 1973 g. (Tomsk, 1973), pp. 12–15; idem, Eskimossko-aleutskie iazyki i ikh otnoshenie k drugim iazykovym sem'iam" [Eskimo-Aleut languages and their relation to other linguistic families], *Voprosy iazykoznaniia*, 1974, no. 1, pp. 46–59.

122. Iu. G. Rychkov and V. A. Sheremet'eva, "Populiatsionnaia genetika aleutov Komandorskikh ostrovov (v sviazi s problemami istorii narodov i adaptatsii naseleniia drevnei Beringii)" [Population genetics of the Aleuts of the Commander Islands (in connection with problems of the history of the peoples and adaptation of the population of ancient Beringia)], *Voprosy antropologii*, v. 40 and 41 (1972).

II. BASIC ECONOMIC OCCUPATIONS
Implements and Means of Maritime Procurement

The type of Aleut economy formed prior to the eighteenth century was closely linked to natural conditions in the islands and with the traditions of a maritime way of life, characteristic, as a whole, for the representatives of the North Pacific basin's cultural-historical region. The apparently severe and inhospitable condition of the region occupied by the Aleuts was in reality favorable for a maritime hunting-fishing-gathering economy. The Bering Sea, washing the chain of islands from the north, was rich in pinnipeds and whales. In the seas surrounding the archipelago, halibut, cod, flounder, herring, Atka mackerel [*Hexogrammus asper*] and *kizhuch* [*Oncorhynchus kisutch*—silver salmon] were found; the salmon entered the islands' streams to spawn. Countless rocky islands with bird rookeries offered opportunities for the hunting of birds and the gathering of eggs. In the littoral zone of the seashore it was possible to gather edible mollusks, echinoderms, crustaceans, etc.

Prior to the time of the arrival of the Russians, the density of the population here was greater than that of the Indians of Florida and the State of New York or New England prior to the arrival of the Europeans.[1, a]

But in order to supply food resources for such a numerous population engaged in hunting and fishing and leading a settled way of life, it was necessary, apart from the natural richness of the region, to maintain a sufficiently high degree of labor productivity which is achieved, as is generally known, by the development of means of production and by the form of work organization. It is reasonable to assume that such a level

---

a. In later studies, Liapunova concluded that these numbers were greatly exaggerated. See R. G. Liapunova, *Aleuty: Ocherki etnicheskoi istorii* [Aleuts: Sketches of ethnic history] (Leningrad: Nauka, 1987); idem, "The Aleuts before contact with the Russians: Some demographic and cultural aspects," *Pacifica* 2, no. 2 (1990), pp. 8–23.—L. B.

85

of labor productivity was maintained among the Aleuts in the mid-eighteenth century. We will try to demonstrate this by examining the tools, the means of labor, the form of the organization of game procurement activities, the norms of the distribution of the catch, and finally, the character of social relations (see below, Chapter 3).

The basis of the Aleut economy in the period under consideration was, as all early sources witness, the hunting of sea mammals. An important addition to it was fishing: both deep sea fishing by hook and line and fishing in rivers during spawning season. The hunting of water and sea birds also played a considerable part in the economy. Collecting in the intertidal zone and also the gathering of edible roots and berries had subsidiary importance.

The sea and seashore were the source of all the necessary means of existence for the Aleuts. From the skins of sea otters, fur seals, seals, and sea lions, they sewed clothing, and used the skins for bedding. For clothing they also used the skins of sea birds. With the [processed] skins of sea lions, fur seals and walrus, they covered their *baidarka*s [kayaks] and *baidara*s [large skin boats]. The meat of sea animals, fish, and birds and gathered products were their food. From driftwood found on the shore they made house frames [supports] and various other items (boat frames, weapon shafts, throwing boards, hunting headgear, and household utensils); from the bones of sea mammals and walrus ivory, they made arrow and spear heads. The ribs and mandibles of large whales were used for dwelling construction.

It is necessary to note that in the territory occupied by the Aleuts there was a natural food supply year round (although there were seasons providing more or less food) since the sea around the Aleutian Islands does not freeze.

The Aleuts' economic life cycle was organized in the following way.

By the end of April the summer birds arrived, the sea mammals—fur seal and sea lion males—appeared near the islands, and the Aleuts began hunting pelagically at that time. Also at the end of April fishing commenced for fish entering the rivers from the sea to spawn. Fish [salmon] of various species continued to run until the autumn (with some differences as to time on various islands).

In May they continued to take male fur seals and sea lions and to fish. From May to July they hunted at sea for sea otters.

In June and July they hunted fur seals (including females which appeared near the islands at the end of May) and sea otters, and fished.

Bird hunting began in the middle of July (at the time when the young were fledging) and continued almost to the time of the birds' migration, that is, until September.

The walrus, in the summer, entered only a few straits near the Alaska Peninsula. Only the very old or very young males came. They were hunted at this time on their hauling-out grounds.

Also in summer they hunted whales which were plentiful in the Bering Sea at that time of year, and also angled for fish in the sea.

In October and November they took fur seals returning from the north and proceeding south.

After the termination of these activities, fishing in the sea [also] ended because of the cold weather and strong winds. The Aleuts lived on a stored supply of fur seal meat, dried fish, fish eggs, [sea mammal] oil, and sarana roots. When the supply of food was depleted, they gathered mollusks in the intertidal zone and sea kelp.

During the winter seals came to the islands from the northern part of the Bering Sea. They were hunted near shore with the aid of decoys. Traditional economic life was reflected in the calendar of the Aleuts, which is cited in the work of I. Veniaminov.[2] He writes that each month had its own name connected mainly with the hunting of animals and birds and with seasonal phenomena. These names were not uniform everywhere, for there existed some differences among the islands in respect to the appearance there of different game, and in species of [available] game animals, etc.

The Aleuts began their calendar in March.

March was called *kadugikh* [*kaduuĝix̂*], "leading," or *qisagunak* [*qisagunax̂*], "the time when they eat skin because of the scarcity of food." In the dictionary of the Aleut-Fox language the term *úliam ílian káĝiq* [*ulam ilan qaĝix̂*], "the time when one eats in the yurta," is given.[3]

April was called *agaliu'igikh qisagunak* [*agaluuĝix̂ qisagunax̂*], "the month in which one eats skin for the last time." It was the time of the arrival of summer birds and sea mammals—fur seals and sea lions. In the dictionary the term *saðagan qáĝiq* [*sadaagan qaĝix̂*] is given, "the time when one eats outside the house."

87

May was called *ichichkhukh* [*iichichxux*] or *chigum tugida* [*chiĝum tugidaa*], "the month of flowers," the time of the sea lion and adult male fur seal hunt. In the dictionary the term given is *sagasanguliuk* [*saĝasangulux*], "the time when one sleeps little."

June was called *chiĝalílim tugida* or *chagaligim tugida* [*chaĝaligim tugidaa*], "the month of nestlings and new-born sea mammals." In the dictionary the term *saɗignam tugidá* is given, "the month in which animals become fat."

July was called s*adignam tugida* [*sadignam tugidaa*], "the month in which young animals become fat." In the dictionary the term given is *chaĝalílim tugidá*, "the month in which seals and other sea mammals are born."

August was called *ugnam* [*uĝnam*] or *úkhnam tugidá* [*ux̂nam tugidaa*], "the warm month in which grasses begin to wilt." At that time the nestlings already fly and the young of the sea mammals become independent. In the dictionary the following explanation of the name of that particular month is given: "the month in which grasses wilt and all animals begin to lose fat."

September was called *chngúlim tugida* [*chngulim tugidaa*], "the month in which the fur of all animals and the feathers of birds become the best" (that is, "the animals are ready to migrate"). The following meaning is given in the dictionary: "the month in which animals change fur."

October was called *kímádĝim tugida* [*kiimadgim tugidaa*], "the month of hunting." In the dictionary the term given is *kimadgim tugida* [*kiimadgim tugidaa*], "the time in which animals, particularly fur seals, are caught."

November was called *kimadgim kangin tugida* [*kiimadgim kingan tugidaa*], "the month after hunting." In the dictionary the term *agal'gáliuq* [*agalĝalux̂*] is given, "the time in which [men] are no longer engaged in catching animals."

December was called *agalgugaq* or *agalgaluq* [*agalĝalux̂*], "the month in which seals are hunted with the help of decoys." In the dictionary this month is called the principal one—"the month of all months" (probably long)[b]—*tugiɗigamaq* [*tugidiigamax*].

---

b. The parenthetical remark was added by Liapunova. It should be noted that ritual festivities began in December and lasted through January—L. B.

January was called *tugidigamaq* [*tugidiigamax*], "the big, important month." In the dictionary the given term is *anulgiliq* [*anulgilix̂*], "the time in which cormorants appear."

February was called *anulgiliaq* [*anulgilax̂*], "cormorant month," because cormorants were caught with snares at that time. In the dictionary the term *kisagúnaq* [*qisagunax̂*] is given, "the time in which straps are eaten very often because of want."

Sea mammals were hunted both in the sea and on the rookeries [hauling-out grounds]. Sea otters were hunted predominately at sea. The hunt on shore was both very dangerous and unproductive (sea otters hauled out only when the sea was very turbulent and at places that were difficult of access). The hunters usually went to sea in groups of three, four, or more baidarkas[4] and maintained such a distance from one another that a sea otter could be spotted between the baidarkas. The first one to sight an otter signaled with a raised paddle and proceeded toward the animal, while the rest tried to encircle it. With each dive of the sea otter the circle tightened (during the first dive a sea otter could remain under water for twenty minutes, after that for an ever shorter period and declining finally, to half a minute). After the first harpoon struck, a second, a third, and so on were thrown. The animal, wounded by the harpoon, was unable to escape because the harpoon head remained in its body, while the shaft was detached. The shaft, tied to the head, was dragged after the animal in the water (perpendicular to the animal's motion since the opposite end of the short line [*maut*] was divided in two and tied to the upper and lower part of the shaft), acting as a brake on its movement, and when the sea otter neared the surface the lighter end of the shaft appeared above the water, indicating the position of the animal. In order to prevent the sea otter from sinking, a harpoon equipped with an inflated bladder was thrown. If there were several sea otters, a large hunting party divided into smaller detachments.

Hunting of otters in the rookeries ("on the rocks") is mentioned in an account by T. I. Shmalev: "The local people hunt in their small baidarkas in which only one man sits, traveling to the rocks, *otpriadyshi* in the Kamchatka usage, no matter how far they were from the island."[5] In the same account, information is given about the ways of hunting sea otters by Russian promyshlenniki, specifically with the aid of nets: "Prior to the arrival of the promyshlenniki, the local people hunted sea otters with arrows, however not with a bow, but by casting them from a small board

89

in such a way that they could kill or wound a sea otter from a distance of fifteen sazhens [ca. 105 feet]. And that is why their catch consists of rather small numbers, but the promyshlenniki, according to their custom, shot the sea otters with rifles first, when they hauled out on the rocks; in this way their catch was considerably greater than that of the local people and now they even have a greater return because they use nets of fine cordage and set them up near [off] the rocks, and since a sea otter on the move often dives, it gets entangled in the nets and soon dies."[6] The assertion sometimes appearing in the literature, that the Aleuts also used nets when hunting sea otters, is disproved by this information.

Similarly, fur seals, sea lions, and other pinnipeds were taken [hunted] at sea.

Fur seals were taken also at their rookeries. The animals were chased farther away from the water, and there they became helpless. The most effective way was group hunting. Several men armed with clubs (*drygalka*, a special club for the killing of fur seals) walked in a line along the shore, separating the fur seals from the water. Having chased them away from the shore, they killed the fur seals with a blow to the nose.

The hunters also went to the seal and fur seal rookeries alone, as mentioned in one of the Aleut tales.[7]

The hunting of sea lions by the drive method was conducted in the same way, only [the hunters] tried to choose a time when there were no males, dangerous even on dry land, with the herd.

Hunters tried to approach the walruses hauled out on shore from the direction of the sea and kill the ones nearest the water with [stabbing] spears; the bodies blocked the way to the sea for the rest [of the walruses], animals very clumsy on dry land.

Seals were hunted in the sea, by the drive method on land, and by means of harpoons cast from the shore.

In the latter case they used decoys, the inflated skin of a seal (Figure 3). The hunter, in concealment on shore, placed the decoy in front of himself and imitated the cry of the female. When a swimming seal came close, the hunter threw a harpoon at it and dragged it onto the shore, where he killed it with a blow of a club or with a spear. Such a method of hunting had the character of an individual enterprise.

Of the many species of whales inhabiting the waters near the Aleutian Islands, the Aleuts hunted the small baleen whale [*polosatik*] called

Figure 3. Decoy made from the skin of a seal, decorated with paints (collection of the MAE, No. 571-37).

aliamak [*alamax*]. A group of hunters or even a solitary one could go to sea to hunt whales. In both cases the hunt had an individual character. The hunter approached the whale from behind and, by means of a throwing board, threw a spear at it, attempting to inflict a wound close to the front flipper, and then hurried away. The same was done with a second, a third and subsequent whales. The obsidian blade of the spear, smeared with vegetable poison (aconite), remained in the body of the whale. In two to three days the wounded whale died and was washed ashore if there was a favorable wind. By such a hunting method, the Aleuts received roughly one whale out of ten wounded ones, but because of their abundance in the Bering Sea and the skill of the hunters, whales were often taken.

From spring to fall the Aleutian Islands are the habitat of a great number of *kaira*[?], Alcidae [*chistiki*], and gulls, which form rookeries on the islands; geese and ducks also come. The Aleuts hunted birds with bird spears [*shatina*] and snares made of baleen. They hunted birds both in groups and individually.

Besides sea hunting and bird hunting, men were also engaged in angling for fish in the sea. Bone hooks tied to a fishing line made of kelp or sinew (Figures 4 and 5) were used. This type of fishing could be undertaken individually.

Fishing [in streams] during the spawning period [of salmon species] was basically a task for women. During this time women formed groups (there were never more than two or three old or sick men included in the group) and settled temporarily at [moved to] certain locations ahead of

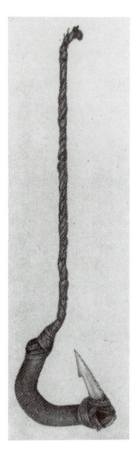

Figure 4. Compound fishhook (collection of the MAE, No. 4087-15).

time. At the time of this type of fishing, stone weirs were erected at stream mouths. The fish were killed with fish spears and caught in sinew dip nets.

Here the women also prepared *iukola* (dried fish). The notes of A. A. Baranov give an idea of the traditional methods of fishing and fishing implements: "...they catch fish in the sea on bone hooks attached to long lines of kelp, but river fish are speared with prongs, also of bone, fixed to shafts, and stone weirs are made where, during large fish runs for which they watch, they scoop them with dip nets."[8]

Gathering, which was also the task of women and children, included the harvesting of gifts from the sea in the tidal zone, the harvesting of various berries and the digging up of *sarana* bulbs [*Fritillaria* or Kamchatka lily] and the roots of *makarsha* [*Polygonum viviparum?*] and [wild] parsley (Figure 14).

The Aleuts' hunting implements, as ethnographic material illustrates, conform to the characteristic features of the traditional economy. Sea hunting implements were the principal ones. A more subsidiary role was allotted to fishing implements (for sea and river fishing), to bows and arrows, used both during hunts on land[c] and in war, and to special clubs for the killing of fur seals in rookeries.

A sufficiently complete presentation of the traditional hunting implements of the Aleuts can be obtained from the written accounts of the early visitors to the islands, and in museum collections.[9] For example, I. G. Voznesenkii compiled an inventory of the contents of one of the boxes of [his] collection. In this inventory, the entire set of Aleut hunting implements was listed. Here is the text of that inventory.

---

c. There was no land prey west of Unimak—W. W. and L. B.

Figure 5. Fishing line made of kelp with compound bone fishhooks and a stone weight (collection of the MAE, No. 4104-29).

A genuine baidarka of the Fox Aleuts in which they set out into the open sea for sea otter hunting. It was constructed according to all the rules of the craft on the island of Akun under the supervision of the toion [chief] of the Fox Islands (the name for baidarka in the Fox language is *ik-khiak* [*iqyax̂*][d]); with it is a full set of hunting implements and other accessories. Spears and other accessories are arranged in the order in which they are kept by the Aleuts on the hunt (on the top of the baidarka).

---

d. Here and below we have added in square brackets the spelling in the modern Aleut orthography, when such could be determined, following Knut Bergsland, compiler, *Aleut Dictionary* (Fairbanks, Alaska: Alaska Native Language Center, University of Alaska Fairbanks, 1994)—L. B.

1) Sea otter spears, in the Fox language *aiakudakhich* [*ayaqudaax*],—nine pieces altogether.

2) Whaling spears, in the Fox language *iglekakh* [*igiqax̂*],—three.

3) A sea otter spear with line and a bladder [float], in the Fox language *aklichikh* [*iglagix̂*], —one.

4) A spear with which they kill sea lions and seals, in the Fox language *agal'chikh* [*agalĝix̂*]; with it a line *(angan)* [*an'gan*] and a bladder *(naiukh)* [*nayux̂*].

5) A spear used exclusively in the sea lion hunt, in the Fox language *akh-chun*; with it a line and a painted bladder *(akh-chun-sa)*.

6) Spears with which they hunt sea birds, in the Fox language *chitasik* [*chataasix̂*],—three pieces.

7) A spear for taking young seals, in the Fox language *chuduk-sek*.

8) A club, in the Fox language *an-nakh* [*anax*]; with it, sea otters are finished off.

9) A spear which served as a decoration for the baidarka, completing the set; it is not used. In the Fox language *katikh*.

10) Throwing board, in the Fox language *as'khukh* [*hasxux̂*]; an Aleut casts spears at the animals with such a board.

11) Seal decoy, in the Fox language *ummagikh* [*umaĝix̂*]; such a decoy is inflated and with it seals are lured close to the baidarka.

12) *Srela (tsrela)*, (a mat—R. L.), in the Fox language *in-kselukkh* [*ixsx̂aĝix̂*]; used as a pad in the baidarka.

13) *Suka* or baidarka covering [drip skirt], in the Fox language *suk-kakh* [*sukax̂*]; with it a line or cord used for drawing it tight, called *kannakh-akh tusian* in the Fox language.

14) A double-bladed paddle, in the Fox language *ak-kkha-dgusak* [*haqadguusix̂*].

15) Carved bone (ivory) representation of a sea otter with a fulmar bird [*glupysh*] used on a baidarka in place of *ukliuchiny* [cord attachers, toggles]; in the Fox language *kiigachinang*.

16) Another item [used] with spears, in the Fox language *takanak*.

17) Fox-Aleut national wooden hat, in the Fox language *kaiatlukh* [*qayaatx̂ux̂*]. A gut *kamleika* [hooded outer garment], [in the Fox language] *chigidakh* [*chigdax̂*]. A carved baleen ornament crowned at the tip with a bone image of a bird (the bone bird is sent separately) is used on the prow, at the bow of the baidarka; called *kangulisik* in the Fox language.[10]

The list of hunting instruments given by their function coincides approximately with that given by G. A. Sarychev. He [the latter] lists five types of throwing implements (or as he calls them, "spears") used by the Aleuts:

The first, measuring up to 4 feet, is for attacking people and large animals; instead of a blade, a similar piece of lava [obsidian?] measuring 1½ inches long by ¾ inch wide is fitted onto the striking end. The second type is smaller than the first and is used for small animals; instead of stone blades these [spears] have bone points attached with sinew cordage. The third type, used for birds, is similar in size to the first type of spear: the striking end is armed with four barbed bone prongs. The fourth type, also for animals, measures 8 feet: at the striking end is a bone blade, attached to a sinew cord, which is split at the other end in two; [these two ends] are tied in a dovetail manner, i.e., in two places to the middle of the shaft; eagle feathers are attached to the butt end. The fifth type is 4 feet 4 inches long, it has a bone point and an inflated bladder is attached to the middle of the spear; this spear is used to keep the dead animal afloat.[11]

I. Veniaminov reports on four types of "spears."

The spears are distinguished in type partly by their size and cord attachments [attached cords], but more so

95

by their points [*noski*]. Sea otter spears have as a rule points of bone (usually inserted into bone heads) approximately 2 inches long and with three barbs; the points [blades] of whale spears are of obsidian, resembling [those of] a lance, also about 2 inches in length; the bird spears have one long point (about 8 inches), barbed, to which three more points of the same length are attached at the sides, their ends spread out, resembling a fish spear; this type of spear almost always has no head. The seal spears are the longest, their heads are from three to five hand spans long and about 5 inches thick, while the points resemble those of sea otter spears but are longer and thicker. Besides these spears, they also have special ones with bladders; in tackle and in point [form], they also resemble sea otter spears, but are longer and bigger; small bladders with a tap or plug for inflating are attached to their shafts. This type of spear is used only when a sea otter or another animal is wounded, to prevent its sinking or to exhaust it more quickly.[12]

A "Note with a description of the implements used by the inhabitants of the Aleutian Islands for hunting and fishing," contains the following information:

...dart No. 4. It is made from light aromatic driftwood, one end of which may be made of walrus ivory or sometimes of whale bone; in it is inserted a bone instead of an iron blade; a sinew cord is attached with one end to the blade, and the other end is secured to the spear [shaft]. When a hunter strikes the animal, the spear [shaft], by means of balance, floats with one end under the water and the other above, thus indicating the location where the wounded animal is to be found; the hunter then continues to discharge additional spears [at the animal]. Such a spear is [represented by] No. 5. Its blade is made of hard stone instead of from iron. A bird spear, No. 6, has one large central and three small barbed prongs. Each of these spears has a [narrow] sinew cord along its [entire] length; it prevents the loss of spear parts should an animal break the spear.

The spear, made of aromatic wood, is used for hunting large sea lions on the rocks and sometimes at sea; a large seal skin bladder is attached to it with a cord of plaited sinew which is wound around the spear, and the other (end—R. L.) is tied to the point, made of stone instead of iron; when the spear is thrown at an animal, the bone point remains in the animal and the attached rope unwinds; the bladder float prevents the animal from escaping into the depths, and so it tires and is caught.[13]

Besides the written information, the sketches of hunting implements that can be found in old publications and archival sources are of significant importance (Figure 2). The most interesting, including those previously unpublished, are shown in this book (Figure 6).[14]

Proceeding from the existing information about Aleut hunting implements and study of the collections of the Museum of Anthropology and Ethnography of the Academy of Science of the USSR (MAE),[e] it is possible to suggest the following classification of the traditional hunting implements of the Aleuts.

I. Implements for hunting sea mammals and water birds.

1) Light non-toggling harpoons ("sea otter spears" in old sources, cast by means of throwing boards; Figure 7). Two types are singled out among them: those with long (24 to 27 centimeters) and thin (about 1.5 centimeters in diameter) socket pieces on the shaft; and those with shorter (about 8 centimeters) but thicker (2.5 centimeters in diameter) socket pieces. The second type was equipped with a bladder float.

The shaft of the harpoon was usually made of Californian *chaga* [cedar] (*Pinus lamberziana* [*sic*]), having the lightest wood. To the thicker end of the shaft a socket piece was attached which was carved

---

e. Now the "Kunstkamera," Museum of Peter the Great—L. B.

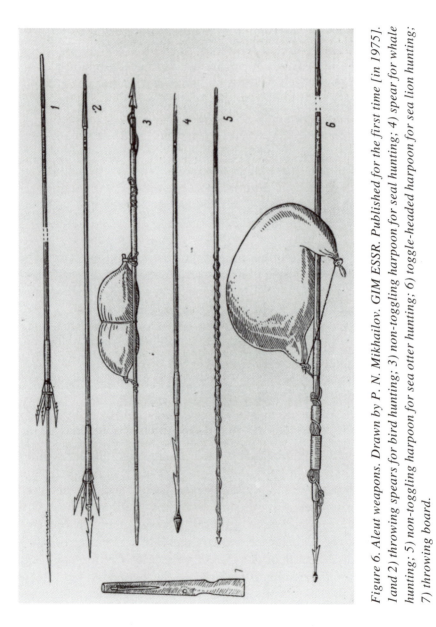

Figure 6. Aleut weapons. Drawn by P. N. Mikhailov. GIM ESSR. Published for the first time [in 1975]. 1 and 2) throwing spears for bird hunting; 3) non-toggling harpoon for seal hunting; 4) spear for whale hunting; 5) non-toggling harpoon for sea otter hunting; 6) toggle-headed harpoon for sea lion hunting; 7) throwing board.

from walrus tusk, whale bone or caribou antler. The head of the harpoon shaft was always made heavier than the rest of the shaft, so that the harpoon would not sink, but remain perpendicular, showing approximately 30 centimeters above the water. A movable head (varying in length from 3 to 14 centimeters) with barbs (two on each side or fewer, down to one on only one of the sides) was inserted into the round or oval opening of the socket piece, which also had a wooden plug. The head was fastened with cord either to the opening in the base, or to a projection. The socket piece was attached to the shaft in the following manner: the wedge-like end of the shaft was inserted into the fork-like (with two prongs) part of the socket piece; a coil of sinew was wound on the outside. The bindings of sinew cord located in several places along the entire length of the shaft functioned to strengthen the shaft and to preserve its broken parts. On some harpoons those bindings were decorated with multicolored strands of wool.

According to Aleut mythology, sea otters are people transformed into animals; therefore, in order to lure them, the Aleuts decorated the "sea otter spears." There are in the collections harpoons with carved and colored bone socket pieces and ornamented shafts.

2) Heavy, non-toggling harpoons for the hunting of sea lions and seals (Figure 8). The hunter usually threw the heavy harpoon at sea mammals from shore, without a throwing board. A second hunter killed the [wounded] animal with a spear or club while the hunter who threw the harpoon held the cord in his hand to prevent the wounded animal from escaping.

The heavy non-toggling harpoons are subdivided into three types: [1] harpoons with a bone socket piece on the shaft, similar to the second type of the light non-toggling harpoons but larger (20 to 30 centimeters in length, proportional to the size of the shaft, 1.2 to 1.3 meters); [2] harpoons with a bone composite socket piece consisting of two long (50 to 60 centimeters) longitudinal halves; and [3] harpoons without a bone socket piece but with a long (2 to 2.2 meters) shaft.

The heads of the heavy non-toggling harpoons are similar to those of the light ones, but are of a larger size (15 to 20 centimeters).

3) Toggle harpoons. These types of harpoons were used by the Aleuts for hunting sea lions, *lakhtak* [harbor seals, *Phoca barbata—morskoi zaiats*] and other sea mammals. They were cast without a throwing

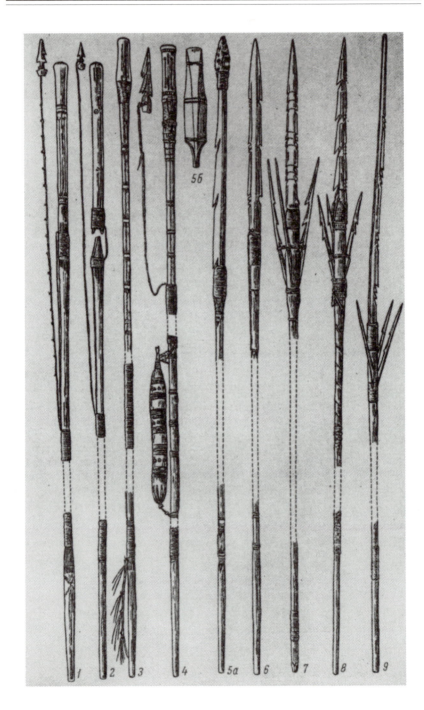

board. The head of the toggle harpoon enters the body of the animals and attaches itself there with a spur; it came off the loose shaft [*kolka*] and turned 90°, remaining in a perpendicular position to the loose shaft (actually functioning, in a sense, as an improved barb of a non-toggling harpoon).

In the MAE collections there are three examples of the heads of toggle harpoons which are characterized by a closed symmetrical socket, a split symmetrical spur, and a slot for an end blade which is parallel to the spur.

4) Throwing spears and lances. With these spears, cast with throwing boards, whales were hunted. At the same time, they were military spears used with a throwing board and as a stabbing weapon. They were also used during the hunts in the rookeries for finishing off wounded animals.

The throwing spears differ from harpoons in that all their parts were fixed and unmovable. Aleut throwing spears and lances are subdivided into two types: with bone heads where an obsidian or slate blade is inserted; and with a sharpened bone tip. Spears of the first type had a shaft (about 1 meter long) to which a barbed bone head (27 to 33 centimeters in length) was secured. Into the slot of the upper end the afore-mentionéd stone blade (6 to 9 centimeters long) was inserted. Some spears of that type have protective cases [blade sheaths] over the heads (about 20 centimeters long, 4 to 5 centimeters wide) made from [two] thin wooden [hollowed out] plates painted red and tied in three places with sinew (Figure 8, item 7e). The spears of the second type were similar, but without a stone blade. According to the descriptions by early authors and existing illustrative materials, whales were hunted only with spears of the first type, that is, those armed with a stone blade.

5) Clubs. They were mainly used for clubbing fur seals on the rookeries, and also for finishing off sea mammals on the shore.

6) Throwing spears for birds *(shatina)*.[15] They were cast with throwing boards. These spears have one main barbed bone prong 25 to 30

Figure 7 (facing page). Hunting implements (from the collection of the MAE). 1 through 4) light, non-toggling harpoons, Nos. 593-89₂, 2868-122, 4270-73, 593-87; 5a) casting spear for whale hunting, Nos. 4270-74; 5b) case for spear heads; 6) casting spear, No. 593-91; 7 through 9) throwing spears for bird hunting, Nos. 4270-75, 2867-27, -21.

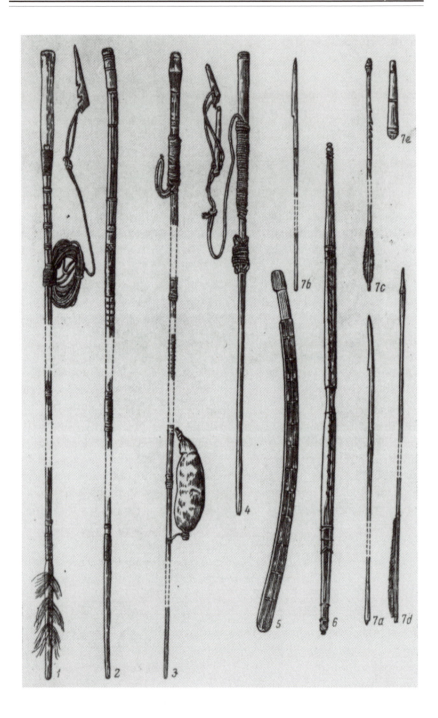

centimeters in length, and, 13 to 15 centimeters below it, three sharp bone side prongs (24 to 27 centimeters) which are attached at a sharp angle [to the central one].

7) Throwing boards (Figure 9). Throwing boards were widely used by Aleuts in the sea mammal hunt at sea, and in war. The spear and harpoon thrown with the aid of a throwing board had their range increased by three to four times; their striking force increased also.[16] The Aleut throwing boards may be classified into two types according to their shape: rectangular and swordlike.

Throwing boards of the first type have the approximate shape of an extended [elongated] rectangle from 44 to 55 centimeters long and from 4.5 to 6 centimeters wide. The handles are marked by a slight palm grip, with an opening for the index finger on the right side, which on the obverse side of the board is often ringed with a carved figure of a whale (stylized). The upper part of the board is smooth, but provided with a groove with a bone rest for the spear; [it is] usually painted red. The obverse side of the board is convex and most often painted black. There are, however, boards painted entirely red or black, as well as unpainted ones.

Throwing boards of the second type are swordlike in shape with more sharply marked hand [palm] grips and indentations for the fingers, Some boards have in addition a bone peg, which serves as a [thumb] rest. As a rule, throwing boards of that type are not painted in entirety but are decorated with a bas-relief image of a sea otter (realistic or stylized) inset with little beads and the teeth of animals.

II. Implements for hunting on land.

Among the Aleuts, these implements are represented by bows and arrows (Figure 8, items 6 and 7a through 7d). Bows and arrows were also their military weapons. Aleut bows are analogous to the bows of the Eskimos, which have the distinguishing feature (characteristic) of a

Figure 8 (facing page). Hunting implements (from the collection of the MAE). 1 through 3) heavy non-toggling harpoons, Nos. 2868-228, 593-82, 2868-119; 4) toggle harpoon, No. 4270-37; 5) club, No. 593-23; 6) bow, No. 2868-186; 7a through 7d) darts, Nos. 4104-119, 4193-23, 2868-2, 4104-16; 7e) case for the head of a spear.

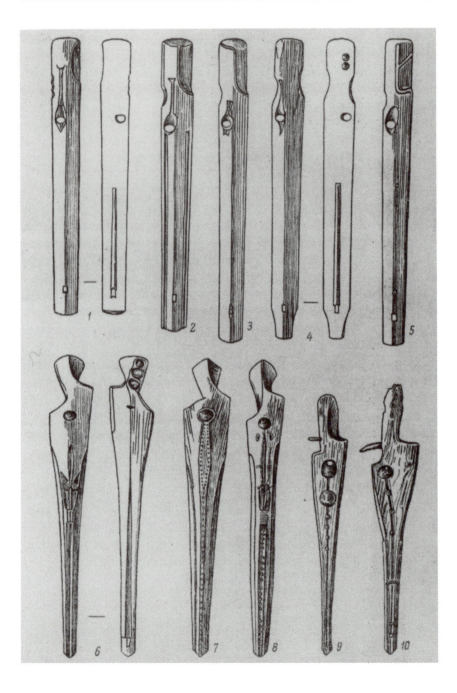

sinew string strung along the outside surface of the bow and laced to it in several places with sinew bindings.

Aleut arrows are also analogous to Eskimo arrows and have sharpened bone heads which are either flat (with one or several barbs) or of a triangular shape (usually with one barb). Some arrows are furnished with obsidian or slate blades (for such blades there are wooden [protective] cases of the type described above, p. 101. Aleuts also used blunt arrows. The tail ends of such arrows are notched to accommodate bow strings and are fletched with two or three split feathers. The heads are attached to the shaft in the same manner as in throwing spears or light non-toggling harpoons.

The Aleut sea hunting implements described here are indicative of the existence of a large variety of means of hunting on the sea and on shore. All sea hunting implements were strictly differentiated according to the species of animals for which they were intended: "sea otter spears," "sea lion spears," "seal spears," and "whale lances." Each type of implement, in accordance with its specialized use, was perfected to the maximum efficiency of its action and application. Even throwing boards were differentiated according to their usage: the swordlike ones were designed for throwing the light non-toggling harpoons in the course of the sea otter hunt; the rectangular ones were for throwing spears while whale hunting. It is necessary also to mention the high artistic level of the Aleut implements, the result of technical and aesthetic mastery.

All these features inherent in the Aleut hunting equipment allow us to speak of such a degree of specialization in maritime procurement, which presupposes a long cultural evolution in the given specific region.

The hunting implements allow determination of the specifics of Aleut maritime procurement activity. Comparing the Aleut and Eskimo sea hunting implements, we find a number of differences. Thus, among the Aleuts non-toggling harpoons constituted the most widely used group of implements, represented in many varieties. Among the Eskimos this

---

Figure 9 (facing page). Throwing boards (from the collection of the MAE). 1 through 5) boards of a rectangular type, Nos. 2868-113,-114,-12, 337-21, 2868-180; 6 through 10) boards of a swordlike type, Nos. 2867-31, -32, 4087-10, 593-67, 4104-22.

harpoon type did not achieve such development. The only exception to the rule were the Pacific Eskimos, neighbors of the Aleuts, who used non-toggling harpoons widely.

At the same time, the toggle harpoons which were the principal weapons of the Eskimos for hunting at sea were used considerably less frequently by the Aleuts.

The light throwing and stabbing spear was entirely unknown to the Eskimos, while among the Aleuts it was, together with non-toggling harpoons, one of the most widespread types, being widely used in whale hunting, in the sea mammal rookeries, and in war.

Archaeological investigations on the Aleutian Islands, which resulted in large finds of non-toggling harpoon heads and spear and lance blades, demonstrate that these types of weapons were prevalent from the rather ancient periods of Aleut history (up to 2,000 B.C.).

The heavy Eskimo spears with leaf-shaped [lanceolate] blades and massive bone heads with an ice pick at the butt end, were unknown in the Aleutian Islands.

Bows and arrows were used comparatively little by the Aleuts, mostly as military weapons. As is known, bows and arrows were not suited for hunting from baidarkas, and hunting for land animals had some significance only among the Aleuts of the Alaska Peninsula [and Unimak]. It should be noted that the bows and arrows of the Aleuts were similar to those of the Eskimos in all aspects.

The [relative] proportion of the various types of Aleut hunting implements preserved in the collections of the MAE is significant. Thus, there are 105 light non-toggling harpoons, but only 3 toggle harpoons, 18 throwing (and stabbing) spears [lances], 9 bird spears, 30 throwing boards, 2 bows and 28 arrows.

The differences in the sea hunting implements of the Aleuts and Eskimos were determined in many ways by the fact that the hunting boat of the Aleuts was exclusively a single-hatch kayak, the baidarka, but among the Eskimos the hunting of large sea mammals, particularly whales, was carried out by means of multipaddle umiaks. The hunting weapons of the Aleuts were adapted for throwing from light, unsteady baidarkas.

According to well-known foreign archaeologists F. Rainey and H. Larsen, Eskimo whale hunting with the aid of umiaks and harpoon floats is associated with a late stage of Eskimo culture and the "whale hunting culture" is defined as being the basis for the formation of contemporary Eskimo culture.[17] They characterized the earlier period as not having clear specialization in maritime [procurement] activity. Consequently, there are many reasons to consider the technique and the implements of Aleut maritime procurement, as well as their methods of whale hunting, to have originated in the Aleutians.

In connection with this, an interesting question arises—whether whale hunting existed on all the Aleutian Islands or whether it was characteristic only of the population of the eastern part. As there is a lack of direct evidence, the following observation by K. T. Khlebnikov deserves attention. He writes that the "Atka Aleuts" (that is, the western) did not hunt whales in the past: "There are plenty of whales near the shores, but the Aleuts particularly fear and never hunt them. Sometimes there are drift whales, but not every year." In a footnote he notes that "Nowadays Atka Aleuts do not fear whales anymore and begin to hunt them."[18] Lacking other information about whale hunting among the western Aleuts, this single direct statement assumes considerable significance. It is possible to assume that whale hunting was typical only for the eastern Aleuts, and that it spread among the western groups only at the beginning of the nineteenth century.*f*

In speaking of the peculiarities of the coastal culture of the Aleuts and its differences from that of the Eskimos, it is necessary to note the following typical trait of the Aleuts: the considerable role of gathering in the tidal zone. Even in a time of lack of those food products which were provided by sea hunting and fishing, the Aleuts could, for a time, subsist on echinoderms, crustaceans, mollusks, kelp, etc. The stability of that tradition is indicated by the circumstance that products of maritime gathering preserved their significance in the food inventory of the Aleuts to the twentieth century as a national, traditional supplement to their food.[19]

The Aleuts' sea hunting implements which have been discussed above illustrate clearly enough the existence among them of an original style of maritime procurement with all its specific implements.

---

f. See also *The Journals of Iakov Netsvetov: The Atkha Years, 1828–1844*, trans. and ed. L. Black (Kingston, Ontario: Limestone Press, 1980), p. 82. The Russian-American Company detailed some Koniag whalers to Atka to teach the local Aleuts whaling—L. B.

Under the conditions of their coastal and insular way of life, boats were the only means of transportation among the Aleuts: single-hatch, two-hatch and three-hatch skin baidarkas, and multipaddle skin boats, baidaras.[20] Baidarkas were hunting boats (Figure 10), but the multipaddle baidaras were used only for transportation from island to island, for the hauling of cargo, and in military raids.

Figure 10. An Aleut in a baidarka. Drawing by M. D. Levashov. TsGAVMF.

In the maritime hunting-fishing orientation of the Aleuts' economy, the baidarka played an especially important role. It was indispensable for supplying the people with the means of subsistence. The sea around the Aleutian Islands did not freeze and almost year round it was the sphere of one or another procurement activity. The Aleuts hunted sea mammals in the open sea also (going out 150 kilometers or more from shore) and on rookeries which could only be reached in baidarkas. They also fished in the sea from baidarkas. In them they set out for the rocky islets to hunt birds and collect eggs.

According to the very apt remark of Veniaminov, the baidarka was for the Aleuts "the most needed means of existence" and "was as necessary as the plough and horse were for the farmer."[21] And indeed, the baidarka had the leading role in the Aleuts' means of production.

The baidarka had the most telling effect in the hunt for sea mammals thanks to its speed and maneuverability, which were decisive for spotting and harpooning [prey]. Its noiselessness in approaching the prey played a large role also.[22]

Museum collections make it possible to make detailed studies of the construction of the Aleut baidarkas, while information about their qualities is found in the early reports of travelers and explorers.[23]

In the collections of the North America Department of the MAE there are one single-hatch baidarka and thirty-two baidarka models made by Aleuts and brought back by Voznesenskii and other Russian travelers and explorers in the first half of the nineteenth century. Three baidarkas (single-hatch, two-hatch, and three-hatch), the frame of a single-hatch baidarka and nine baidarka models are in the collection of the Central Naval Museum in Leningrad [St. Petersburg].

The baidarka models supplement our knowledge of that particular type of boat considerably. Most of them reproduce the original baidarkas in all details with amazing accuracy. Moreover, they give an idea about the equipment of the hunter and his garments which is not given in an accurate enough form in literature sources.

The Aleuts had three types of baidarkas: the single-hatch *(iqakh)* [*iqyax̂*], the principal form of hunting boat; the two-hatch *(ulliukhtadak)* [*ulux̂taadax̂*], used by an old man accompanied by a boy to go to sea for the purpose of training the latter, or for the transportation of a woman, old man or child; and the three-hatch *(ulliukhtak)* [*ulux̂tax̂*].[24] After the introduction of firearms among the Aleuts, the two-hatch baidarkas became more necessary for hunting than before because the recoil while shooting could overturn the light single-hatch baidarka, which had very little stability. In the two-hatch baidarka the paddler sits in the rear hatch. They began to build three-hatch baidarkas at the time of the arrival of the Russians and used them primarily as a means of transportation (the paddlers sat in the first and third hatches and the passenger in the middle).

A hunter in a baidarka was obliged to wear over his garments a hooded *kamleika* [outer shirt] made of intestines. A wide drip skirt made out of strips of intestines *(tsuki)* was stretched around the hatch of the baidarka and around the hunter under his arms by means of a sinew cord (with a strap over the left shoulder), linking the hunter and baidarka into a single unit. On his head, over the hood, the hunter wore a painted wooden hat with a bill or a visor extending forward; it protected the eyes from the sun's rays and from the spray of water. Veniaminov wrote that the Aleuts are somewhat clumsy on dry land, but that they had "a beautiful and majestic appearance" in baidarkas, and "it seems that he (the Aleut—R. L.) was created for the baidarka or the baidarka for him in order to show him in the best possible light."[25]

The explorers and voyagers of the nineteenth century noted the high technical quality of the Aleut baidarka and the exceptional dexterity of the Aleuts in controlling it. Veniaminov writes: "It seems to me that the Aleut baidarka is so perfected in its type that even a mathematician cannot add much, if anything, to perfect its seaworthiness." And in another place: "At that time, the excellent riders [*ezdok*] had [baidarkas] so light in their motion that they kept up with birds (skimming the water with the aid of their feet and wings before taking off), so narrow and with such a sharp keel that without a rider they could not maintain an upright position in the water, and were so light that a seven-year-old child was able to move it from place to place without strain."[26] However, these words referred to baidarkas of earlier years (probably prior to the arrival of the Russians), and during Veniaminov's stay in the Aleutian Islands some decline in the technique of their construction was already observed. G. Sarychev notes the great art of the Aleuts in controlling the baidarka, and its speed: "The islanders (Aleuts—R. L.) in their baidarkas travel so speedily that no light ship's boat is able to overtake them. We observed that when our vessel sailed at four miles per hour, even then they overtook it."[27]

The Aleuts amazed the Russians with their indefatigability in baidarka travel; they were able to paddle for ten and twelve hours without rest. Veniaminov writes: "I had occasion to travel with them several times from fourteen and to even twenty hours without touching shore, and in all that time they stopped no more than once and for no longer than fifteen minutes." And farther: "When captains Krenitsyn and Levashov were here, one Aleut, from among the best baidarka riders, was sent from Kapitanskaia Gavan' [Captains Bay, Unalaska] to Issanakh Strait [Isanotski Strait] with important news, who in 25 or 30 hours covered a distance of about 200 versts …And also it happened many times that in

12 to 18 hours they traveled from Ugamak to Sannakh (about 120 versts)."[28]

The best of the Aleut baidarkas could sail against the swiftest current in the straits.

The qualities needed by first-rate baidarka riders and sea hunters were taught among the Aleuts from early childhood. The youngsters were "trained to operate the baidarka: they were taught to be skillful both in the launching and the landing of the baidarka, how to manage it in heavy surf, and how to save themselves and others in dangerous circumstances, but especially how to be skillful in hunting and fishing."[29] Their education encompassed everyday training exercises: how to sit straight with legs outstretched forward and to be able at the same time to bend the arm in the proper manner for harpoon throwing. Little girls were trained how to equip hunters going to sea: to sew skin baidarka coverings and sew waterproof garments from intestines.

The Aleuts went many tens of versts out to sea and returned home in any weather without going off course, recognizing the correct direction by the flight of birds and other signs. If the wind became stronger and there was surf at the shore, they waited for an approaching wave and its crest carried them to shore; when the wave receded, they managed to pull the baidarka farther inland to prevent it from being carried back into the sea by a new wave. When the sea was running strong, they attached inflated bladders (a seal or sea lion stomach) to the sides of the baidarka, or if several baidarkas were at sea they tied them in twos or threes in a row and in between they attached to the sides inflated bladders (so the sides of the baidarkas would not rub when they pitched); they pointed the bows toward the waves and waited for the calm. The bladder *(sanguk)* [*sangux̂*] was an indispensable accessory for each baidarka. If the skin cover of a baidarka was torn, the hunter could, by leaning on the bladder, get out of the baidarka, float on the water with its assistance, repair the baidarka and get in again using the bladder for support. However, this could only be done in calm weather; during a storm the bladder was put into the baidarka and blown up as much as possible; it kept the boat afloat even if it was filled with water. There existed also another method for repairing the baidarka at sea (if there were three or more of them): the damaged baidarka was raised out of the water and placed across the other two. When a leak appeared in the baidarka seams, the latter were smeared with sea mammal oil.

Hollow bones or wooden tubes were used to bail water out of a baidarka.[30] They also used sea sponges to bail out the water.

The paddles *(akadgusik)* [*haqadguusîx̂*] used with baidarkas had two blades and were about 2.5 meters in length. The blades of the paddle were oval with sharpened ends and with a longitudinal rib on both flat surfaces; the shaft was round. When the baidarka tipped over the skilled hunters could, without getting out, right it with the aid of the paddle. They also carried out other difficult maneuvers with the aid of the paddle. Loss of a paddle was the greatest misfortune at sea.

The Aleut baidarkas had the following dimensions (in meters):

	Single-hatch	Two-hatch	Three-hatch
Length	4.2 to 6	5.6 to 7	7 to 8.5
Width	0.42 to 0.54	0.6 to 0.8	0.72 to 0.85
Height	0.27 to 0.4	0.38 to 0.54	0.4 to 0.55

The amount of material (excluding wood) used in the construction of a baidarka (and the hunting outfit) is apparent from the standard determined in 1816 by the Russian-American Company for issue to the Aleuts:[31]

For a two-man baidarka

6 laftaks of bachelors [32]	3 rubles each	18r.
2 gut kamleias	5 rubles each	10r.
7 funts of baleen for tying,		
whale sinews for sewing,		
portion of whale blubber		2r.

The principal part of the baidarka was the wooden latticed frame usually made from Californian chaga [cedar], the lightest and strongest wood. According to the information of Veniaminov, up to sixty bone parts were inserted in the frame of old baidarkas built for speed in order that each part of the baidarka "had movement" during use. The frames of the baidarkas in the nineteenth century were already entirely of wood. All parts of the frame were connected (tied) with strips of baleen.

The frame of the baidarka consisted of several parts (Figure 11).[33]

1) Upper frame with longitudinal details: side planks or planchettes, a middle plank or midsection (from the bow portion to the hatch and from the hatch to the stern), and cross pieces or beams (three to four in the bow portion and two to three in the stern). The bow and stern ends

of the frame were formed by the widening ends of the side planks; sometimes between the latter were inserted cross planks—a *breshtuk* and a stern thwart. Baleen fibers joining the parts were threaded through drilled openings or wound around the separate parts. At the top of the frame toward the stern, they secured to neighboring beams (with baleen fibers) a ring made of a bent wooden strip, a coaming, forming an opening for the baidarka hatch. In two-hatch and three-hatch baidarkas the coamings were also placed closer to the center and to the stern.

2) The keel (rather, keel plank or "false keel" because a keel in the true sense did not exist in the baidarka) was always assembled from three parts (in order to make the frame of the baidarka less brittle) and tied together with baleen fibers. The rear part of the keel plank, expanding almost to the height of the baidarka, formed the stern projection or stern post. In the front part the keel plank, expanding to approximately double, formed the lower part of the split bow of the baidarka, the stem.

3) The upper part of the stem, formed by a wooden plate, was joined at one end to the frame; the opposite, front, end was pointed and could be either straight or upturned. The upper half of the bow was attached to the lower half with baleen strips laced through drilled openings. Aleut baidarkas had bifid bows of two types: an upturned one and a straight one.

4) The stern projection of the baidarka, the stern post, had the shape of an irregular rectangle (it slanted from the frame) with a cutout where the end of the frame fit it.

5) Along the keel along the sides of the baidarka ran longitudinal planks (round or rectangular [in cross section]) or stringers (two, three, four on each side).

6) On the stringers from the inside were placed cross-framing ribs, made of bent sticks round or rectangular in cross-section. Each juncture of the stringers with the ribs was tied with baleen fibers. The pointed ends of the ribs fitted into round openings in the lower part of the side planks or planchettes.

7) The hatch was framed by a bent wooden plank.

The entire frame was painted red, sometimes with additions of blue stripes. The completed frame of the baidarka was fitted with a skin cover which was stretched also over the top of the boat, the deck, excluding the hatches. Sea lion skins were considered the best for these purposes and

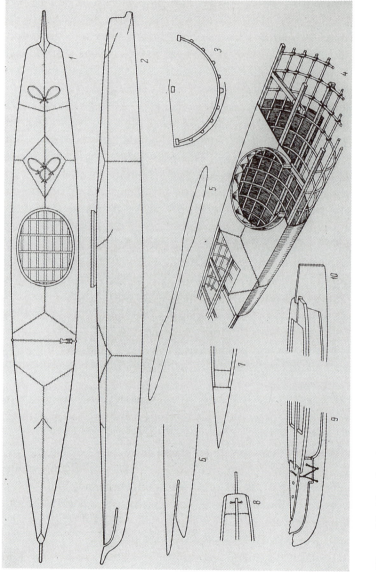

Figure 11. Aleut baidarkas (from the collection of the MAE). 1) top view; 2) side view; 3) cross-section; 4) detail of frame with cover; 5) paddle; 6) stem with cover (side view); 7) stem (frame, top view); 8) stem (frame, top view); 9) stern (frame, side view); 10) stern (frame, side view).

were used for covering the baidarkas as well as baidaras. Seal skin was used for covering smaller baidarkas. When sea lion skins were lacking, walrus skins were used (most often for baidaras), but these were too thick and required too much effort to process them (splitting the skin). A baidarka cover was sewn from two, three, or four whole skins with inserts between them. The cover was cut over the frame by the men, and the women sewed it (using small running stitches[g] with thread made of twisted sinew). Then the men fitted the cover onto the frame and sewed (also with running stitches) the last seam from the hatch to the stern and across the stern in the single-hatch baidarka, and from the front hatch to the stern and across the stern in the two-hatch and three-hatch baidarkas. All seams on the baidarka, except the last one, were internal; the last seam was external. In the completed baidarka the seams were carefully smeared with sea mammal oil to waterproof them. The upper seams were decorated with tiny bird feathers and long strands of wool inserted into the seam. After the arrival of the Russians, multicolored pieces of wool thread, 0.5 to 1 centimeter in length, instead of feathers, were inserted into the seams; they also decorated the seams with large beads [*korol'ki*] and glass seed beads [*stekliarus*] of various colors. Preparing to go to sea, the hunters lined the bottom of the baidarka with an old skin, on top of which they placed grass mats; then [the craft] was loaded (with provisions, water and stones for ballast).

In front of the hatch where the hunter sits and behind it one or two strips of baleen or thin sinew cord were tied across the baidarka; under these cords hunting equipment was secured. At the sides of these strips were often placed decorative carved bone images of sea otters. Behind the hatch on many baidarkas were thong loops (one pair and sometimes two). These apparently served for the transportation of game.

The baidarka skin covers were changed every year or even more frequently (they did not last longer than a year). To prevent the skin from swelling in the water and from drying out on land, it was periodically greased with [sea mammal] oil. The frame of the baidarka, with repairs of course, could remain serviceable for several years.

The baidarka and baidara construction was carried out by special masters whose art was highly valued; [but] every Aleut could repair a baidarka.

---

g. Smetochnyi shov, literally "running stitch," but may mean overcast stitch— L. B.

The materials used for baidarka construction encompassed all the means presented by the natural resources of the islands, which were utilized with maximum efficiency: wood washed onto the shore by the sea; skins, sinews and oil of sea mammals; baleen [and] bone. The baidarka decorations illustrate the aesthetic inclinations of the Aleuts and some aspects of their world view connected with hunting.

The type of skin-covered hunting boat with a wooden frame with a closed deck excluding only the hatch for the paddler-hunter, was widely distributed along the entire northern seaboard of North America, including the northwestern part, the coast of Greenland, and also Northeast Asia (among the Eskimo, Chukchi, and Koriak). Within this region many variations of skin boats of special local forms, typical of one or another region or tribal group, are found.[34] But the principal features of a single type of construction are preserved everywhere: a wooden frame consisting of an upper part with longitudinal (planchettes, midsections) and cross (beams) details; "false keel"; stringers; ribs; and sea mammal skin covers, leaving open only the hatch.

The character of the skin boats was conditioned first of all by the specific area where they were to be used (on the open sea, in the coastal zone, encircled with ice, in a river, in a lake), and then by their function in the economy.

Thus, the construction of the baidarkas of the Aleuts, an island people among whom sea hunting was the chief branch of the economy, achieved the highest perfection. They were excellently adapted to their use in the open sea—they had the longest length in conjunction with a narrow width and sharp keels, and possessed speed and maneuverability; Aleut baidarkas had pointed bows and a truncated stern with a stern projection (stern post). The kayaks of the Eskimos (including even the Pacific Eskimo group), Chukchi and Koriak basically had an identically pointed bow and stern. The latter [feature] permitted, while navigating through ice, movement in both directions without turning. The Aleuts had no need to reduce the seaworthiness of their baidarkas by use of such features because the sea was open the whole year round. The bifid bow of the Aleut baidarkas also should be attributed, apparently, to the achievements of Aleut boat construction. This [feature], together with the compound [composite] keel plank, gave the baidarka the ability "to bend on the wave." And moreover, apparently, such a bow slicing a side wave was better protected from breaking. On the whole, it is possible fully to agree with the words of Laughlin who characterized the baidarka as the "engineering triumph" of the Aleuts.[35]

Veniaminov, characterizing the baidarkas of the eastern Aleuts, declares that "the perfection of the baidarkas belongs to the Aleuts, this is indisputable; one has only to look at the baidarkas of the Kodiak Islanders, Aglegmiuts, and other inhabitants of the north, and even their compatriots, the Aleuts living on the islands nearest to Kamchatka, to note at first glance the superiority of the local baidarkas in comparison with all others."[36]

It is natural that the degree of perfection of these boats and their construction features reflect in each separate case the specialization of the economy. As is known, in the economy of the [northern] Eskimos a considerable role was played not only by sea hunting, but also by winter hunting for seals by means of "creeping up" to the breathing holes, with nets, and by land hunting for caribou and other land animal species. River and lake fishing had great importance. Moreover, not only the kayak but also a multipaddle skin boat, the umiak, was used in sea hunting by the [northern] Eskimos (and also by the Chukchi and Koriak). Thus, whales and other large sea mammals were hunted by large groups of hunters from an umiak, while the Aleuts hunted even whales from their baidarkas.

It becomes apparent that the technical perfection of the Aleut baidarkas was connected first of all with the specialization of their economy for sea hunting and fishing, and secondly with the specific features of their maritime activities, principally open sea hunting.

If the discussion concerns the differences between the baidarkas of the eastern and western Aleuts, then besides the above-mentioned remarks of Veniaminov about the superiority in quality of the baidarkas of the Aleuts of the Fox Islands (eastern) over the baidarkas of the more western Aleuts, there is nothing to add; we were unable to establish any differences in construction.[h]

The multipaddle skin boats, baidaras, were an integral part of the Aleut way of life prior to the arrival of the Russians. Thus, for example, I. Solov'ev reports a meeting with the inhabitants of the island of

---

h. See, however, the journal of Litke, who noted considerable differences in 1828 (F. Litke, *A Voyage Around the World, 1826–1829*, tr. R. Marshall, ed. R. A. Pierce, Kingston, Ontario: Limestone Press, 1987, p. 119)—L. B.

Sannakh [Sanak] (eastern Aleutian Islands) on a small neighboring island.[37] The Sannakh people came here with the entire settlement for "the preparation [putting up] of food for the winter" and informed him that they "always summered here, but during the winter they lived in their settlements on Sannakh." Five *toions* and fifty-one men of their "command" (that is, the male hunters), were here accompanied by wives and children. Each Aleut hunter had his single-seater "small baidarka." Besides that, they had five "large baidaras, capable of transporting entire families."

The question of the baidaras' construction is somewhat confused. In the museum collections there are no Aleut baidaras, nor models of them. Therefore, written sources and sketches assume great significance in determining the shape of these boats. In the literature, they are mentioned only briefly; detailed descriptions or sketches are lacking. Soon after the arrival of the Russians on the islands, the typical Aleut baidaras became very rare, and later they disappeared entirely. Another type of multipaddle skin boat appeared, baidaras used by Russian promyshlenniki. These baidaras were made on the Koriak model. F. I. Soimonov mentioned such boats.[38] T. I. Shmalev dwelt in detail on their characteristics:

> ...at first the Russian promyshlenniki carried with them small plank [wooden] boats, but nowadays they have dropped their use entirely and are using boats resembling the local baidaras; the frames, which resemble those of a small boat or yawl, that is, the keel, bow and stern post, thin ribs [*kokorki*] and strips [*barkhoty*], are all made on Kamchatka, then are disassembled and carried aboard the vessel and on reaching the islands, are assembled without any use of iron nails, but for the most part with thongs, instead of planks the [boats] are covered with sea lion or fur seal skins [from which] the fur has been scraped; these will not get soaked for a considerable length of time; these [baidaras] are so strong that the water can even be seen through them from the inside; they are made so large that up to six to eight men can travel in them. Between hunts, they

are always dragged up on the shore and dried out; because of their light weight they can be dragged out without much effort, after the hunting is done. [39]

Further [Shmalev writes that]:

1) As mentioned above, all frame components are made of wood, namely: (1) the keel, 8 arshins[i] long, 4 vershoks[j] wide, and 3 vershoks thick; (2) the lower ends of the stems, each not thicker than 4 vershoks, which are usually attached by their lower ends to the keel ends, while ribs, attached with nails, are placed on top; (3) along the entire keel, bars 3 vershoks wide are placed at intervals of 1 arshin, each bar nailed in the middle with two nails; ribs [*kokorki*] 5 and 6 vershoks long are attached at the bent ends of each bar; directly on the keel, bent ribs [extending] from the cross bars to the same height as the side [the gunwales], are attached with baleen the thickness of a goose quill; on the upper end are placed bars or thin poles [forming] gunwales; instead of thwarts five or six small planks are placed across, the ends of which are then attached to standing ribs with baleen, and these serve as thwarts for the oarsmen.

2) After all of the above-described [features] have been fastened, the sewn skins of sea lion or sea cow are placed under the keel, the edge[s] are pulled over the gunwale, and those skins or covers are attached to the internal bar[s] or round rod[s] below the gunwales by means of cords or sinews, in the same manner as sails are sewn with double seams; the entire architecture of those baidaras consists of the above-described.[40]

---

i. One arshin equals 28 inches—Trans.

j. One vershok equals 1³/₄ inches—Trans.

The information cited here indicates that Russian promyshlenniki at first carried [wooden] plank boats with them; later they carried only their wooden frames, and only after arrival in the islands assembled the frames and covered them with sea lion, fur seal, and sea cow skins. Some scholars consider as the Aleut type of baidara precisely this boat of the Russian promyshlenniki, which is basically of the Koriak type.[41] The sketches from the album of M. D. Levashov[42] help to resolve the question. In one of them we can see the representation of a baidara of the promyshlenniki with the notation "baidara or skin boat" (Figure 12, item 2). It has a rounded bow and stern, typical of the Koriak baidaras, but has a rudder and oarlocks for the oars and eight small benches for oarsmen, which are missing in the genuine Koriak baidaras. In the second sketch a traditional Aleut baidara is undoubtedly depicted, although there is no inscription (Figure 12, item 1). That baidara has the pointed and bifid bow that is also typical of the Aleut baidarkas. The stern is also pointed. Benches are absent; there are only narrow cross beams (in early reports it is mentioned that the Aleuts sat directly on the bottom [of the baidara] and not on benches). Levashov's drawing is of great value because it helps to establish the true shape of the traditional Aleut baidara.

It is necessary to note that the illustrations provided in the work of V. I. Iokhel'son represent the type of Aleut baidaras in existence at the beginning of the twentieth century.[43] In their construction are elements of traditional Aleut baidaras and elements introduced by the Russians. These baidaras have a pointed bow, but it [the bow] is not bifid; the stern is almost vertical, and there are benches.

Having examined the Aleut watercraft, we have had the opportunity to note that in the island [archipelago] environment, the Aleuts became excellent seafarers, equipped with highly developed means of seagoing transport. Of course, this required a long period of adaptation in this particular region.

Let us now briefly consider the tools used by Aleut men in the manufacture of hunting implements, weapons, baidarkas, and other items; [let us also consider] basic women's tools. Ethnographic data on this subject are extremely meager, as the use of traditional Aleut tools was discontinued in short order. Prior to Russian arrival, materials used for tools were stone, bone, and wood. Metals entered the Aleutian

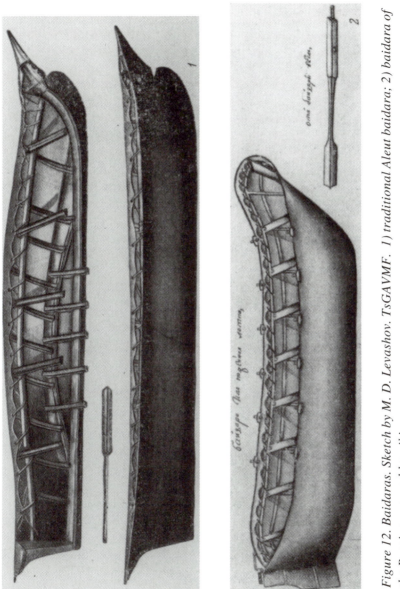

Figure 12. Baidaras. Sketch by M. D. Levashov. TsGAVMF. 1) traditional Aleut baidara; 2) baidara of the Russian promyshlenniki.

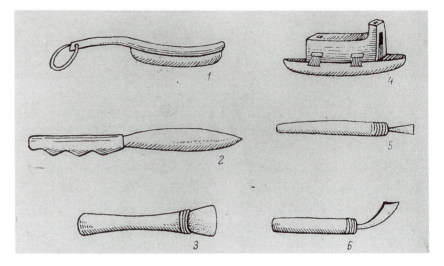

Figure 13. Men's tools (after M. D. Levashov).

Islands only in small quantities (either through barter via Alaska or imbedded in wood from wrecked vessels). Knives and projectile blades [points] were produced by cold hammering [from such drift iron].

In woodworking, the Aleuts' main tool was a bone wedge by means of which they split the logs. The finishing was done with axes [adzes]. Aleut axes resembled adzes [*shliakhty*], hewing tools: the shafts were secured [to the blades] in a manner which resulted in the blade being perpendicular to the shaft. The stone blade was secured to the wooden shaft with thongs and sinew.[44] Further working of wood was accomplished with smaller tools. A unique representation of Aleut tools of the eighteenth century is in the album of M. D. Levashov—"a set of instruments for making baidarkas and spears" (Figures 2 and 13).[45] Out of six objects, four (Figure 13, items 3 through 6) have notations that can be read, though with difficulty. Figure 13, items 1 and 2, are varieties of knives; their handles, judging by the coloring on Levashov's sketch, are wooden. Figure 13, item 3, is a tool of the chisel type ("for finishing of spears" is written above it in the original). Figure 13, item 4, is a retoucher (notation [reads] "with this they work stones for spears"; "wood" is written above the handle, and near the lower working end part is written "bone"). Tools of that type were described in detail by Iokhel'son.[46] He provides a sketch of the model of such an instrument which was made by one old Aleut on his request.[47] Figure 13, item 5, is a cutter [*rezets*, burin] (under it is the notation "drill, with this they made holes"). Figure 13, item 6, is also a cutter, but curved (beside its handle

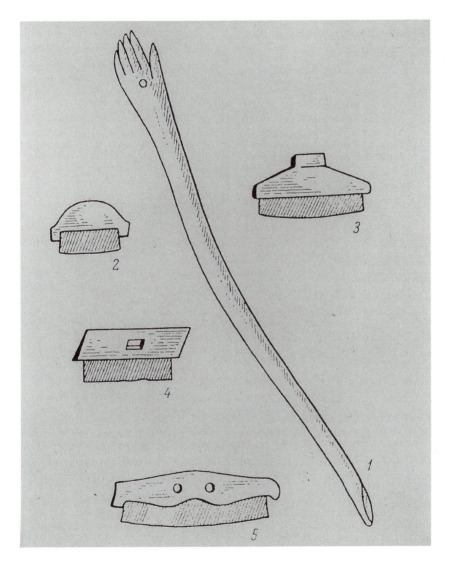

Figure 14. Women's tools (after M. D. Levashov).

123

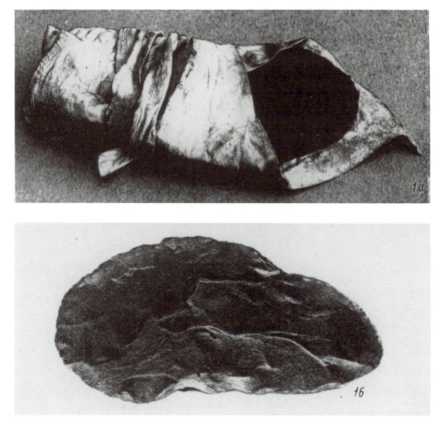

Figure 15. Women's tools (from the collection of the MAE). 1a, top, and 1b) knife, No. 4104-137.

"wood" is written, and by the working part is written "animal tooth"; the notation under the instrument [reads] "with it they made grooves in wood for some purpose").

The tools which were used by women were connected with gathering and with the preparation of skins, etc. (Figure 14). The digging stick, *koparulka*, is for digging up edible roots; broad slate knives with wooden handles at the butt end, *pekulki* [ulus], are for cutting skins, etc. These objects are pictured after Levashov's drawings. In the collection of the MAE there is an obsidian knife, used without a handle (Figure 15, item 1). Oval in shape, it is more rounded at one end and more pointed at the other. The knife is wrapped in a strip of thin white skin. Such knives are mentioned by Iokhel'son, who illustrates some examples thereof.[48] There are two scrapers for scraping skins (Figure 15, items 2 and 3) in the collection of the MAE. Both of them, besides providing evidence on the type of Aleut scrapers, illustrate highly artistic bone carving.

The tools examined above demonstrate the differentiation of labor between men and women in Aleut society, connected with the different character of their part in economic life.

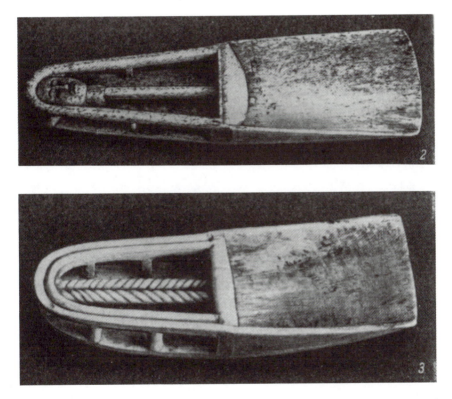

Figure 15 (continued). 2 and 3) scrapers, Nos. 4104-55, 2937-17.

CITATIONS AND NOTES

1. H. B. Collins, A. H. Clark, and E. H. Walker, *The Aleutian Islands: Their People and Natural History* (Washington, 1945), p. 2.

2. I. Veniaminov, *Zapiski ob ostrovakh Unalashkinskogo otdela* [Notes on the islands of the Unalaska district], vol. 2 (St. Petersburg, 1840), pp. 256–258.

3. Here and below the first meaning is given according to I. Veniaminov, *Zapiski...*, vol. 2, pp. 256–258, and the second ["in the dictionary"] according to I. Veniaminov, *Opyt grammatiki aleutsko-lis'evskogo iazyka* [Tentative grammar of the Aleut-Fox language] (St. Petersburg, 1846), pp. 2–69. [The additions within square brackets are in the modern Aleut orthography, after Knut Bergsland, compiler, *Aleut Dictionary* (Fairbanks: Alaska Native Language Center, University of Alaska Fairbanks, 1994)—L. B.]

4. The reports in the literature about large hunting parties of Aleuts (up to 100 to 200 baidarkas) setting out to hunt sea otters, refer to the period of the existence of Russian trading companies on the islands. The initiative in organizing such hunting parties belonged entirely to the Russian promyshlenniki, and later, to the Russian-American Company.

5. TsGADA, f. 199, d. 528, ch. 2, l. 10–10 ob. T. I. Shmalev sent academician G. F. Müller materials compiled on the basis of reports and journals of the promyshlenniki.

6. TsGADA, f. 199, d. 528, ch. 2, l. 10–10 ob.

7. I. Veniaminov, *Zapiski ob ostrovakh Unalashkinskogo otdela,* vol. 3 (St. Petersburg, 1840), p. 23.

8. After K. T. Khlebnikov, "Zapiski o koloniiakh v Amerike" [Notes on the colonies in America], part 3, ALOII, koll. 115, d. 344.

9. For details see R. G. Liapunova, "Orudiia okhoty aleutov" [Aleut hunting implements], *Sbornik Muzeia antropologii i etnografii im. Petra I*, t. 21 (1963).

10. I. G. Voznesenskii archive, LOAAN, f. 2, 1845, no. 12.

11. G. A. Sarychev, *Puteshestvie po severo-vostochnoi chasti Sibiri, Ledovitomu moriu i Vostochnomu okeanu* [Voyage to the northeastern part of Siberia, the Arctic Sea, and the Eastern Ocean] (Moscow, 1952), p. 213.

12. I. Veniaminov, *Zapiski...*, part 2, p. 246.

13. M. M. Bulgakov collection, AVPR, f. 339, op. 808, d. 733, l. 1 ob., 2 (rough drafts of Bulgakov's reports to the Academy of Sciences about the forwarding of curiosities found by the Russian-American Company, 26 November 1816).

14. The author of the sketch, P. N. Mikhailov, was a participant in the round-the-world expedition of 1826–1829 on the vessels *Seniavin* and *Moller* under the command of F. P. Litke and M. I. Staniukovich.

15. We were unable to single out fish spears based on the ethnographic materials, but it is feasible to assume that they were those of the "bird darts" which have side points bent toward the central prong rather sharply (for firmer seizure of the fish; Figure 7, item 7). It is also possible that the fish were taken with spears with sharply pointed barbed bone heads.

16. On Aleut throwing boards, see also: O. A. Girshfel'd, "Kop'emetalki po materialam etnograficheskikh myzeev Leningrada i Moskvy" [Spear-throwers according to the materials of the ethnographic museums of Leningrad and Moscow], *Sbornik Muzeia antropologii i etnografii im. Petra I,* t. 14 (1953), pp. 98–118; O. T. Mason, "Throwing-sticks in the National Museum," *Report of the United States National Museum for 1884,* pt. 2 (Washinton: Government Printing Office, 1885), pp. 279–289.

17. H. Larsen and F. Rainey, "Ipiutak and the Arctic Whale Hunting culture," *Anthropological Papers of the American Museum of Natural History* 42 (1948).

18. K. T. Khlebnikov, "Zapiski o koloniiakh v Amerike," part 4, ALOII, koll. 115, d. 447, l. 120 ob., 121.

19. J. E. Ransom, "Aleut natural-food economy," *American Anthropologist,* n.s., 48 (1946), pp. 607–623.

20. The Russian promyshlenniki called the Aleut single-, two-, and three-hatch boats "baidarkas," and the multi-paddle ones "baidaras"; these names for the designation of Aleut boats entered the literature. For the Eskimo boats, their local names were preserved in the literature: "kayak" for the single-hatch and "umiak" for the multipaddle ones.

21. I. Veniaminov, *Zapiski...,*vol. 2, p. 240.

22. The remarkable aptitude of the Aleuts for sea hunting was utilized in the eighteenth and nineteenth centuries by the Russians, who forced them [the Aleuts] to hunt for fur-bearing sea animals (sea otters and fur seal), first for various trading companies, and later for the Russian-American Company.

23. R. G. Liapunova, "Aleutskie baidarki" [Aleut baidarkas], *Sbornik Muzeia antropologii i etnografii,* t. 22 (1964).

24. I. Veniaminov, *Opyt grammatiki...,*pp. 62, 63.

25. I. Veniaminov, *Zapiski...,* vol. 2, p. 7.

26. Ibid., pp. 220, 222.

27. G. A. Sarychev, *Puteshestvie...*, p. 214.

28. I. Veniaminov, *Zapiski...*, vol. 2, pp. 12, 221–222.

29. Ibid., p. 72.

30. H. C. Fassett, "The Aleut sea otter hunt in the late nineteenth century," ed. R. F. Heizer, *Anthropological Papers of the University of Alaska* 8, no. 2 (1960), p. 133.

31. K. Khlebnikov, "Materialy dlia istorii russkikh zaselenii po beregam Vostochnogo okeana (zapiski K. Khlebnikova ob Amerike)" [Materials for the history of Russian settlement along the shores of the Eastern Ocean (notes of K. Khlebnikov about America)], in *Prilozhenie k Morskomu sborniku* [Supplement to *Morskoi sbornik*], no. 3 (St. Petersburg, 1861), p. 66.

32. "Laftak" here means a skin; "bachelor" refers to a two- to three-year-old [non-breeding] male sea lion or fur seal, *lakhtak*.

33. The names of the parts are given by analogy with boat terminology, but they do not correspond to it fully.

34. *Istoriko-etnograficheskii atlas Sibiri* [Historical-ethnographic atlas of Siberia], ed. M. G. Levin and L. P. Potapov (Moscow and Leningrad, 1961), pp. 107–130; K. Birket-Smith, *The Eskimos* (London: Methuen, 1936), pp. 83–89; idem, *The Caribou Eskimos: Material and Social Life and their Cultural Position, Report of the Fifth Thule Expedition 1921–24*, vol. 5 (1–2) (Copenhagen, 1929), pp. 172–175; F. Boas, "The Eskimo of Baffin Land and Hudson Bay," *Bulletin of the American Museum of Natural History* 15 (1901), pp. 9–13, 76–78; idem, "The Central Eskimo," *Sixth Annual Report of the Bureau of American Ethnology for the Years 1884–1885* (1888), pp. 390–669.

35. W. S. Laughlin, "Human migration and permanent occupation in the Bering Sea area," in *The Bering Land Bridge*, ed. D. M. Hopkins (Stanford: Stanford University Press, 1967), p. 425.

36. I. Veniaminov, *Zapiski...*, vol. 2, p. 220.

37. N. N. Ogloblin, "Putevye zametki morekhoda I. M. Solov'eva, 1770–1775. Epizod iz istorii russkikh otkrytii v Vostochnom okeane" [Travel notes of navigator I. M. Solov'ev, 1770–1775. An episode from the history of Russian discoveries in the Eastern Ocean], *Russkaia starina*, book 9 (1892), pp. 744–762.

38. F. I. Soimonov, "K drevnei poslovitse - Sibir - zolotoe dno" [To the ancient saying—Siberia—a gold mine], *Sobranie sochinenii k pol'ze i uveseleniiu sluzhashchikh,* 1761, November-January.

39. T. I. Shmalev, "Pribavleniia k zhurnalu tainogo sovetnika i sibirskogo gubernatora Fedora Ivanovicha Soimonova" [Supplements to the journal of Privy Councilor and Governor of Siberia Fedor Ivanovich Soimonov], TsGADA, f. 199, no. 528, ch. 2, d. 10, l. 10 ob.

40. Ibid., AVPR, f. RAK, op. 888, d. 2, l. 157–158.

41. B. Durham, *Canoes and Kayaks of Western America* (Seattle, 1960), p. 21.

42. See R. G. Liapunova, "Etnograficheskoe znachenie ekspeditsii kapitanov P. K. Krenitsyna i M. D. Levashova na Aleutskie ostrova (1764–1769 gg.)" [Ethnographic significance of the expedition of captains P. K. Krenitsyn and M. D. Levashov to the Aleutian Islands (1764–1769)], *Sovetskaia etnografiia,* 1971, no. 6.

43. W. I. Jochelson, *History, Ethnology and Anthropology of the Aleuts, Carnegie Institution of Washington Publication* 432 (Washington, 1933), pp. 56, 58.

44. W. I. Jochelson, *Archaeological Investigations in the Aleutian Islands, Carnegie Institution of Washington Publication* 367 (Washington, 1925), pp. 32, 57, 58, 90, 120; I. Veniaminov, *Zapiski...,* vol. 2, p. 249.

45. Figure 13 was made from M. D. Levashov's watercolor.

46. W. I. Jochelson, *Archaeological Investigations...,* p. 71.

47. Ibid., p. 70.

48. Ibid., p. 63.

III. SOCIO-ECONOMIC RELATIONS

Having examined the Aleut economy, we now confront the question of relations of production expressed in attitudes toward property, and the question of socio-economic relations which existed among the Aleuts on the basis of the particular level of development of the forces of production of their society. Because of a lack of material, only partial examination of these questions is possible, but examination seems to be highly necessary for a [valid] characterization of Aleut society up to the time when Russians encountered them.

The work of I. Veniaminov is the principal source of information concerning the social structure of the Aleuts.[1] The description he compiled of the Aleuts inhabiting the eastern part of the islands contains an attempt at the reconstruction of Aleut society in the first half of the eighteenth century (by the time of Veniaminov's arrival on the islands, the social structure of the Aleuts had already undergone considerable change). But Veniaminov's information, regrettably, is far from comprehensive, and a number of his statements require verification. He does not define, naturally, the character of the social structure of the Aleuts. Veniaminov's general appraisal of the Aleuts' level of development is evident only in the following remark: "The Aleuts are above the Indians because the locality forces them to devise a means of subsistence and, consequently, to improve their cleverness."[2]

Analyzing the information provided by Veniaminov, M. V. Stepanova came to the following conclusion: "The society which Veniaminov paints for us is undergoing a transition from the stage of a kinship-based tribal system to a 'military democracy'....[a] If one ought to see in the Tlingits the prototype [sic] of Tacitus's Germans, then Veniaminov's

---

a. Liapunova was writing in a period when scholarship was constrained and had to follow a Marxist line. The concept of the military democracy as a stage in the development of society is derived from the Marx and Engels interpretation of Lewis Henry Morgan's *Ancient Society*—L. B.

eastern Aleuts resemble the Scandinavians prior to the time of the Vikings."[3]

The question of the social structure of the Aleuts as a part of the general problem of the social structure of the Eskimos and Aleuts was studied by L. A. Fainberg.[4] He focused primarily on the proof for the existence of matrilineal clans among the Aleuts in the past. He defines Aleut society at the end of the eighteenth century as being transitional from a matrilineal clan organization to a patrilineal one, with the presence of "at least a formal kinship-based [clan-based] tribal organization" concomitantly with incipient property [inequality] and social stratification.[5]

Until recently, foreign specialists seldom touched upon the question of the social structure of the Aleuts. Only W. S. Laughlin, subscribing to the popular theory current among western investigators about the originally clanless society of the Eskimos, expressed the hypothesis that among the Aleuts, clan [lineage] developed at a comparatively late date, as was supposedly the case among the Eskimos of St. Lawrence Island.[6] G. Berreman also does not concede the existence in the past of a clan [lineage] organization among the Aleuts, and proceeds from the position that a conjugal pair was the initial social and economic unit among the Aleuts from earliest times, and the village was the largest and ultimate unit. Of interest is Berreman's conclusion concerning individualism as one of the remarkable features of the Aleut character.[7] Only in 1970, in response to the special interest in latter years in the Aleuts as a people linking the chain of cultures of the Old and New Worlds, did there appear the large [extensive] work of American scholar M. Lantis on the social organization of Aleuts in the period 1750–1810, derived from early historical sources.[8]

This work, naturally, is based mainly on old Russian publications. It is necessary to note its broad scope and thoroughness of characterization [assessment]. In the main part of her work, the author cites materials classified according to the following headings: population of the islands; settlements; dwellings; domestic economy; domestic life; customs relating to birth, coming of age, marriage, death; and social system—kinship, partnership, secret societies, classes and castes, political authority and government, property, and trade. Summing up, Lantis emphasizes that the data cited by her should serve as a basis for the elucidation of "the cultural and historical place of the Aleuts, [which] is still something of a mystery," in the "North Pacific and Bering Sea cultural histories." This, in her opinion, should be fulfilled in the future by the comparative study of the Aleut culture and the cultures to the west and east, that is, [cultures] on the Asiatic and American shores of the Pacific Ocean.

We have attempted to bring to the investigation of the socio-economic relations formed among the Aleuts toward the middle of the eighteenth century, data collected in the first decades after the discovery of the islands by the Russians. These are "testimonies" [*skaski*], "tales," and "reports" of the Russian merchants and promyshlenniki who visited the Aleutian Islands in the second half of the eighteenth century, the materials of the governmental expeditions of 1764–1769 (Krenitsyn-Levashov) and 1785–1793 (Billings-Sarychev), and also the notes of A. A. Baranov about Unalaska, dating to 1790. Some of these materials have been published, and part have been extracted from archives.

Despite the fact that the scant material available does not permit complete elucidation of some aspects of the relations of production and character of the social institutions, the available information allows us to see the original features of Aleut society and the specific historical peculiarity [historical predication] of its development.

Examining the economic pursuits of the Aleuts, we noted that their principal procurement activities (hunting of sea mammals, fishing at sea, and bird hunting) were tied in many cases to cooperative work as a means to increase productivity. But this cooperation did not have by then an obligatory character. Alongside the collective, individual procurement activities were also widely practiced. The utilization of the single-hatch baidarka and not the multipaddle baidara as a hunting vessel played a special role in this. The baidarka, with its excellent seafaring qualities, in many ways determined the character of undertakings.

It is very important that this type of hunting boat permitted individual hunting. A baidarka could be launched on the water and also brought onto the shore with only the effort of a single hunter. An Aleut hunter in his baidarka could go hunting without needing the aid of any hunting companions. Information about such [individual] forays are found in the folklore of the Aleuts. The catch brought in by the hunter was substantial enough: 100 to 200 kilograms in the baidarka and hundreds of kilograms in tow (for the transportation of game, special seal skin floats were on hand). It follows that the baidarka allowed the hunter and his family to maintain an individual existence without the obligatory cooperation of the entire community or even of several of its members.

The hunting implements of the Aleuts, as we have seen, were exceptionally well suited to the peculiarities of their maritime procurement activity.

In general it can be said that the highly perfected means of production and the elevated skills of the hunters achieved during many centuries of carrying on that type of economy, assisted, among the Aleuts, the development of a rather high productivity of labor, given the high efficiency of their activities of production. In these conditions, cooperative labor as a means of increasing productivity was not necessary. The role of individual hunting activity and, accordingly, individual hunters, promyshlenniki, was considerable.

However, cooperative labor was obligatory in catching and putting up fish at the streams during the spawning season. Women were engaged in this work. It is known that at this season they, with the children, gathered into groups and moved to predetermined locations. But unfortunately, we only have information that these groups were formed of women either from the entire village or from several families.

Gathering was also the activity of women and children. Cooperation is not registered [noted] here.

The latter forms of activity were not considered the principal ones in the Aleut economy during the period examined; they played only a subsidiary role.

The single-hatch baidarka and the hunting implements were the property of a single hunter, that is, the principal means of production were subject to individual ownership. This [such ownership], together with the individual hunting activity practice, testifies to the economic independence of individual families, each led by a pater familias-hunter. The character of the norms of distribution of material goods in the Aleut society of the period examined also testifies to this: the individualization of labor led to the individualization of appropriation and the separation of nuclear family from the community collective. As is known, the collective character of production in the primitive communal system conditioned also the collective character of consumption.

Among the Aleuts there existed the practice of individual appropriation of the catch obtained by individual hunting, but with the survival of collective distribution phenomena.

This is indicated by a number of customs. Among the Aleuts, as well as among some groups of Eskimos, a custom is noted which is a survival of collective distribution, which existed earlier: "From the beginning of the hunt, the owner distributes the meat of the first animal killed to all the Aleuts in his village, a part to each."[9]

Besides that, Aleuts had a definite form of economic association based on fraternal kinship. It should be noted that these were fictive fraternal connections. This is indicated by the term *agitudak* [*agiitudax̂*],[b] "brother," "comrade."[10] Apparently it is this custom which is reflected in the account that during the hunting of sea otters the first man who hit the animal with a spear and got it, never retained it for himself but gave it to his closest relative, who in turn acted in the same manner.[11] These economic relations between individual families which have replaced the collective ones once again point to the absence of collective norms of distribution.

The accounts dating to the second half of the eighteenth century, available in archives, confirm that among the Aleuts there existed a considerable number of individual procurement activities, the products of which were retained by individual families and not distributed to everyone. For example, in the notes of A. A. Baranov we read: "...as a community they do not recognize either poverty or profit, but are attached to property; even in hunting, it often happens that, when one wounds a seal or fur seal with a spear, another seizes it and seldom shares unless it is a large animal, if they get a sea lion or a whale washes ashore, but even then each one tries to grab as much as possible for himself."[12]

From the reports about the sorry state of orphans in the community, who were forced to feed themselves only by gathering in the tidal zone or with the gnawed bones left by others, it is possible to draw a conclusion concerning the absence of collective norms of distribution.[13]

---

b. Here and below we have added in square brackets the spelling in the modern Aleut orthography, when such could be determined, following Knut Bergsland, compiler, *Aleut Dictionary* (Fairbanks, Alaska: Alaska Native Language Center, University of Alaska Fairbanks, 1994)—L. B.

Age-old traditions of collective distribution of food among all members of the community preserved their significance only in the case of extreme shortage.[14]

Certain norms existed for the distribution of the catch. The greatest equality was observed in the process of the distribution of [drift] whales that were washed ashore. The man who was the first to locate [such] a whale had the right to take half of the membrane from the tongue, half of the intestines and sinew, "the rest was divided by the *toion* of the settlement among the Aleuts equally."[15] If a wound with a spear point embedded in it was found in the whale, then according to the ownership mark on the point, it was determined who had wounded the animal. If the whale was wounded by a hunter from another settlement, its inhabitants were notified and the catch was divided in common. The better parts belonged to the owner of the spear; the rest the head of the community divided equally.

Distribution of the spoils of the collective hunt was always done according to strictly established rules. A sea lion carcass was distributed in the following manner: the first [man] who hit the animal with a spear with an attached bladder float received half the skin and half the intestines, and had the right to assign to anyone (of the participants in the hunt) the second half of the skin and intestines; the second [man] who hit the animal with a spear received the esophagus and the remaining intestines; the third received the bladder; the fourth and fifth received the front flippers; the sixth and seventh received the rear flippers; and the meat was divided among the entire hunting party. In the hunt for fur seals, the skin of the animal belonged to the one whose dart with an inflated bladder float hit the animal first. The meat was divided among all who participated in the hunt. In the hunt for sea otter, the skin (which was the most valuable part of the animal) belonged to the hunter who hit the animal first with a harpoon. If several harpoons hit the animal at once, then the skin belonged to the hunter whose harpoon was closest to the head if the mortal wound was in the back; if such a wound was in the belly, then the skin belonged to the hunter whose harpoon was closest to the tail (on all the harpoons there were ownership marks). The rest of the hunting party received a fixed share of meat.[16]

Information about food storage by each family individually is in concordance with the above-mentioned rules for distribution of the catch. In the large communal dwellings of the Aleuts, spaces existed for each family where their belongings "and food reserves" were stored. Besides that, "the well-to-do husbandmen sometimes made inside the wall special storerooms *(agaiaq)* [*agayax̂*] to the side of their compartments, where they stored their belongings and food."[17] The summer dwellings *(uliaq)* [*ulax̂*], which to be sure did not exist on all islands, were already not communal, but separate for each family. Year round, the family stored hunting and fishing equipment, food reserves, and other belongings in them.

In the communal dwellings, meals were taken not in common, but by each family in its own space.[18]

The hunting and fishing grounds among the Aleuts were the collective property of their community-settlements: "...each settlement had its own separate hunting and fishing grounds...The leaders of the settlement were obliged to defend them and...not permit outsiders to hunt or fish within another's boundaries."[19]

Information in early Russian sources (I. Solov'ev's "report") confirms this: "And where one has a dwelling, no other has the right to hunt animals or to collect that which was washed ashore, unless he has permission."[20] Or: "...each hut or homestead protects its place on the shore. Outsiders requiring food dare not pick up even a dead fish, but must first beg for it as for charity; otherwise, they will not get away with their heads intact...the uninhabited islands belong to all equally; on the inhabited ones outsiders are either guests or enemies."[21]

In Aleut folklore we encounter the motif that people who infringe on this rule are punished by death.[22]

Besides the ownership of specific areas by individual communities, there was apparently also ownership of land by the alliance of several community-settlements (for instance, those of one island). A toion who headed an alliance of several related settlements and their leaders or toions was considered "the ruler of his island or district" and he had the right to a share "of everything cast up" (sea mammals, fish, wood, etc., washed ashore) in this territory, while the settlement toions did not have such rights in the grounds of their own communities.[23]

In a report of the merchant V. Shilov (1767), one can also see indications of the existence of such procurement grounds "...they (Russian promyshlenniki—R. L.) never saw the inhabitants of one island wage a war between themselves, but they saw battles fought for possession of hunting grounds between one island and another by collective force."[24]

Some sources note the struggle between individual communities for hunting grounds. "The weakest and the poorest" were forced "to seek for their means of existence in other places, becoming opponents and even enemies of their former oppressors, and later of all fellow tribesmen."[25] Apparently, this was reflected in the names of the separate groups of the population. Thus, the eastern Aleuts called the inhabitants of the Near Islands "exiles from the island."[26]

In determining the economic relationships within the domestic community of the Aleuts, it is necessary to take into account first of all the fact that they were formed by the dominant role of men in all spheres of economic life. Among the Aleuts, a clear division of labor existed between the sexes. Men were engaged in the hunting of sea mammals, fishing in the sea, hunting for birds, stockpiling wood (driftwood), making hunting baidarkas and baidaras, hunting implements and weapons, wooden hunting headgear, and stone and wooden dishes, and erecting dwellings. Women's work, which was shameful for the men to do, was catching fish in the streams, putting up fish stores, digging roots and gathering berries, gathering in the tidal zone, sewing, weaving, and the manufacture of sinew threads. Thus, thanks to the labor of men, the Aleuts were supplied with the main food product, meat, with material for garments and means of production, with implements [tools] and some household articles, and with dwellings. In accordance with this, the men were owners of the principal means of production. The work of women, although important, still played an auxiliary role in economic life.

The existing relations of production and relations in the sphere of distribution created the preconditions for social stratification in the Aleut community. In the early sources there is information that among the Aleuts property differentiation and the initial forms of exploitation of men by men had already appeared. Patriarchal slavery was already solidly entrenched in their lives and was reflected in their ideology.

According to Veniaminov, there were three "estates" among the Aleuts: "notables," "commoners" and "*kalgas*" (slaves).

"Toions and their children and nephews formed the highest class; [those] distinguished in military deeds and in the art of hunting, and their descendants, constituted the so-called notables proper; all the ordinary Aleuts made up the class of commoners, those who did not distinguish themselves in anything, and emancipated slaves; and the *kalga*s were prisoners of war and their descendants."[27]

But even according to Veniaminov's own materials, it turns out that more than three subdivisions existed in Aleut society.

The toions, their children, and nephews represented, apparently, the highest category of hereditary lineage [clan] aristocracy (Figure 16).[28] This was a socially and materially distinctive group. It was accorded a special space in the long house: the toion's family always occupied the front, the eastern, part of the dwelling (they built dwellings oriented from east to west; the east was specially regarded by the Aleuts). If there were several dwellings in the settlement, the leader and his family lived in the largest one. This group was distinguished by the nature of burial, its garments, and the presence of slaves for service.

The "notables proper" was probably a newly formed wealthy stratum and military elite. They, too, could own slaves: "Only the notables had the right to own slaves, the ordinary people very rarely."[29]

The two above-mentioned categories differed from the others in that they were better supplied with food and had the opportunity to accumulate wealth: the best baidarkas, stone knives and daggers, richly adorned wooden headgear, well-made implements and weapons, festive parkas, kamleikas, various pigments, and finally, bone facial decorations and the most expensive adornments—amber and *tsukli* (dentaliaum shells). Products from hunting and fishing were not accumulated as wealth by the Aleuts (in contrast to the Indians of the northwest coast of North America).

The third category constituted "commoners," the rank-and-file members of a community.

The fourth category was that of so-called Aleuts without kin. Freed slaves and immigrants from other islands belonged to it. This was an economically dependent category. The position [situation] of these "kinless Aleuts" is attested by a song that was, to judge by the text, composed by one of them: "As I am a poor (working) man, I must be thankful and happy against my will."[30]

And finally, the slaves, "kalgas," occupied the lowest rung on the social ladder.

139

Figure 16. Toion from the Fox Islands. Watercolor by M. T. Tikhanov reproduced here in black and white. Museum of the Academy of Arts of the USSR.

Slavery among the Aleuts was still widespread at the end of the eighteenth century. Some Aleuts had up to twenty slaves. The wealth of a man was measured by the number of his slaves. The slaves were considered the private property of the toions, members of their families, and other "notable" Aleuts. From Aleut folklore it is evident that slaves were in the personal service of each family member. Among the Aleuts, the terms "slave" and "servant" were expressed by the same word: *taliak* [*tahlax̂*]—"slave," "servant," *aiagam taliagana* [*ayagam tahlaĝanaa*]— "[serving] maid," "female slave."[31] The female slaves often became concubines.

The slave was entirely in the power of the master. The punishments of the slaves were clearly defined: "...for disobedience they cut off the ears, for carrying tales from the master's household, lips were cut off, and if the slave persisted [in spreading gossip], especially if hostility arose as a consequence of his [loose] tongue, then death was inevitably his fate. For the first attempt to escape corporal punishment was inflicted, that is, he was beaten with whatever was at hand; for the second attempt, his hands were tied behind him and he was kept for some time in such a position; for the third, they cut the calf [tendon] of the leg; for the fourth, punishment was death. The form of the death penalty for the kalgas was completely different: they were not shot like the others, but strangled with sticks."[32] There existed a custom of killing the slaves after the death of the master.

Slaves were units of exchange. "The price of the kalga was such: for a baidarka or for a good parka they gave a pair of kalgas, a man and wife; for a stone knife, for a pair of tsukli, or for a sea otter parka[c] they gave one kalga."[33]

Levashov made a note characterizing the institution of slavery among the Aleuts: "The above-mentioned leaders do not make anything themselves, either their baidarkas, or the equipment that goes with it, but everything is done by their slaves whom they called kalgas."[34]

Cook describes the following scene: "I was once present, when the Chief of Oonalashka made his dinner of the raw head of a large halibut, just caught... two of his servants eat the gills...This done, one of them cut off the head of the fish, took it to the sea and washed it...He then cut large pieces of the cheeks, and laid these within the reach of the great

---

c. Sea otter parkas were worn by women—L. B.

141

man, who swallowed them with as much satisfaction as we should do raw oysters. When he had done, the remains of the head were cut in pieces, and given to the attendants, who tore off the meat with their teeth, and gnawed the bones...."[35]

Hunting and other implements and baidarkas used by the slaves belonged to the masters: "the kalga could not own his own property; everything acquired by him belongs to his master."[36]

In the everyday life of the Aleuts, the work of the slaves supplemented the work of the free men. They carried out principally domestic, chiefly women's, work. The task of slaves was "to look after cleanliness and household duties." The Aleuts did not train their children for this type of work, "stating that their children were not of the kalga lineage."[37] There are, however, indications that slaves made stone lamps, and of their participation in hunting and military sea expeditions.

Sometimes the slaves were given their freedom, which was considered to be an honorable and worthy deed. The children of slaves inherited the slavery status from their parents, but the children of a slave woman and a free man became free.

Judging overall, slavery among the Aleuts had a patriarchal character, was a developed institution, and had considerable antiquity.

Slaves were acquired not only in war, but also by purchase from the Kodiak Islanders, Chugach, Tlingit, and Kenaitsy [Tanaina, Dena'ina] during maritime expeditions.

The discoverer of the Andreanof Islands, A. Tolstykh, reporting about his voyage in 1764, noted that during military clashes the Aleuts captured their enemies and "bringing them to their settlement, divide them among the lineages and, keeping them in isolation, use them for hard work and treat them badly."[38]

Levashov writes that the Aleuts of Unalaska brought from the Alaska Peninsula "through barter and war, women, girls, and boys as slaves [*kholopy*] for themselves, called by them *kalga*s."[39]

The above-quoted information concerns in the first instance the western Aleuts, in the second, the eastern, that is, slavery was characteristic of both Aleut subdivisions.

Together with the exploitation of slaves in Aleut society, the exploitation of poor kinsmen also existed. Thus, orphans, in order not to die from hunger, passed into dependency on some rich man and worked for him for food and clothing. The owner who brought up an orphan could sell him to whomever he wished.[40] Several instances of selling orphans into slavery are described in the diaries of Levashov. For example: "...noticed among the inhabitants of this island (Unalaska—R. L.) in various yurtas many poor little children, completely naked and living in extreme filth; through the interpreter it was learned that they were helpless orphans who survive only by gathering mussels at low tide and the remains of fish bones left by adults. Our captain-lieutenant asked

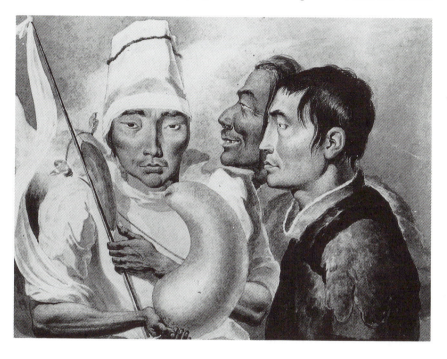

Figure 17. Aleuts of Unimak Island. Watercolor by M. T. Tikhanov reproduced here in black and white. Museum of the Academy of Arts of the USSR.

them through the interpreter whether the toions in whose yurtas the aforesaid young orphans lived, might sell them for clothes and shirts, to which they willingly agreed, and that is why our commander bought two of the above-mentioned orphans for clothing and footwear."[41]

Apparently, the exploitation of the poorest kinsmen is reflected in the report of S. Cherepanov as well: "Toions kept the wives and children of their dead relatives in servitude, but they called the toion father."[42, d]

---

d. This may be an indication of the levirate—L. B.

Thus, the composition of the Aleut settlement-communities was far from uniform (Figures 16 and 17). Besides kinsmen, a considerable number of foreigners lived among them: slaves and "kinless Aleuts." Even kinsmen were differentiated according to property and social criteria.

The domestic community of the Aleuts apparently should be viewed as being already patriarchal, although some local peculiarities obviously existed on individual islands.

There is somewhat diverse information about the nature of the settlements of the western and eastern halves of the Aleutian chain at the time of their discovery. According to S. Cherepanov, in the settlements on the Near Islands there were "yurtas" in which one, two, or three men lived, but also there was one large yurta in which "the toion and his closest kinsmen" lived.[43] About the Andreanof Islands there is A. Tolstykh's information that there were dwellings where "each who was married and his family" lived.[44] These two reports concern the western Aleuts.

The very first reports about the eastern Aleuts contain data on the fact that there were settlements with large communal dwellings. Thus, on the island of Unalaska a settlement was found with two "yurtas," inhabited by about three hundred persons, which had three toions, a settlement with one "yurta" where there were thirty persons and one toion, a settlement with one yurta inhabited by four hundred persons with two toions, and a settlement with "one large yurta" where there were four toions.[45] The travelers at the end of the eighteenth century and at the very beginning of the nineteenth century (Levashov, Cook, Langsdorff, Sarychev and others) report the presence of the same sorts of settlements and dwellings in the eastern chain of islands, but primarily with one toion. Veniaminov also speaks of settlements with one toion.

The inhabitants of a single collective dwelling with one toion apparently constituted one patriarchal domestic community, while the inhabitants of the settlements with several toions formed an enlarged patriarchal domestic community set, with new independent units budding off. The same applies to the settlements with several large dwellings. The settlements with several patriarchal community units could be viewed as emerging territorial-neighborhood communities. Apparently, such [territorial] communities existed only in the eastern part of the archipelago on Unalaska and Umnak, the largest islands in the chain. The greatest population density was noted there and it is possible to postulate that the social development in this area was proceeding more rapidly [than elsewhere]. The inhabitants of the above-mentioned islands were the most warlike of them all. In these communities, to a greater degree than elsewhere, the kinship relationships yielded to territorial ones based on private property and social stratification.

But, the nucleus of an Aleut settlement consisted of a group of consanguineal and affinal kin. This society Veniaminov termed "kinsmen" [*rodniki*] and cited the Aleut term for it, *sgan* [*sxax̂*]. For designation of the inhabitants of a single dwelling, "household members," he provides another term, *uliakilianak* [*ulax̂ ilan anaa*] or *ulianakak* [*ilan aqax̂*], which has the meaning of "home" [house], "family" [*sem'ia*], "family members" [*semeistvo*].[46] The kinsmen [*rodniki*] constituted a definite social unit during military and trade expeditions, and when changing residence. The broadening of the category *sgan* by means of marriages of the representatives of the community elite with women from other settlements had great significance (the rest of the marriages were endogamous). However, the traditions of matrilocal lineage organization were still strong in Aleut society. This especially concerned marriage relations and the kinship system.

Marriage relationships were characterized by a diversity typical of a transitional period. The desirable form of marriage was marriage with the daughter of an uncle on the mother's side; [the practice] was connected with the norms of a matrilineal form of organization. Bride service existed,[47] which is typical of the transitional period from a matriliny to a patriarchal family. Matrilocal and patrilocal forms of [postmarital residence] coexisted.[48] Matrilocality often was represented in the form of marriage by visitation (a survival), or by temporary matrilocality until the birth of the first child. Fraternal polyandry also existed,[49] and polygyny was also developed. This is reported by Levashov, and the entry indicates also the heterogeneity of Aleut society "according to wealth": "They have wives according to their wealth, one, two, three, four, and more...A man can have as many wives as he is able to make parkas for... And if a husband does not love his wife, he can sell or exchange her, but most often, when hungry, he gives her away for a bladder of whale oil."[50]

The newborn "was given an ancestral name from the father's or mother's side, and sometimes both,"[51] that is, matrilineal, patrilineal, and bilateral filiation were combined. Parallel with this, there existed the custom of returning children to the mother's lineage, and the avunculate: the mother's brother played a larger role in the children's upbringing than did the father (often a nephew was brought up by an uncle on the mother's side).

The analysis of the kinship terms by Fainberg revealed the presence of matrilineality among the Aleuts.*e* In their kinship terminology, the distinction of persons belonging to the father's and mother's lineages, typical for the kinship-organized society, was clearly indicated. There were kinship terms indicating the dual character [*sic*] of exogamy.*f* The theme of love affairs between nephews and the wives of their uncles on the mother's side is frequent in Aleut folklore. Only according to the norms of matrilineal clan [lineage] organization are such relations possible, for in this case the nephew and wife of the uncle belong to different lineages. The sororate and levirate also existed, the first being typical of a matrilineal clan structure, and the second appearing only with the formation of the patriarchal family.[52]

There is scant information about the rules of inheritance. There is only a mention that inheritance from the father was divided by the kin: the wife and children received the larger part, and the others took the remainder.[53]

Thus, the basic features of the Aleut domestic community were those of the patriarchal family with some survivals of matrilineal clan society.

The stage of development of the Aleut domestic community seems to be fully comparable with the state of its development among the Indians of the northwest coast of North America, about which Iu. P. Averkieva writes: "It is appropriate to consider that already at the beginning of the eighteenth century among all the tribes of the coast the matrilineal clan community yielded to a more or less formed patriarchal family community with the accompanying characteristic dualism of a transitional institution from a clan [-based] society to a patriarchal family."[54]

The authority of a toion could already be hereditary, from father to son or nephew, but such inheritance was still regulated by "the ancestral traditions and the decisions of the notables."[55] Alongside information about the nonhereditary [nature] of power [authority] ("...he who has

---

e. Fainberg's analysis does not demonstrate matriliny—L. B.

f. Liapunova here follows Fainberg, who hypothesized that there were exogamous moieties among the Aleuts, as they practiced the sister-exchange form of marriage—L. B.

many children is the toion, but after a father's death his son is not appointed in his place if he lacks support; he who is stronger and more apt in all their undertakings becomes the toion"[56]), there is also information about the inheritance of [such power].[57]

In the choice of leaders of the community, the principle of seniority often was superseded by that of wealth. It is impossible to agree with Veniaminov when he writes: "Each settlement consisted without fail of kinsmen and constituted almost a single family, where the elder of the lineage, called the toion *(tukkuk)* [*tukux̂*], had power over everyone."[58]

His own explanation and other materials make it clear that they deviated from that rule. The toions of the settlements were not necessarily the eldest in the family. A man could only be leader if he had famous ancestors and earned the reputation of being a skillful hunter and [brave] warrior and possessed considerable wealth. In the language of the Aleuts, the words *tukkuk* or *tukuk* (toion) and *tukugasik* [*tukuĝaasix̂*] (wealth, power) are very close.[59] Thus the Aleut words for "toion" and "wealthy," ascending to one lexical stem, were almost synonyms.

There is information that the toions were chosen from among the wealthiest, and that a son inherited from the father. If there was no son, then they chose someone else as toion.[60]

The power of the toion in the settlement was quite limited: he could not punish anyone by his own decision; for this the approval of all the "notables" of the settlement was required.

There are indications that the toion of a settlement was first of all the military leader, that he and his nearest kinsmen, children and nephews, played a leading role in organization of military and trade expeditions and constituted a privileged part of the settlement [population] at the division of the spoils following these expeditions. In the everyday economic life of the settlement the toion did not enjoy any economic advantages. The first Russian observations testify to this as follows: "In each dwelling there is an elder [*starshina*]—*tuku* or toions [*sic*]—one or two, who do not have further power over the inhabitants, but work alongside the others."[61] Further: "Their toions, so called by the Russians, are superiors over [in] each settlement and over everyone, but those they call *tukguk* are lineage heads, and those are stronger [more powerful] who have more relatives, brothers, children, nephews, but they have no power, no advantages, and mete out neither judgments nor punishments; they earn their living the same way as others and if they do not bring in the catch, they will go hungry, no portion will be assigned to him from the others' shares; and the toion has no advantage except for the title of *toion*."[62]

On the basis of Veniaminov's information, one can conclude that among the Aleuts there were present the remains of a lineage [clan] organization or territorial alliance: "Several settlements tracing their descent [being descended] from one forefather or one generation, constituted states [*shtaty*], or a society, where the head toion, descending in a direct line from his forefather [male ancestor] who had settled this island or, for the lack of such ancestor, chosen from among the toions...had the same authority over all the toions and settlements making up their society as a particular toion had over his [own] settlement."[63] The head toion dealt singly with trade and military ties with other tribes. Questions of war and peace were decided by the head toion in agreement with the settlements' toions. He had judicial authority, limited by the council of "notables." The influence of the head toion of the tribe over his tribesmen, and over the neighboring tribes as well, depended on the accumulation of wealth in his hands. The head toion had the right to a part "of everything washed ashore" within his territory.[64]

Names cited by Veniaminov for the Aleut subdivisions apparently refer to these tribal or territorial alliances. "The inhabitants of Unga and the others [other islands] up to Unimak are called *qagan taiagungin* [*Qagaan tayaĝungin*], that is, people or men of the east; the inhabitants of Unimak are called *unimgin* [in modern orthography the same]; the inhabitants of the Krenitzin Islands and the first settlements of Unalaska up to Veselovskoe [Reese Bay] are called *qigigun* [*Qigiiĝun*], that is, the northeastern[ers]; the other inhabitants of Unalaska and all the inhabitants of Umnak are called *kauliangin* [*Qawalangin*][65] or *kaguliangin*; the inhabitants of the Islands of the Four Mountains were called *akugan* or *akugun* [*Akuuĝun*], that is, the locals; the inhabitants of Atka are called *nigugin* [*Niiĝuĝin*] or *niiagungin*; the Rat Islanders are *kagun* [*Qaĝun*], and those closest to Kamchatka are *sasignan* [in modern orthography the same].[66] All the inhabitants of the Andreanof Islands[67] as a whole are sometimes called *namigun* [*Naahmiĝun*], that is, western."[68]

The ethnonyms cited above were apparently based primarily on the idea of four directions of the world, with the center in the region of Unalaska and Umnak; they resemble more the names of territorial alliances than tribal [clan] names. It is very interesting that the determination of this center according to the names of the Aleut territorial groups coincides with the determination of the center of the formation of Aleut culture according to the latest data of archaeological investigations on the Aleutian Islands. Such a center is now considered to be the region of Umnak Island, where the early sites of Anangula and Chaluka are located.

The general ethnic consciousness of the Aleuts is reflected in the existence of the term *unangan*, but up to now the question still remains open as to whether the word *unangan* is an autonym of all the Aleuts, or only of their eastern, stronger and more numerous group. It is also possible that the western Aleuts were pressed by the eastern Aleut group and thus held names corresponding to the situation, which are translated as "exiles from the islands" and "prisoners of war" (see p. 136, above, and notes 66 and 67 to this chapter).

The presence of barter was also characteristic of Aleut society at the end of the eighteenth and beginning of the nineteenth century; [it] developed on the basis of the division of handicraft labor between the inhabitants of the eastern and western parts of the Aleutian chain and also between the maritime hunters of the Bering Sea, to whom the Aleuts belong, and the tribes of fishermen of Alaska and the Pacific coast of North America.

The possibility of exchange between the inhabitants of the eastern and western parts of the Aleutian Islands arose because of some differences in [availability of] game animals. Among the western islands the sea otters were plentiful; from the skin of these, women's parkas were made prior to the arrival of the Russians, but among the eastern islands there were walruses (which did not enter the regions of the western islands), providing walrus ivory (tusks) for [various] articles. And only from the easternmost islands and from the Alaska Peninsula was it possible to obtain a kamleika made from bear intestines, deemed to be the best.

Already present among the Aleuts was incipient social division of labor, an emergence of handicrafts. "The handicrafts of the former Aleuts," writes Veniaminov, "were confined only to tool-making but, of course, not everyone was able to make every article for himself, especially a baidarka or sea otter spears; there were and there still are special masters for this among them."[69] The items of [material] culture

149

preserved in museums that are representative of the Aleut way of life for the period examined, many of which are remarkable works of art and handicraft, convincingly testify to handicraft professionalism.

The works of masters were highly prized. Thus, for a baidarka and a good parka they paid a pair of slaves for each, and for the best wooden headgear, up to three slaves.[70]

There existed a specificity in the manufactured articles of the western and eastern Aleutian Islands. Thus, the inhabitants of the eastern islands and the Alaska Peninsula were famous for their art of carving bone (and they had for this the necessary material, walrus tusks), while the inhabitants of the Alaska Peninsula were very good at working skins. The women of the western islands were very artful in weaving, and the women of the eastern islands were famous for their "embroidery" with caribou hair, and also for the sewing of kamleikas.

The Aleuts, being excellent seafarers, participated in the exchange between the tribes of the Bering Sea region and the northwest coast of North America. They sent whole flotillas to foreign lands in search of spoils, but only now and then, and then only the most easterly islands, were visited by the neighboring tribes, "comrades in trade."[71]

Particularly well developed was the armed barter,[72] which frequently turned into military clashes.

There exists a whole body of information about articles of non-Aleut origin commonly found among the Aleuts, and about exchange with foreign tribes. About amber adornments it is mentioned: "...amber...they obtain from the island of Aliaksa in exchange for spears and kamleikas, but more often by war."[73]

By means of barter the Aleuts obtained caribou and bear parkas from [mainland] Alaska, and marmot parkas from the Kenaitsy and Chugach.[74] Besides that, the Aleuts bought ground squirrel parkas from the Alaskan Eskimos and sold them gut kamleikas. In order to obtain adornments, "dare-devils with great difficulty and even with danger to their lives undertook voyages to distant lands (they even visited the Kenaitsy and the Chugach) solely to obtain by purchase or by bravery *tsukli* [dentalium shells] or something similar for their beloved."[75]

Barter within communities already existed among the Aleuts also. Veniaminov describes "the most ancient method of barter" among the Aleuts through a mediator called *tauianak* [*taaguyanax̂*] and chosen from among the young people. One who had some superfluous or unnecessary article sent it with the mediator into another *barabora* (dwelling) or, more often, to visiting guests, asking [in exchange] for it a certain article or whatever they would give for it. The mediator came into the barabora or to the guests and said "this is for sale," but the name of the owner of the article was not mentioned. The person who wished to buy retained the article and sent an item of his own with the mediator in exchange. The business was closed if the seller was satisfied with the [exchange] article. Otherwise, he sent it back and asked either for something in addition or for a replacement. The buyer either added something to it or refused the item [first offered]. In such a case, another [man] started to buy.[76]

Barter within the community was characterized by Engels as characteristic of the later stages of primitive communal formation: "We all know that at the beginnings of society products are used by the producers themselves, these producers living in indigenous communities that are organized more or less on a communist basis; that the exchange of their surplus products with foreigners, which introduces the transformation of products into commodities, is of later date. It takes place first of all simply between individual communities of different tribes and only later does it come to prevail within the community, where it makes a decisive contribution to the dissolution of this community into larger or smaller family groups."[77]

Counteraction to the growth of property differentiation among the Aleuts existed in the form of the potlatch. It had the same basic features as the potlatch among the Indians of northwestern America, an analysis of which was provided in the works of Iu. P. Averkieva.[78] But apparently among the Aleuts, as among the Kodiak Islanders, there was an archaic form of potlatch. It was expressed in ritual entertainments, dances, and the distribution of gifts.[79] Among the Aleuts, food and gifts were most often distributed to their guests and not among the members of their own settlement.

Veniaminov describes such a potlatch under the title "festive celebrations" or "plays" [*igrushki*, games]. Igrushki took place in each settlement in turn during the winter period. All the inhabitants took part in their organization. "The festive celebrations consisted of stage performances which always took place in winter and in turn, first in one

151

and then in another settlement, and the entire settlement [population] attended and every individual gave everything he had, especially food, so that after such an event almost everyone experienced hunger in the full meaning of the word. Such hunger was not only not considered as something negative, but was [considered] glorious."[80] At the end of the festivities, which continued for several days, "they presented the guests with gifts that they had made. Everyone in general tried to entertain them to the fullest and gifted them generously."[81] Apparently, one can attribute the following information supplied by Veniaminov as pertaining to the potlatch among the Aleuts: "A man never lives out his life in the same condition, and among the best tribes many were famous and wealthy, but also as many were beggars and poor, but many a time [they] could change their status in one day."[82]

There also existed a funeral potlatch among the Aleuts. The deceased was mourned by relatives for forty days, "after that elapsed they held as elaborate (i.e. replete) a funeral feast as possible. At these feasts all the food provisions that could be found in the dwelling of the deceased were set before the guests, who were all those living in the settlement, to entertain them for one, two, and three days, that is, until the entire food supply was exhausted. On the last day of the funeral feast the relatives of the deceased presented the guests with gifts in memory of the deceased, various articles which were either given according to the will [testament] of the deceased, or by the judgment of the relatives."[83] The food and gifts in this case were received by the inhabitants of the settlement. In an account about the Atkan Aleuts, it is indicated that the relatives of the deceased "distributed articles to strangers in his memory."[84]

The custom existed of killing slaves during the funeral and at the funeral feast. The number of slaves to be killed was indeterminate: a husband, wife, and all their children could be killed, or only the husband and wife, or the personal servants, but this was not considered obligatory in the years prior to the arrival of the Russians. Sometimes, in contradiction to the will of the deceased, slaves were not killed, which was "the consequence of calculations." This is indicative of the further development of forms of property, when a slave was retained as wealth. Sometimes a "wealthy dying man" willed the slaves to be given their freedom and even for them to be sent back to their native land, giving them baidarkas and everything required for the journey.[85]

The potlatch among the Aleuts, as is the case among other peoples where it was recorded, reflects the stage of development of relations of private property in their society. The existence of such relations under conditions of the disintegration of [tribal] kinship-based society necessitated the emergence of this institution of redistribution of wealth.

The contradictions inherent in the potlatch, being the most typical characteristic of the institution, have been pointed out by Iu. P. Averkieva: "The dialectical essence of the potlatch consists in that, in helping to form relations of ownership, it at the same time delays that process, preventing the gathering of a large quantity of wealth in a single pair of hands. It serves the role of an institution for the redistribution and equalization of that wealth."[86]

Thus, the potlatch, among the Aleuts as everywhere, is connected with the development of forces of production and relations of production, with the formation of private ownership relationships. It reflects the property contradiction which appears within the decaying tribal kinship-based society at the transitional stage of [its transformation into] a class [stratified] society.

The great significance of wars in the social life of the Aleuts brings them closer to that stage of development which was typical of the Nootka and of the other tribes of northwestern America which, according to the definition of Iu. P. Averkieva, were passing through the epoch of the developing military democracy.[87, g] War among the Aleuts was an important and honorable means of acquiring wealth and slaves. "The foreign wars or military campaigns [raids] *(alitkhuk tkhidin italik)* were considered to be a hunt and a craft as profitable as it was renowned."[88]

Distant sea voyages were undertaken with the aim of armed barter [see note 72 of this chapter], military raids, and, partly, in search of new hunting grounds and natural deposits providing materials for the manufacture of spear tips, daggers, etc. Constant raids were made on Eskimo tribes on the coast of the Alaska Peninsula, and particularly on the Kodiak Islanders. In the course of one such seagoing raid, the Aleuts, according to Veniaminov, supposedly reached the "northernmost tip of America," calling it "Northern Head."[89]

The organization of the military campaigns was in the hands of the toion and the notables of the community. They recruited detachments

---

g. See note *a.* of this chapter.

from consanguineal and affinal kinsmen, and also from volunteers, frequently beyond the limits of their own settlements, tempting them with [prospects of] glory and booty. The leader had from four to eight aides, something like a personal fighting body [*druzhina*], consisting of "nearest kinsmen or experienced famous warriors who commanded the military units entrusted to them and together constituted a military council."[90] During a successful raid they killed the older men and women, but took the young into slavery. A surviving remark indicates that the heads of enemies were placed on poles outside the dwellings as military trophies.

The rise of a military elite among the Aleuts and the structure of their military organization are clearly shown by Veniaminov in the description of "military law" connected with the division of the spoils. The booty was at first received by the chief and he divided it all according to the social position of the warriors and according to the estimated value of [a portion of] the booty. The captives and *tsukli* [dentalium shells] (the most valuable adornments of the Aleuts) were given to the warriors of the privileged "estate," while the warriors from "the commoners," "kinless Aleuts," and slaves received only a share of the everyday articles and weapons.[91]

Besides foreign wars, the Aleuts also fought internecine wars, between inhabitants of individual islands or island groups for hunting grounds or natural [mineral] resources. The consequence of such wars was hostility which was maintained from generation to generation. The captives of such wars were either killed or enslaved.

The data presented here, characteristic of the socio-economic basis of the social structure of the Aleuts of the pre-Russian period, allow one to consider the social relations of the Aleuts in the mid eighteenth century as being in the latter stage of primitive communal formation.

An examination of the implements and the means of hunting and fishing together with the materials concerning socio-economic relations has shown that, although the Aleut economy was based on hunting, fishing, and gathering, utilizing only the products of nature, it was highly productive. Such labor productivity created a possibility for accumulation of some types of wealth, which was the economic basis for the emergence of property inequality and social differentiation and exploitation.

The specific historical peculiarity of the development of social relations among the Aleuts consisted in that the process of the decomposition of primitive tribal relations and the appearance of the foundations of a class society occurred among them not on the basis of changes in the means of production necessary for subsistence, well known among peoples of the Old and New World (i.e., the introduction of pottery, the domestication of animals, the transition to agriculture, the smelting and working of metals, etc.), but on the basis of the specialization and the perfection of their [hunter-gatherer] economy, which was the sole possible mode due to the ecological conditions of their territory. In this unique situation, but in full concordance with [correspondence to] the level of development of productive forces, the development of relations of production and social institutions occurred among the Aleuts.

The social relations among the Aleuts seem most likely to be comparable with the social relations among the Indians of the northwest coast of North America insofar as the levels of development of the productive forces of their societies were similar. For this reason, though the Aleuts had their own specific peculiarities, the same basic features of social structure are apparent among the Aleuts. Among them there also existed matrilineal clans, an ancient form of organization which was preserved up to the eighteenth century only in a survival form, [while] the patriarchal community united people unequal in their social and property status, including slaves. Also characteristic of Aleut society was an incipient division of labor, barter, the potlatch, and a military organization which was similar to a military democracy.

Thus, at the time the Russians encountered them, the Aleuts were in a stage of transition from a preclass to a class society. During the millennia of independent development in conditions of insular isolation, they traversed the path of tribal kinship-based society and reached the stage of its decay.

The Aleut example demonstrates that when a sea hunting and fishing economy reaches a sufficiently high level of development, preconditions for the appearance of a class society are also created. Such a high level of development of both the economy of the Aleuts and the socio-economic relations and social institutions corresponding to it, could be achieved in the given ecological environment only as a result of the extremely long period of mastering the same.

CITATIONS AND NOTES

1. I. Veniaminov, *Zapiski ob ostrovakh Unalashkinskogo otdela* [Notes on the islands of the Unalaska district], vols. 1–3 (St. Petersburg, 1840).

2. I. Veniaminov, *Zapiski...*, vol. 2, p. 18. Here he has in mind the Indians of northwestern America, who were also the object of his study.

3. M. V. Stepanova, "I. Veniaminov kak etnograf," *Trudy Instituta etnografii*, n.s., t. 2 (1947), pp. 298–300.

4. L. A. Fainberg, "K voprosu o rodovom stroe u aleutov" [Toward the question of clan structure among the Aleuts], *Kratkie soobshcheniia Instituta etnografii*, t. 23 (1955); idem, *Obshchestvennyi stroi eskimosov i aleutov* [Social structure of the Eskimos and Aleuts] (Moscow, 1964).

5. L. A. Fainberg, *Obshchestvennyi stroi...*, pp. 151–160, 208–213, 244.

6. W. S. Laughlin, "Eskimos and Aleuts: Their origins and evolution," *Science* 142, no. 3593 (1963), pp. 633–645; C. Hughes, "An Eskimo deviant from 'Eskimo' type of social organization," *American Anthropologist* 60, no. 6 (1958), pp. 1140–1147.

7. G. Berreman, "Inquiry into community integration in an Aleutian village," *American Anthropologist* 57, no. 1 (1955), pp. 49–59; idem, "Effects of a technological change in an Aleutian village," *Arctic* 7, no. 2 (1954), pp. 102–107.

8. M. Lantis, "The Aleut social system, 1750 to 1810, from early historical sources," in *Ethnohistory in Southwestern Alaska and the Southern Yukon,* ed. M. Lantis (Lexington: University of Kentucky Press, 1970), pp. 139–301.

9. G. A. Sarychev, *Puteshestvie po severo-vostochnoi chasti Sibiri, Ledovitomu moriu i Vostochnomy okeanu* [Voyage to the northeastern part of Siberia, the Arctic Sea, and the Eastern Ocean] (Moscow, 1952), p. 197.

10. I. Veniaminov, *Zapiski...*, vol. 3, p. 23; idem, *Opyt grammatiki aleutsko-lis'evskogo iazyka* [Tentative grammar of the Aleut-Fox language] (St. Petersburg, 1846), p. 4

11. A. Jacobi, "Carl Heinrich Mercks ethnographische Beobachtungen über die Völker des Beringsmeers, 1789–1791," *Baessler-Archiv*, 1937, Bd. 20, Hf. 3–4, p. 120.

12. After K. T. Khlebnikov, "Zapiski o koloniiakh v Amerike" [Notes on the colonies in America], part 3, ALOII, f. 115, d. 344, l. 14 ob.

13. "Zhurnal ekspeditisii Krenitsyna-Levashova" [Journal of the Krenitsyn-Levashov expedition], TsGAVMF, f. 172, op. 1, d. 408, ch. 1, l. 252 ob.

14. I. Veniaminov, *Zapiski...*, vol. 2, p. 56.

15. G. A. Sarychev, *Puteshestvie...*, p. 201.

16. Ibid., pp. 196–197.

17. I. Veniaminov, *Zapiski...*, vol. 2, p. 207.

18. A. Jacobi, "Carl Heinrich Mercks...," p. 121.

19. I. Veniaminov, *Zapiski...*, vol. 2, p. 166.

20. *Russkie otkrytiia v Tikhom okeane i Severnoi Amerike v XVIII v.* [Russian discoveries in the Pacific Ocean and North America in the eighteenth century], ed. A. I. Andreev (Moscow, 1948), pp. 167–168.

21. I. Georgi, *Opisanie vsekh obitaiushchikh v Rossiiskom gosudarstve narodov* [Description of all the peoples living in the Russian state], part 3 (St. Petersburg, 1799), p. 92.

22. I. Veniaminov, *Zapiski...*, vol. 2, pp. 280–282.

23. Ibid., pp. 166–168.

24. *Russkie otkrytiia...*, 1948, p. 177.

25. I. Veniaminov, *Zapiski...*, vol. 2, pp. 94–95.

26. A. Jacobi, "Carl Heinrich Mercks...," p. 116.

27. I. Veniaminov, *Zapiski...*, vol. 2, pp. 164–165.

28. Illustration by M. T. Tikhanov, member of the round-the-world expedition of 1817–1819 on the sloop *Kamchatka* under the command of V. M. Golovnin.

29. I. Veniaminov, *Zapiski...*, vol. 2, pp. 164–165.

30. Ibid., p. 303.

31. I. Veniaminov, *Opyt grammatiki...*, p. 56.

32. I. Veniaminov, *Zapiski...*, vol. 2, p. 170.

33. Ibid., p. 165.

34. "Zhurnal ekspeditsii Krenitsyna-Levashova," l. 241 ob.

35. James Cook, *A Voyage to the Pacific Ocean*, vol. 2 (London, 1785), p. 510.

36. I. Veniaminov, *Zapiski...*, part 2, p. 165.

37. Ibid., p. 73.

38. TsGADA, f. 538, ch. 1, l. 236–265.

39. After A. P. Sokolov, "Ekspeditsiia k Aleutskim ostrovam kapitanov Krenitsyna i Levashova, 1764–1769 gg." [Expedition by captains Krenitsyn and Levashov to the Aleutian Islands, 1764–1769], *Zapiski Gridograficheskogo departamenta Morskogo ministerstva,* part 10 (1852), p. 99.

40. G. A. Sarychev, *Puteshestvie...*, p. 216.

41. TsGAVMF, f. 172, op. 1, d. 408, ch. 1, l. 252 ob.

42. *Russkie otkrytiia...*, 1948, p. 115.

43. Ibid.

44. After L. S. Berg, "Iz istorii otkrytiia Aleutskikh ostrovov" [From the history of the discovery of the Aleutian Islands], *Zemlevedenie,* t. 26, v. 1–2 (1924), p. 13.

45. *Russkie otkrytiia...*, 1948, pp. 123–126.

46. I. Veniaminov, *Zapiski...*, vol. 2, p. 279; idem, *Opyt grammatiki...*, pp. 31, 63.

47. I. Veniaminov, *Zapiski...*, vol. 2, p. 75.

48. G. A. Sarychev, *Puteshestvie...*, p. 216.

49. I. Veniaminov, *Zapiski...*, part 2, pp. 76, 78, 282.

50. After A. P. Sokolov, "Ekspeditsiia k Aleutskim ostrovam...," p. 99.

51. I. Veniaminov, *Zapiski...*, vol. 2, p. 78.

52. L. A. Fainberg, *Obshchestvennyi stroi...*, pp. 156–159.

53. G. A. Sarychev, *Puteshestvie...*, p. 217.

54. Iu. P. Averkieva, *Razlozhenie rodovoi obshchiny i formirovanie ranneklassovykh otnoshenii v obshchestve indeitsev severo-zapadnogo poberezh'ia Severnoi Ameriki* [The dissolution of clan structure and the formation of early class relations in the Indian society of the northwest coast of North America] (Moscow, 1961), p. 261.

55. I. Veniaminov, *Zapiski...*, vol. 2, pp. 99, 164–165; vol. 3, p. 13.

56. "Zhurnal Levashova" [Levashov's journal], TsGAVMF, f. 172, op. 1, d. 131, l. 126 ob.

57. A. Jacobi, "Carl Heinrich Mercks...," p. 121.

58. I. Veniaminov, *Zapiski...*, vol. 2, p. 166.

59. I. Veniaminov, *Opyt grammatiki...*, p. 58.

60. A. Jacobi, "Carl Heinrich Mercks...," p. 121.

61. "Zhurnal Levashova," l. 326 ob.

62. After K. T. Khlebnikov, "Zapiski...," part 3, l. 15.

63. I. Veniaminov, *Zapiski...*, vol. 2, p. 167.

64. Ibid., p. 168.

65. In Merck's manuscript is given the translation "the region of sea lions" (after A. Jacobi, "Carl Heinrich Mercks...," p. 116).

66. In Merck this term relates to the Aleuts of the Near Islands "evicted from the island" (after A. Jacobi, "Carl Heinrich Mercks...," p. 116).

67. In Merck's manuscript the inhabitants of the Andreanof Islands are called *negbo,* "prisoners of war" (after A. Jacobi, "Carl Heinrich Mercks...," p. 116).

68. I. Veniaminov, *Zapiski...*, vol. 2, pp. 2–3. In general the names in Veniaminov's report approximately coincide with the names indicated in Merck's work, and also with those cited by Levashov: "The people of those islands—the islands of Unalaska—are called *kagolagi,* those of the island of Akutan and the islands farther (to the east—R. L.) as far as Unimak are called *kigigusy,* and those of Unimak Island and Alaska (the Alaska Peninsula—R. L.) are called *katagaschuki*" ("Zhurnal Levashova," l. 326).

69. I. Veniaminov, *Zapiski...*, vol. 2, p. 253.

70. Ibid., p. 165.

71. Ibid., pp. 99, 252, 253.

72. An armed (or military) exchange: a form of exchange consisting in that the trading parties, in full military armament, offered their goods to each other. In the case of mutual satisfaction the exchange took place, otherwise an armed conflict began. See N. I. Ziber, *Ocherki pervobytnoi ekonomicheskoi kul'tury* [Sketches of a primitive economic culture] (Moscow, 1937) p. 343; V. G. Bogoraz-Tan, *Chukchi,* vol. 1, (Leningrad,1934), p. 79.

73. After A. P. Sokolov, "Ekspeditsiia k Aleutskim ostrovam…," p. 99.

74. A. Polonskii, "Promyshlenniki na Aleutskikh ostrovakh (1743–1800 gg.)" [Promyshlenniki on the Aleutian Islands (1743–1800)], AGO, r. 60, op. 1, d. 3, l. 30.

75. A. Jacobi, "Carl Heinrich Mercks…," p. 126.

76. I. Veniaminov, *Zapiski*…, vol. 2, pp. 110–111.

77. F. Engels, "Dopolneniia k III tomu *Kapitala*" [Supplement to volume III of *Capital*], in K. Marx and F. Engels, *Sochineniia* [Works], vol. 25, part 2, p. 471. [English version of quote taken from K. Marx, *Capital*, vol. 3, tr. D. Fernbach (New York: Vintage Books, 1981), p. 1034.]

78. Iu. P. Averkieva, "K istorii obshchestvennogo stroia u indeitsev severo-zapadnogo poberezh'ia Severnoi Ameriki" [Toward a history of the social system of the Indians of the northwest coast of America], in *Amerikanskii etnograficheskii sbornik* [American ethnographic anthology], *Trudy Instituta etnografii*, n.s. vol. 58 (1960), pp. 5–126.; idem, "Razlozhenie rodovoi obshchiny…."

79. Iu. P. Averkieva, "K istorii…," p. 47.

80. I. Veniaminov, *Zapiski*…, vol. 2, pp. 85–86.

81. Ibid., p. 90.

82. Ibid., pp. 137–138.

83. Ibid., pp. 81–82.

84. Ibid., vol. 3, pp. 11–12.

85. Ibid., vol. 2, pp. 84, 100.

86. Iu. P. Averkieva, "K istorii…," pp. 74–75.

87. Iu. P. Averkieva, "Razlozhenie rodovoi obshchiny…," pp. 196–201.

88. I. Veniaminov, *Zapiski*…, vol. 2, p. 99.

89. Ibid., p. 272.

90. Ibid., p. 100.

91. Ibid., pp. 103–104.

IV. MATERIAL CULTURE

Settlements and Dwellings

The Aleutian Islands up to the time of the arrival of the Russians, as we have already noted, had a relatively dense settled population, particularly in the part occupied by the eastern Aleuts. This territory— the Fox Islands, the southwestern part of the Alaska Peninsula, and the islands adjacent to it—was singled out by the Russian administration as a special district, the Unalaska (named after the principal island of the Fox group, Unalaska, where the district administrative center was located). Another district, Atka, included all islands of the Aleutian chain to the west of the Unalaska district: the Andreanof [island] group, the Rat Islands, and the Near and Commander [islands] (after the latter were settled by Aleuts on the initiative of the Russian-American Company). The western Aleuts lived there. The administrative center of the Atka district was located on the island of Atka. Thus, when organizing the districts, the Russian administration emphasized the existing division of Aleuts into the eastern and western [populations].

According to Veniaminov, in the Unalaska district prior to the arrival of the Russians, almost every island and almost every place suitable for habitation on an island was settled. He estimated that there were approximately 120 settlements there. In each settlement there were over forty single-hatch baidarkas and consequently, over forty male hunters.[1] On this basis, Veniaminov determined that the population of the Unalaska district consisted of approximately twelve to fifteen thousand persons.[2]

The numerical strength of the population of the Atka district at the time of the arrival of the Russians, judging by various sources, was approximately 5,000.[a]

Already in the first quarter of the nineteenth century, numerous ancient Aleut settlements were abandoned either because the number of

---

a. In later work Liapunova revised these estimates downward drastically. See note a. of Chapter 2—L. B.

inhabitants was considerably decreased, or because the inhabitants changed their place of residence. The settlements which appeared after the arrival of the Russians on the islands began to be located near harbors convenient for [large] vessels, at the mouth of rivers where seasonal fish entered and where it was possible to catch them in larger quantities, and primarily closer to the fur animal hunting grounds.

The principle of choosing places for settlements was different in the pre-Russian period. Aleut settlements were located mainly along the Bering Sea coast of the Aleutian archipelago, rich in fish, sea mammals (especially whales), and driftwood. The remains of ancient settlements were located by the investigators of the nineteenth and twentieth centuries by [noting] ruins of dwellings and depressions in the ground with an especially rich growth of vegetation at the sites of ancient semi-subterranean houses.[3] Based on these data, Iokhel'son indicates the conditions determining the selection of the site for a settlement.

The settlements were usually established on capes [promontories] or on isthmuses, between two bays, so that at the approach of enemies it would be easy to carry the baidarka from one bay to another. The settlement would be located on a relatively high [elevated] open place from which it would be possible to watch the sea whence either enemy baidarkas or the baidarkas of returning hunters appeared, and also sea mammals which the Aleuts hunted. Moreover, near the settlement there would be a source of fresh water, a stream, a waterfall, or a lake. [In] earlier [times] the mouths of rivers were never chosen for permanent settlement because they were vulnerable to sudden attacks.[4]

In addition to the above, of course, subsistence resources had to be nearby: sea mammal rookeries, a rich tidal zone, fishing grounds (in the sea and in streams), bird nesting grounds, and also places for gathering wild roots and berries.

We find information about settlements of the Aleutian Islands in the second half of the eighteenth to the beginning of the nineteenth century, and about their inhabitants, in the reports of promyshlenniki and navigators; such information was also collected by Veniaminov. We will begin with the Unalaska district.

In the "report" of I. Korovin about the voyage to the islands of Unalaska and Umnak in 1762–1765, it is written that on Unalaska a settlement with two "earthen yurtas" with 300 inhabitants of both sexes was found.[5] Then still another settlement was found, consisting of one "yurta" where there were "up to six tens of people, for the most part women and children, while the men were few." In the third settlement there was also one "yurta" in which, of inhabitants there were, "according to the number of baidaras approximately up to two hundred of male and female gender together."[6] In the fourth settlement "one dwelling was found, 35 sazhens [245 feet] in length with approximately four hundred people, females and children for the most part, and few men; the toion said that the men had dispersed for hunting."[7]

In the journals of M. D. Levashov (1768–1769) the following is reported about the population of the island of Unalaska: "On it there are in various places sixteen settlements, in which there are up to five hundred persons of the male sex and of the female many more...allegedly this island earlier had many people [but] at the time of their attacks on the Russian promyshlennye vessels they suffered many losses,[b] and a great number of them died of hunger in the year [1]761."[8]

In the notes of A. A. Baranov concerning Unalaska, dating to 1791, there is an "inventory of Aleut settlements, the number of inhabitants and baidarkas on Unalaska and the adjacent islands." It mentions sixteen settlements on Unalaska, five settlements on the neighboring small islands (Borka, Ukalga [*sic*] and others), and five settlements on the island of Umnak (one of these on a neighboring islet[c]).[9]

According to the information of G. A. Sarychev [1790–1791], there were fourteen settlements with 323 male inhabitants on Unalaska.[d] Those settlements were located on the [island's] northern, eastern and western coasts.[10]

Veniaminov writes that on Unalaska Island (*Ayan Alakhskha* or *Nayan Alakhskha* [*Nawan-Alaxsxa*][e]) the second island of the chain in size, prior to the arrival of the Russians there were twenty-four large

---

b. Refers to the "war" of 1763–1766—L. B.

c. Most likely Samalga—L. B.

d. This census has since been located in manuscript. The figures differ (TsGADA, f. 24, op. 1, d. 67; TsGAVMF, f. 214, op. 1, d. 89)—L. B.

e. Here and below we have added in square brackets the spelling in the modern Aleut orthography, when such could be determined, following Knut Bergsland, compiler, *Aleut Dictionary* (Fairbanks, Alaska: Alaska Native Language Center, University of Alaska Fairbanks, 1994)—L. B.

settlements, in 1805 there were fifteen settlements with 800 inhabitants, and in his time (1824–1839 [*sic*; 1834]) there remained only ten settlements with 470 inhabitants, which were located on the northern and northeastern sides of the island. On the island of Bor'ka (Sedanka) in Veniaminov's time there was a settlement consisting of six dwellings ("yurtas") with 44 inhabitants, on the island of Amaknak prior to the arrival of the Russians there were three settlements, but later there remained none; on Hog Island (Uknadak) prior to the arrival of the Russians there was also a settlement.[11]

Most information pertains to the island of Unalaska, where the most convenient harbors for Russian vessels were found. Information about the rest of the islands is more meager.

On Umnak Island prior to the arrival of the Russians there were twenty settlements with a large number of inhabitants, but in Veniaminov's time only two settlements remained, in the eastern and southeastern parts of the island, with 109 inhabitants. A. A. Baranov [1790] speaks of five settlements on Umnak Island. At the settlement located on the eastern end of Umnak Island, by Umnak Pass (Tulikskoe settlement), writes Veniaminov, the remains of an old dwelling, con-structed with the ribs of large whales, were found. On the small island adjacent to Umnak, Tanginakh (now called Ship Rock) in Umak Pass, there was a cave located on the southern side of the island with the mummified corpses of Aleuts in a flexed position. On the other neigh-boring small island, Samalga, there was a settlement until 1764, with no fewer than 400 inhabitants.[12]

Veniaminov reports the following about the rest of the islands of the Unalaska district.[13]

On Kagamil Island in the Islands of the Four Mountains group, there were signs of a large settlement on the southeastern part, and on the western side of the island in a cave "even up to the present the corpses of some kind of people hanging in cradles can still be seen; beside them are all their belongings—*tserely* (grass mats), parkas, sea otter spears, some kind of bundles, etc."

On the southeastern side of the Chuginadak Island (Tanak Anunak) [*Tanax̂ Angunax̂*], in the same group of islands, traces of previous dwellings were also seen. Until 1764, writes Veniaminov, approxi-mately one hundred Aleuts lived there, but the men died in clashes with the Russians, and some of the women and children died of hunger and

some migrated to Umnak Island.*f* On Carlisle Island (Uliagan) [*Ulâĝa,*
Uliaga I.], also in the Islands of the Four Mountains, there existed up to
1764 a small settlement located on the southeastern part, and on the
islands Herbert and Yunaska (Chagulak) [*Chiĝulax̂,* Herbert I.] two
settlements were earlier found on each. In Veniaminov's time all of the
islands in the Islands of the Four Mountains group were uninhabited.

The Krenitzin Islands (Unalga, Akutan, Akun, Golyi [Rootok],
Avatanak, Tigalda and Ugamak) were all inhabited earlier, but by
Veniaminov's time two of them—Golyi and Ugamak—had lost their
inhabitants. On the southern side of Unalga Island in Veniaminov's time there was
a single settlement. On Akutan Island there were previously seven
settlements, the inhabitants numbering not fewer than 600, but in
Veniaminov's time there remained only one settlement. On Akun Island
there had been eight settlements with 500 inhabitants, but only three
settlements remained, located on the southwest, north and southeast of
the island, with eighty-five inhabitants. On Golyi Island [Rootok] there
had been one settlement with thirty inhabitants. On Avatanak Island
there were three settlements previously; in Veniaminov's time, only one
remained (on the northern side of the island) with forty-nine inhabitants.
On Tigalda Island in "previous times" there were five settlements with
a total of no fewer than 500 inhabitants. In Veniaminov's time there was
only one settlement (on the northern side of the island), and there "were
evident the signs of the yurta of the previous inhabitants, the length of
which extends to not less than 30 sazhens [210 feet]." There was also a
settlement on Ugamak Island, but in 1826 the remainder of its population (eighteen persons) resettled on Tigalda Island.

Unimak, the largest island of the Aleutian chain, was the most
populous of all the islands prior to the arrival of the Russians. According
to Veniaminov, at the end of the eighteenth century there were still
twelve settlements on it, and some of them were of considerable size.
Those settlements were located on the northwestern, northern and even

---

f. Confirmation of resettlement is found in the 1790–1791 census. Veniaminov's
date is wrong. On Ocheredin's attack on the Islands of the Four Mountains in
1769–1770, see JLS, *Neue Nachrichten von denen neuentdekten Inseln in der
See zwischen Asien und Amerika; aus mitgetheilten Urkunden und Auszügen
verfasset von JLS* (Hamburg and Leipzig, 1776).—L. B.

the southern shores of the island. In Veniaminov's time there was one settlement, Shishaldin (Sisaguk) [*Sisagux̂*], on the northern side of the island. Prior to the arrival of the Russians, an Aleut settlement was located on this site; later it was moved farther to the east, but in 1831, because of possible eruptions of the Shishaldin volcano ("which was burning then"), it was moved back to the previous location.

On the Alaska Peninsula "there are not as many signs of settlements as on the islands; as far as is known, there were no more than ten of them, even in the most propitious of times, with the greatest number located on the southern side." In Veniaminov's time three settlements were located here [on the peninsula], with 206 inhabitants: Morzhovskoe, Bel'kovskoe and Pavlovskoe. The Morzhovskoe settlement was located on the northwestern side of the peninsula (up to 1808 its inhabitants lived in a large settlement on the southern side on the cape not far from Issanakh [Isanotski] Strait). Bel'kovskoe was situated on the southern side (there was no settlement on that site up to 1832 [1823]; its inhabitants were moved from Sanak Island by order of the Russian-American Company in order "to increase the quantity of sea otters" on Sanak Island). The Pavlovskoe settlement was situated at the middle of the eastern shore of Pavlof Bay (Tachik) [*Tachix̂*].

There were inhabitants on Amak Island on the northern side of the Alaska Peninsula up to 1823. Veniaminov writes "There were a number of settlements in ancient times, but they were not very populous.

On the Shumagin Islands (Kagigun) [*Qagiiĝun*] in previous times there were twelve settlements which were located on six islands, but in the course of time those settlements disappeared, "partly because of feuds, partly because of Russians, and most of all as a result of clashes with the Eskimos[g] from Kodiak Island." In the 1830s only Unga Island was inhabited, where, instead of four once well-populated settlements, only one remained in the eastern part. Earlier there had been one settlement on Popof Island, and three on Nagai Island. On the western side of Simeonof Island there had been one settlement; one settlement had also been on a small neighboring island. Two settlements had been on Chernabura Island.

---

g. Sic. The phrase "the Eskimos" is interpolated by Liapunova. Veniaminov actually says "the Koniags, i.e. Kodiak Islanders"—L. B.

There was no population on the Pribilof Islands (St. George and St. Paul) prior to the arrival of the Russians. The Russian-American Company transported Aleuts there from Unalaska for hunting and placed them in two settlements: Gavanskoe, on the southwestern end of the island, and Stoshnoe (Eastern) on the southeastern end [of St. Paul Island].[h]

The following early reports testify to the relatively dense population of the islands to the west of the Fox [group] (the area of the western Aleuts), that is, the Atka district.

In the "testimony" [*skaska*] of S. Cherepanov about the Near Islands (Attu, Agattu, Semichi) it is stated that all of them were populated and that there were about forty male Aleuts "and more females."[14]

In the descriptions of the Andreanof Islands, composed from the words of the cossacks M. Lazarev and P. Vasiutinskii (1764), six islands visited by them are enumerated and the approximate population number is indicated. Concerning the largest of the islands, Adak (Aiakha, Aiaga), it is stated that the number of inhabitants "cannot possibly be stated definitely because they move with all their households in large baidaras from island to island, crossing the straits, and live in localities they like."[15] On Kanaga Island there were approximately 200 inhabitants; on the island of Sitkin (Chetkhina), up to 400 families;[16] on Tagalak Island, up to 400[i] families; on Atka Island, up to 60 persons; and on Amlia Island, up to 600 persons.

K. T. Khlebnikov reports that at the beginning of the nineteenth century the islands Atka, Adak, Attu, Amchitka, Chugul, and Bering were inhabited.[17]

On Atka Island prior to the arrival of the Russians the settlement was located on a mountain slope, but in 1826 it was moved onto the cape, closer to the sea. On Attu Island the Aleut settlement was located in Massacre Bay [*Ubiennaia bukhta*], where it was left alone by the Russians because of its convenience for the putting up of fish. The

---

h. The settlement of the Pribilofs proceeded in stages. This is only one stage in a complex process—L. B.

i. The figures of 400 families each for Sitkin and Tagalak islands appear to be in error. The JLS publication of 1776 (*Neue nachrichten...*, p. 66) specifies only four families on each of these islands—L. B.

settlement for the Russian promyshlenniki and the Aleuts in the service of the company was established in Chichagof Harbor. On Amchitka Island Khlebnikov mentions only the abandoned settlement with "company yurta" (built by the company). Its inhabitants, as well as the inhabitants from Kiska Island, moved to the settlement on Attu Island, located in Chichagof Harbor. After this the islands of Amchitka and Kiska remained uninhabited.

According to the earliest reports, the settlement character in the western and eastern halves of the Aleutian chain in the pre-Russian period apparently was somewhat different.

On the Near Islands there were "yurtas" in the settlements where men lived in ones, twos, and threes, and also one big "yurta" which was occupied by the toion and his closest relatives. In the "testimony" of S. Cherepanov about the Near Islands it was stated: "They live in earthen yurtas such as the Kamchadal have; they enter [the dwellings] through the roof, and men live there by twos, threes, and singly; there is also one large earthen yurta in which their toion lives with his nearest relatives... And when they return safely from their endeavors or otherwise wish to make merry, they all get together in that one large yurta and celebrate... They live in the above-described yurtas in the winter, but in the summer they do not know any shelter or rest, but wander around the entire island to hunt; each lives where he hunts."[18]

On the Andreanof Islands there were dwellings for individual families. A. Tolstykh reports about this: "For the most part in the winter, but not in the summer, their earthen yurtas made as dwellings are heated, while in summer they have a fire during the night for light only. They burn oil of any animal they happened to take in hunting. They sleep in those yurtas. Each married man with his family, having dug out as much space as appropriate, places in the hole moss and grass, and here they lie down in flexed position, and cover themselves with their [rather] small parkas and over that with *chirely* made for this purpose out of grass and resembling bast matting."[19]

These two reports relate to the western Aleuts.

From the information about the eastern Aleuts, we learn that among them large communal dwellings were in use. Thus the first Russians (I. Korovin) on the islands of Unalaska and Umnak found a settlement with two "yurtas" where about 300 persons lived; a settlement with one "yurta" in which 30 persons lived; a settlement with one "yurta" with 400 inhabitants; and a settlement with "one large yurta."[20] The travelers at the end of the eighteenth century and at the very beginning of the nineteenth century (M. D. Levashov, J. Cook, G. H. Langsdorff, G. A. Sarychev, and others) also report on communal dwellings in the eastern chain of islands.

Thus, the settlements of the western Aleuts apparently consisted of individual dwellings for each separate (small) family and one communal dwelling, the principal one where the toion of the settlement lived with his relatives. The settlements of the eastern Aleuts, on the other hand, consisted of one or two large communal dwellings occupied by large familial communities.

The dwelling construction itself, however, was the same among both the western and eastern Aleuts, judging by everything, and they only differed in their dimensions. We do not have a detailed description of the dwellings of the western Aleuts (except the above-mentioned description by Cherepanov), but there are excellent descriptions of the old dwellings of the eastern Aleuts. Thus Korovin writes:

> They did not have any large buildings besides the yurtas. Yurtas are constructed [in the following manner]: first having excavated pits in the ground, they place along the edges sawhorse-shaped trestles [supports] as well as firmly secured posts of larch, spruce, or poplar wood; [over these] they place shingles of split poles; these are covered first with grass and then with earth; here they live. On the top of the yurta an entry is made and a ladder put in, and this they use for entering and leaving the yurta. The size of these yurtas may extend up to 10, 15, 25 or even more sazhens. These yurtas may contain approximately 50, 100 or 150 or even more people, men, women and children. Those people, in comparison to the local Kamchadal, maintain outstanding cleanliness and have the following appointments in their yurtas: they never heat [their yurtas] at any time and do not use any wood as firewood... And some of them in the winter, returning to their dwellings

from hunting or fishing or from other places, after [exposure to] most severe and hard to bear cold, warm themselves by burning grass, all sorts of which was stored during the summer; they put on long sea otter or bird skin parkas, and place under them between their legs the smoldering grass; they stand over it until they get warm, then move away. Women also warm themselves in the same way... some of them have grass mats which are used instead of bedding, which they [also] put over their parkas.[21]

The "report" of I. Solov'ev (1764–1766) also contains a description of the dwellings of the eastern Aleuts:

And the yurtas are made from driftwood, larch, spruce, or other kinds, in the same manner as do the local iasak-paying Kamchadal: they pile the earth up from the bottom toward the top but not too high; first they cover it with grass; every year new grass is put on; they live this way until the upright [standing] posts rot and break from the pressure on top; in length the yurtas are up to five, ten, fifteen and [over] thirty sazhens, in width from three to four *pochatnye*[j] sazhens, and in height from two to three sazhens. They enter from the roof. In small yurtas there are from two to five, and in large ones up to ten hatches; to the [main room] are attached separate compartments, entered from the main yurta. Sometimes the side compartments have their own hatches. Other [compartments] are secret ones. There are no stoves [fireplaces] in the yurtas nor do they make fires within; if somebody wants to get warm, they set fire to some soft grass and stand over it dressed in their parkas, then lie down and sleep in the same clothing which they usually wear, they do not have bedding as such... If the men happen to be en route from one settlement to another, when they stop, they sleep under their baidarkas.[22]

---

j. There were several types of sazhen measurements. Here Solov'ev specifies the official "seal" sazhen—L. B.

I. Georgi cites the following information about the Aleut dwellings:

Their dwellings are similar to Kamchatkan ones, but for the most part more spacious.[23] The winter semi-subterranean one *(ullaa)* [*ulaa*], which also resembles that of Greenland where it is called iglol [*sic*], ranges from 10 to 50 sazhens in length, from 3 to 5 sazhens in width and is dug to the depth of 1½ sazhens into the earth; inside, it is divided by poles, at the top it is latticed and [the lattice] is covered with grass, over which earth is piled up. Such lattices are made of poles made of driftwood. In this ceiling there are from four to six openings, and sometimes even more, for entry by ladder and for passage of smoke and light; inside, in the very middle, one can see one or more places for fire between the poles, but in all [dwellings] the number of such is very small; that is the reason why they seldom start fires in their semi-subterranean dwellings. Sleeping places are covered with grass mats or warm skins. For the illumination of this long grave there are lamps placed [on] the dividing posts, made out of pieces of stone in which the fire is maintained with fish oil. In such a hut [*khizhina*] lives a small or large work crew [*artel'*] consisting of related families, which may number generally 50, 100, 200 and sometimes even 300 souls... On some islands,[24] in part due to ancient tradition and in part for reason of the rocky terrain, there are also small semi-subterranean dwellings approximately three feet deep in which only single families live. The majority of the islanders[25] have in addition summer dwellings (barabora), which are also similar to those of the Kamchadal. They are larger, stand above the ground, and are full of people.[26]

In Levashov's album (1768–1769) there are three drawings [pictorial representations] of Aleut dwellings on Unalaska Island (Figure 18). They provide excellent material for the reconstruction of the Aleut dwellings.[27]

171

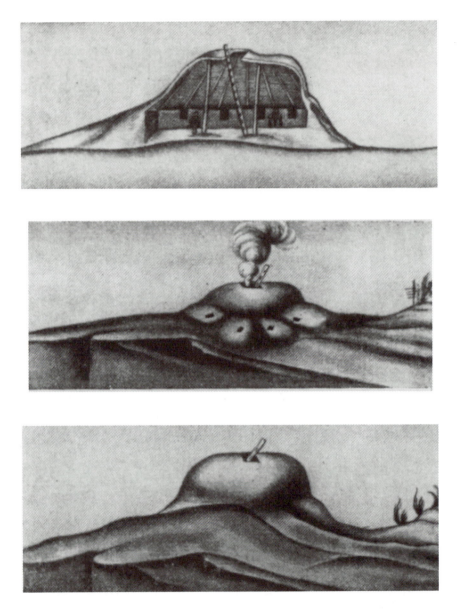

Figure 18. Dwellings of the Aleuts. Drawings by M. D. Levashov. TsGAVMF.

Figure 19. Interior view of an Aleut dwelling on Unalaska Island.

A detailed description of the construction and an internal view of the dwellings of the eastern Aleuts (Unalaska Island) are [found] in Cook's book. There is also an illustration of such a dwelling (Figure 19).[28]

Sarychev, too, provides a description of the Aleut dwellings on Unalaska:

> Each settlement consists of two or three semi-subterranean dwellings of various sizes, of which the largest may be nine sazhens in length and three sazhens in width. The base of such a semi-subterranean dwelling is dug slightly into the ground. Its [the dwelling's] top is formed by a flat roof made from driftwood, covered with grass, then sod, and earth. At the very top several rectangular openings are left through which light passes into the semi-subterranean dwelling, and through which the inhabitants enter by means of a ladder made from logs with steps cut into them. About seven feet toward the center from the dwelling's side [outer wall], posts

supporting the roof are placed. They also serve to separate each family space, where instead of bedding, grass mats are laid; during the day they sit on them, engaging in handiwork, and during the night they sleep on them, covering themselves with their parkas. The islanders empty out their slops and other refuse in the middle of their subterranean dwellings, which causes dampness and filth, and if there were no openings at the top of the yurtas through which the dampness and stale air are drawn out, then it would be impossible to remain inside for very long. Each family stores urine, used both to dye grass and for washing, in special wooden containers in front of its compartment.[29]

Information about Aleut dwellings on Unalaska Island is also provided by Merck. He speaks of the existence of summer dwellings *(sakudaktschaluk)* *[saaqudaxchalux̂]* and winter dwellings *(kamuktschaluk)* *[qanaxchalux̂]* among them. The latter were made warmer for the winter. In both, storage rooms were made from the inside, with a narrower and lower entrance. In these storage rooms stomachs of sea mammals filled with seal and fish oil, dried fish, fish roe, etc., were stored. On the outside, the storage rooms and entries into them were covered with sod. The winter dwellings were rectangular in shape with somewhat oblique corners. The floor was sunk several feet into the earth, and along the sides low earthen banks were erected. In the middle of the dwelling stood four logs sunk into the ground, also forming a rectangle. In the larger dwellings four additional logs were placed, making them longer. Across these log posts, logs of lesser thickness were placed, with supports which rested on the earthen banks. The side walls were formed of slanted poles or thin logs. Such a construction was covered from above with dry grass or grass mats, on top of which they placed sod and then piled up earth. The interior of the dwelling was divided into compartments for sitting and sleeping. The floor in these sections was slightly lowered and covered with mats. In the roof there were two openings. The smaller served as an entry and a notched log instead of a ladder was placed in it. Through the other, in the autumn, they brought in the boats for drying.[30]

These early data and illustrations have great significance for the reconstruction of the number and the character of the Aleut settlements and dwellings of the eighteenth and beginning of the nineteenth century, because with the arrival of the Russians the picture quickly began to change: some settlements disappeared, some were moved to other locations, and dwellings began to be built somewhat differently. Already Veniaminov, during his study of the Aleuts of the Unalaska district, resorted to reconstruction according to information still preserved in his time in order to characterize the settlements and dwellings of the eighteenth century. Veniaminov's data are supplemented with other early information about the settlements and dwellings of the Aleuts. Of course, his materials relate only to the eastern Aleuts.

The ancient settlements of the Aleuts, writes Veniaminov, usually consisted of one, two and sometimes six communal dwellings called *uliagamakh [ulaagamax]*, each holding from ten to forty families.[31] Veniaminov notes that the dwellings were built running lengthwise from east to west: "And as much as I had the chance to see the remaining traces of the former yurtas, they were almost always built running lengthwise from east to west and, it seems, not always along the direction of the stronger winds."[32]

The semi-subterranean dwelling *(uliagamakh)* among the eastern Aleuts was the principal type of structure. They did not have special communal structures ("kazhims" as among the Eskimos). The dwelling itself served as a communal hall for various kinds of festivities, meetings, ceremonies, etc.

Among the western Aleuts, as we saw in the early reports cited above, the role of the communal house was fulfilled by the largest dwelling in the settlement, where the toion lived.

Besides these dwellings, which were predominately winter ones, there were among the Aleuts, although not everywhere, also summer dwellings, *uliak [ulax̂]* which were not communal, but separate for each family.[33] In them they stored their hunting equipment, food reserves, and some belongings all year round. Information on summer dwellings is scarce in the literature. Probably, they were huts constructed from whale bone or driftwood, and less deeply excavated into the ground and less warmly roofed than the semi-subterranean dwellings.

Among the western Aleuts, apparently, there were no summer dwellings. In the above-cited reports it was stated that during the summer the Aleuts often did not live in a permanent place. During their travels and distant undertakings, they spent the nights as separate families in pits lined with moss and grass, and covered themselves with parkas and mats. They also spent the nights under baidarkas and structures made of baidaras, paddles, and long poles covered with skins.

In almost every settlement of the eastern Aleuts, writes Veniaminov, there were strongholds, *attagin* [*ataagin*], for defense in case of attack by enemies. They were built upon elevated sites and consisted of a large pit, fenced around with boards the height of a man.[34]

On the seashore not far from the settlements were supports of bone or wood for baidarkas and baidaras. Hunting implements and weapons were always left on the baidarkas in case of an unexpected attack by enemies or the appearance of animals in the sea.

The winter dwellings, according to Veniaminov, were from 20 to 60 meters in length (and even more) and from 8 to 14 meters in width. The construction of dwellings was carried out in the following manner. A pit from 1½ to 3 meters in depth was dug according to the size of the dwelling. Then four rows of posts were placed lengthwise: two rows along the edges of the pit, level with the ground, at about 1-sazhen intervals, and two rows [of posts] twice the length of the first [set] at a distance of 2 to 4 meters from the wall and with 4- to 6-meter intervals between the poles. On all four rows of poles along the structure they placed crosspieces (of round logs) and across the latter, rafters (split or round poles). In the dwellings constructed with the ribs of whales, one end of the rib was dug into the ground along the walls, and between the upper ends of the ribs they placed spreaders, tying them with thongs. On top of them they placed and secured a row of logs longitudinally, on which they later placed split or round poles. On the top, in the middle, they left several rectangular openings: some of them served for entry and exit, for lighting and fulfilling the function of a smokehole, and some only for light and ventilation. They made from one to five of the first (according to the size of the dwelling) and of the second, "as many as could fit." Then the roof was covered with thick woven grass mats, with dry and fresh grass, with piled-up earth, and with sod. When finishing the interior trim of the dwelling made from whale ribs, a second row of posts was erected (as in dwellings made with wooden frames); these posts served as the dividers [between] areas for separate families. Between the posts and the walls there ran low partitions, the bottom of which was of boards, and the top of mats. They separated the familial compartments. Low partitions of boards, *aiuk* [*hayux̂*], (less than one meter in height) were also made in the front in order to separate family compartments from the center of the dwelling. Along the walls of the dwelling, within the family compartments, shelves *(kikhian)* [*qixyan*] were made from poles and sticks, the height of a man. These were covered with mats, and during the winter they kept their food supplies on them. Above these shelves they made other small shelves *(itgúsin)* [*itxuusin*] where each family kept its belongings.

At the front of the dwelling, on the eastern side, the toion lived with his wives and children; then in accordance with their status, other families took their places, each family with their belongings in a separate compartment. They came in and went out by means of a log in which were made notches which served as steps.

Sometimes separate families dug out in their wall a special compartment *(agáiak)* [*agayax̂*], either large or small in size. It could be used as storage, as a sleeping place for children, etc. Sometimes they made hatches for light there. Entrances into such compartments were very small and often very skillfully concealed, so that in case of unexpected enemy attacks they could hide in them and wait out the danger.

The dwelling was not heated; the oil lamps were used only for light (the Aleuts often did not cook meat and fish, but ate them raw).

The construction of large dwellings and the move into them was always accompanied with a celebration. When the pit for the future dwelling was ready, the toion or the elder of the lineage [clan] organized a feast on that place for all the future inhabitants of the dwelling. At that time, the place where each family would live was indicated (by seniority). After that, further construction commenced; the head of each family prepared his compartment. After the completion of the dwelling everyone moved in at once, but in turns according to their status, beginning with the toion, because each had to give a feast, *kangulialik*, and entertain all the inhabitants of the settlement. After everyone had moved in, a communal celebration, *ukámak* [*ukamax̂*], was organized, to which inhabitants of neighboring settlements were invited. This celebration was held each year when the people moved from individual summer dwellings into communal ones.[35]

177

With the arrival of the Russians, the dwellings and even the settlements of the Aleuts changed. Already in the first quarter of the nineteenth century, Aleut settlements consisted of a larger number of dwellings (from two to ten) and in each only one family lived (or two, but not more); these dwellings correspondingly were no more than twenty meters in length. The construction of dwellings also changed. The Russians considered it more practical to build "yurtas" which were sunk into the ground to a lesser depth. The Russian-American Company started to build such dwellings. New settlements with dwellings of a somewhat different type appeared; however, these dwellings still preserved the basic construction of the former Aleut dwellings. The new "yurtas" were not large; they were sunk not more than seventy centimeters into the ground. Instead of entry and light hatches at the top, they often began to cut windows in the front wall, and in the opposite wall, a very narrow and low door. True, sometimes they still made hatches in the top for light. Those hatches, as well as windows, were covered with sea lion or whale intestines instead of glass. They curtained off the doors with the skins of sea lions and other marine mammals. They sometimes made the entrance at the side of the "yurtas" via a low lean-to, resembling a Russian foreroom [*seni*].

The data on the settlements and dwelling of the Aleuts are very important for the solution of many problems connected with the early history of the Aleuts.

When discussing the Aleut dwelling type, it is necessary to recognize, following Iokhel'son, their great similarity first of all with the semisubterranean dwellings of the Paleo-Asiatics and then with the dwellings of the North American Indians (the northwestern Indian tribes, Athabaskans, the Indians of British Columbia and California).[36]

Iokhel'son, basing [his argument] on a great number of comparative materials, came to the conclusion that the dwellings of the above-mentioned peoples are not only the product of similar cultures, but that they probably spread by borrowing [diffusion]. He maintains that the common features of those dwellings are the following:

1) The location of the dwelling pit, from one to two meters in depth, usually on a hill in order to provide for the drainage of rain water.

2) Wall construction out of logs placed in the pit vertically, forming a rectangle, irregular octagon, or circle, half or one-third of its [the log's] length protruding above the excavation [pit]; and the use of a bank

around the above-ground portion of these walls, utilizing for it the earth removed from the pit.

3) Roof installation on four or more posts standing in the middle of the dwelling, sloping toward the walls.

4) The use of square openings in the roof as doors, windows and smoke holes (for entry into the dwelling, a notched log was utilized).

Arguing from the fact that similar features appear in the dwellings of tribes very distant from one another, Iokhel'son advances a hypothesis of the existence in the distant past of contacts between those tribes, simultaneously pointing out several other [similar or identical] features of material culture, mythology, and decorative art.

Subsequent excavations by Iokhel'son in the Aleutian Islands indicated the presence, together with the remains of rectangular structures, of earlier intermediate forms with rounded corners. In the most ancient layers the ground plan of such structures approached an oval and even a circle.[37] This gives support to the conclusions expressed earlier by Iokhel'son about the similarity of the semi-subterranean dwellings of the inhabitants of Northeast Asia and northwestern America.

The materials from excavations of recent decades have added new information, corroborating the point of view that there are common original traditions underlying the dwellings of northern Asia and North America. Such a discovery was made in the most ancient site of the Aleutian Islands, Anangula: a dwelling representing the remains of a semi-subterranean structure of circular form with a hearth of a thin stone slab laid out in the center, very close in type to the Paleolithic dwelling of the Ustinovka site, discovered in Primor'e by A. P. Okladnikov.[38] The dwelling excavated by A. Hrdlička on Umnak Island also was semi-subterranean and circular in form.[39] The dwellings of the Chaluka site, investigated by Laughlin's group, are different. Also round in outline, they were, however, dug into the ground only slightly (ten to fifteen centimeters), indicating that these were almost certainly above-ground structures; their walls were made of stonework. Such a dwelling type is analogous only to that in the north among the Eskimo.[40] It remains unclear how and when that type of dwelling appeared among the Aleuts and when and how it disappeared. Or, perhaps they were the remains of summer dwellings.

All the excavated ancient dwellings in the Aleutian Islands mentioned above are small. The long houses of the eastern Aleuts which accommodated several family groups, well-known from ethnographic materials, more likely reflect their social structure, formed before the eighteenth century. The smaller dwellings of the ancient inhabitants of the Aleutian Islands, just as the dwellings of the western Aleuts of the eighteenth century, reflect a more archaic type of social organization than among the eastern groups.

The character of the Aleut settlements of the eighteenth century (especially eastern ones), in combination with their larger number, illustrates remarkable density of population for a hunting and fishing economy. This serves as an indicator, on the one hand, of the ecological wealth of the territory occupied by them, and, on the other hand, of the excellent mastery of it [the environment] and the achievement of quite a high level of economic development that could only occur as a result of a long adaptation to the specific harsh conditions of the given region and achievement of quite a high level of economic development.[k]

Weaving

Woven articles occupied an important place in the household inventory of the Aleuts (Figure 20). Mats were very widely used. Along with skins, they served as bedding and floor covering. The bottoms of baidarkas were lined with them. They were hung to divide the living space for individual families. The dead were wrapped in them. Woven bags and baskets were of various forms and [served] a variety of purposes: [they were] large and small, flat and cylindrical, for the storage of small and large articles and food supplies, and for carrying heavy objects. In the burial caves on the Aleutian Islands, a large number of child mummies were found in woven cradles.

Aleut woven products, according to the numerous testimonies of travelers and investigators, are distinguished among the products of the neighboring peoples (of Northeast Asia and northwestern America) by their great skill in execution.

As ethnographic data indicate, the Aleuts preserved the traditional methods and materials of weaving almost to the twentieth century: articles found in burial caves and articles [produced] at the end of the nineteenth and beginning of the twentieth century are almost identical. The only innovations were in decorative materials (wool, cotton, and

---

k. *Sic*. Phrase repeated in original text.—L. B.

Figure 20. Woven articles (from the collection of the MAE). 1) mat, No. 2868-230; 2) large soft basket for the transportation and storage of small articles, No. 4104-99.

Figure 20 (continued). 3) basket, No. 2868-238.

silk threads) and some article forms produced for sale (purses, wallets, and cigar cases).

The western Aleuts were especially famous for their weaving.

For all the woven articles of the Aleuts the vertical warp was characteristically plaited with the weft (twined work), a variation of woven wicker (woven basketry). A second type of weaving was coil or spiral (coiled basketry) based on the sewing together (sewed work) of spiral warps; it had wide distribution on the American continent, but the Aleuts (and their neighbors the southern Eskimos, Tlingit, and Nootka) did not use it.[41]

The twining of a vertical base with a weft (twined basketry)[l] consists in that strands of the vertical base (warps) are twined in most cases with

---

l. In this discussion of weaving techniques, the terms in parentheses are those used by O.T. Mason in his "American aboriginal basketry," *Report of the United States National Museum for 1902* (Washington, 1904). In the Russian text, Liapunova includes this English-language terminology in parentheses—L. B.

182

paired strands of weft, but sometimes with three strands. On the basis of this technique, there are several types of weaving known among the American aborigines.

I. Simple twining (plain twined weaving) with a two-strand weft on a vertical warp.

II. Diagonal twining (diagonal or twilled twined weaving) with a two-strand weft on two or more vertical warps.

III. Wrapped twining (wrapped twined weaving or bird-cage, or fish-trap style), in which one weft element is fastened in a horizontal position, and the other weft is wrapped around the crossing of the first weft and the strands of the vertical warp.

IV. Twining on a latticed warp (lattice-twined work or tee, or hudson stitch) where, as in the previous variant, one weft element is fastened in a horizontal position, forming the horizontal part of the lattice warp (its other part is the vertical), but the twining is done with two other wefts. This method could be viewed as a variant of method III.

V. Three-strand twining. Twining of the vertical warp with three wefts (three-strand twined).

O. T. Mason, basing his conclusions about Aleut weaving on studies of the collection of the U.S. National Museum, noted the existence among the Aleuts of only type I weaving on a vertical warp, but in five variants, characterized on the whole by the various positions of the warp.

The first variant is simple twining on a vertical warp (plain twined weaving). The weft, consisting of two elements, twines with every strand of the parallel warps as if braiding a two-stranded rope. Each consecutive row repeats the foregoing, and the rows come together tightly. This weaving is called "close together" by the Tlingit.

The second variant [involves] the same [method of] weaving as in the first variant, only with open spaces between the weft rows (open twined work).

The third variant is the same [method of] weaving, but on warps consisting of two elements, one inclined to the right, the other to the left, crossed at an angle (crossed warp). After twining the warp with the weft, a series of hexagonal openings are formed.

The fourth variant is the same [method of] weaving, but on a divided warp (divided warp). Here each strand of the warp consists of paired stalks or of two [paired] split strips of stalk. In weaving, each left half of one pair (of warps) is twined with half of the adjoining pair. In the following row the old [previously divided] pairs are united. Thus a series of triangular openings were formed. The open variant of this [type of] weaving (openwork) created the impression of drawn-work [*merezhka*] (that was reflected in its English term "hemstitch").[42]

The fifth variant involves the same weaving, but on angled warps (diverted warp). Here the strands of the warp are diverted from the perpendicular (the vertical) for some distance, and then returned [to the previous position]. Woven geometric figures result on the surface. The basket with a cover published by Mason illustrates the technique of this variant in combination with the second variant.[43]

It is necessary to add to Mason's characterization of Aleut weaving the results of later studies of Aleut weaving obtained on the basis of newly discovered material.

Thus, A. Hrdlička's expedition found in the Kagamil mummy cave one basket made by the technique of wrapped twined weaving, type III in the classification cited above.[44] In this technique, one element of weft remains inside the basket (or, on the contrary, on the outside) and the other is wrapped around the intersection of the vertical warp and the horizontally placed first element of the weft.[45] Aleut baskets made entirely by this technique are also in the MAE (Nos. 4104-98, -99, -101). In these baskets the weft, placed horizontally, is on the outside of the basket.

P. Gebhard and K. Kent, authors of an article on the woven items from the burial caves on the islands of Kagamil and Ship Rock in Unimak [*sic*; Umnak] Pass, consider that they were executed by the technique of diagonal twining of the weft on a vertical warp (diagonal or twilled twined work).[46]

In the collections of the MAE are a number of articles (Nos. 337-4; 633-11; 2868-53, -230,-238; 4104-100) on which the separate rows are executed with three-strand twining (three-strand twined weaving). In this technique, each strand of the weft (consisting of three strands) covers two rows of the warp on the outside and winds round only one row of the warp on the inside. On the exterior of the article, this results in elongated close stitches, while on the inside the texture appears like that resulting from simple two-strand twining (plain twined work). Three-strand weft is also employed, but in a somewhat different technique (for this see below, p. 186), to achieve [create] an ornamentation found on Aleut articles which is known under the name "false embroidery."

Besides the methods already mentioned, which are variations of twining on vertical warps (twined work), there is on one of the baskets in the MAE (No. 2868-238; Figure 20, item 3) a band executed in the technique of diagonal weaving on equal warps (twilled weaving or twilled plaiting).[47] Here, in diagonal plaiting each element of weft passes through two strands of the warp. Though this technique was not noted earlier on the Aleutian Islands, attribution of the above article to the Aleuts is without doubt. Mason notes that the distribution of the technique of diagonal weaving (twill work) encompasses both the northwestern and the southern states of the United States, and was also excellently developed in Peru, Guiana, and Ecuador.

Summarizing all the material at our disposal, it is possible to propose the following inventory of weaving techniques which were known to the Aleuts (Figure 21).

Type I is simple twining with two-strand weft on vertical warps (plain twined weaving).

The first variant is simple twining with two-strand weft and vertical and parallel warps. It could be with compact rows of weft ("close together") or lace-work (openwork). According to Mason's classifications, these are [his] variants 1 and 2. Examples of such weaving are widely represented in the publications and collections of the MAE (Figure 21, items 1a and 1b).

The second variant is the same, but on crossing warps (crossed warp), variant 3 according to Mason. There are no such examples found in publications, but they are present in the collections of the MAE (Nos. 2868-21; 4104-11, -12, -25, -28; see Figure 21, item 2).

The third variant is the same, but on divided warps (divided warp), variant 4 according to Mason. It is represented in other publications and by a large number [of articles] in the collections of the MAE (Figure 21, item 3).

The fourth variant is the same, but on deviating warps (diverted warp), variant 5 according to Mason (Figure 21, items 4a and 4b). No such examples are found either in other publications or in the collections of the MAE.

Type II is diagonal interlacing of the weft with a vertical warp (diagonal twined work). Examples are given in publications

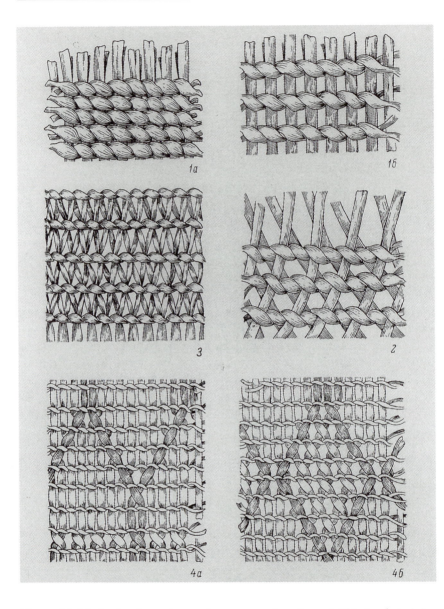

Figure 21. Methods of weaving and ornamentation. 1a and 1b) simple twining with two-strand weft on vertical warps (1a close, 1b open); 2) twining with two-strand weft on crossed warps; 3) twining with two-strand weft on divided warps; 4a and 4b) twining with two-strand weft on diverted warps.

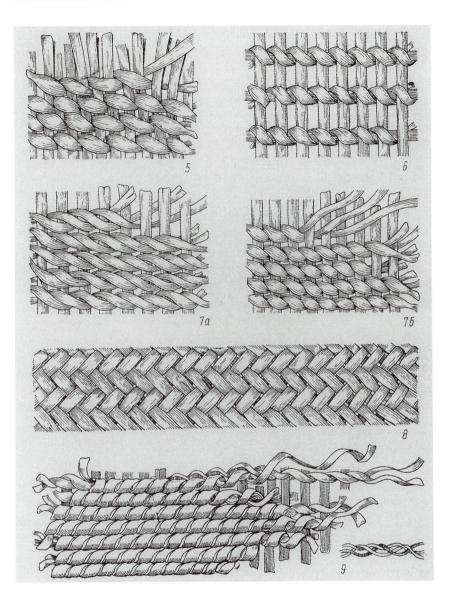

Figure 21 (continued). 5) diagonal interweaving of weft on vertical warps; 6) wrapped twining on vertical warps; 7a and 7b) three-strand twining on vertical warps; 8) diagonal twining on equal warps; 9) ornamentation by the method of "false embroidery."

187

representing woven articles from the burial caves on the islands of Kagamil and Ship Rock (Figure 21, item 5).[48]

Type III is wrapped twining (wrapped twined weaving). It is twining with one weft on a vertical warp at the same time as the second weft is fastened horizontally, that is, perpendicular to a vertical warp (forming a horizontal warp). Examples are found in the materials of A. Hrdlička and in the collections of the MAE (Figure 21, item 6).

Type IV is three-strand twining (three-strand twined) on a vertical warp. Examples are in the collections of the MAE (Figure 21, items 7a and 7b).

Besides that, there is basis for the hypothesis that the Aleuts also knew the technique of diagonal weaving on equal warps (twill work; Figure 21, item 8).

The enumeration of these techniques demonstrates the fact that all the basic types of basketry weaving on a vertical warp (twined weaving) noted by Mason on the American continent were [also] present among the Aleuts.

The woven articles were ornamented by the method known as "false embroidery" (Figure 21, item 9).[49] The same method was also used by the Tlingit. To the ordinary two-strand twining, a third, decorative (usually dyed), strand was added which interlaced with only the external stitch of the weft. The direction of the decorative stitch was opposite to the direction of the stitches of the main structure. The decorative strand was not visible on the inside.

In addition, there is mention of another method of ornamentation, arrasene work, though it was not widespread. Two strands of dyed straw were interlaced over the strands of the principal weave by means of a special type of "false embroidery." On every half-turn, one of the strands was fastened under the winding. This ornamentation creates a distinctive raised effect on the outside of an article. On the inside, just as with "false embroidery," it was not visible.[50] Unfortunately, such a technique of ornamentation is absent in the collections of the MAE (nor did we find it illustrated).

The upper rim of the article was usually finished with a woven three-strand braid. On bags, after this row, a row was made of large cells, the loops: the jutting ends of the bundles of warps were woven into columns of three-strand braids, and then were woven into a rim of the same kind of weaving (three-strand braid). A cord was passed through the loops.

The technique of weaving was conditioned on one hand by the cultural traditions of a people, and on the other by the natural resources of the area.

The only material suitable for weaving found on the islands was soft grasses. Mason and Dall named wild rye *(Elymus mollis)* as the material for Aleut weaving. Iokhel'son gives quite a long list of the names of grasses for weaving; the principal ones he considers to be wild rye and the wild pea *(Lathyrus maritimus).*[51]

M. L. Kissel, who published [a picture of] a single Aleut basket, named the only suitable material for weaving on the islands as wild rye (among the Aleuts, "beach grass").[52]

In another publication, it is stated that according to a botanical analysis of the remains of weaving found in burial caves, they were made from wild rye, and that the dark ornamental fibers belong to a plant similar to *Scirpus.*[53]

As a result of an analysis of the weaving material obtained by Hrdlička's expedition from the Kagamil mummy caves,[54] the conclusion was drawn that the principal weaving material was "beach grass," wild rye. Some fibers had leaf and some had stem and root structure. It follows that they [the Aleuts] used the leaves, stems, and roots of wild rye for weaving. In some specimens, stems and leaves were used without any preliminary processing. But some specimens bore traces of considerable treatment for the strengthening of the fibers. In preparing ornamental strips, the Aleuts made special efforts to make them thin, narrow, and glossy, but at the same time durable. For the ornamental strips of black color they used in most cases either the roots of the Sitka spruce *(Picea sitchensis),* or the roots of wild rye. In one case, ornamentation with strips of baleen was noted. Articles with small feathers inserted were also found.

The articles in the collection of the MAE are ornamented with the same materials. There is one basket decorated with baleen strips (No. 2868-238) and there are specimens with small feathers inserted. Besides that, there are examples of weft strands made from strips of sea lion esophagus (No. 4104-27) and sinew threads (No. 337-1/5).

The weaving process involved two preparatory stages which were very important and occupied much of the women's time. These were the gathering of material and its processing.

Every year, beginning in July, groups of women went out to gather grass, wild rye. This tall grass, with leaves about sixty centimeters long and two centimeters wide, grows abundantly along the coast and on hills. The stems were cut with a knife. For the manufacture of delicate articles, the entire stems were not needed, but only two or three young, thin leaves, therefore the gathering was a long and tedious task. Grass gathered in the middle of July acquired a yellow color after processing. It [the grass] was spread on the ground in the shade to dry, and turned over often. This drying stage lasted for two weeks. Then the grass was sorted according to size. The larger leaves were split into three parts, and the middle part was discarded. The thin leaves were left whole, since they were too delicate for such treatment. After this, the entire supply was tied into bundles and brought into the dwellings, but for the course of a month on dry cloudy days it was brought out and hung on a rope. The final drying was carried out inside the dwelling.

To obtain stems that were white in color, the entire grass stem was cut in November. Then the bundles were hung to dry near the dwellings with the tops down. The final drying was done inside.

If they wanted to have green stems, they processed them in the same way as the ones gathered in July, but for the first two weeks they kept [the cut grass] in the shade of the thick grass usually growing beside the dwellings. After this, the drying continued inside the house. Under no circumstances were the sun's rays allowed to fall on the grass in the process of drying, which lasted a month or more. The grass supplies were stored in dry caves.

Grass prepared for weaving was divided into small bunches (the thickness of a finger), the ends of which were lightly braided in order that the strands of grass did not get tangled when they were pulled out of the bunch.

The weaving was done during the winter months. Before weaving, the stems were pulled out and, with a thumbnail specially grown out for the purpose, were split (if necessary) into thinner strips which were then used in the work.

The Aleut women did not have any tools for weaving. The function of a tool was fulfilled by the specially grown and sharpened thumbnail. With that nail they split the stems, leaves and roots, pulled through strips of baleen and decorative threads, and fastened small feathers (and later bundles of [imported] threads) under the strands.

In weaving, they always turned the glossy side of the split stems to the outside of the article being made. When weaving mats and flat bags, the warps were arranged along the width. When weaving a basket broadening toward the top or a semi-circular flap for a flat bag, new warps were added to the existing ones. Sometimes the number of warps was increased by splitting them. The baskets were woven in a hanging position with the bottoms up (and the opening down). First they wove the bottom of the basket, then it was hung on a stick stuck in the wall, ceiling, or roof (if they were weaving outside the dwelling), and they continued weaving, keeping the bottom up. There is an illustration in Iokhel'son which shows a somewhat different method: an Aleut woman is weaving a basket, having put it on a post.[55]

The weaving of articles with the opening down is dictated by the fact that the warps and wefts of Aleut weaving are soft. The Tlingit (and also the Californian Indians and others), who weave with firmer warps, keep the article on the ground with the opening up in the process of manufacture.

As a rule, in simple twining the weave spiral went from left to right (counterclockwise), but, depending on the position of the basket during weaving, the direction of the spiral changed. Among the Aleuts and Haidas, who in the process of weaving kept the basket upside down, the direction of the spiral became clockwise when they turned the basket bottom down; among the Tlingit, who wove with the opening up, the weave spiral was counterclockwise. But, this rule has exceptions. Thus, the weave spiral on one of the published Aleut specimens ("B") from the Kagamil cave is counterclockwise.[56] We see the same on basket No. 2868-238 in the MAE.

The direction of the stitches on the outside surface of the completed article reflects the method of interlacing the wefts. This interlacing can be of two kinds: in the direction toward the worker or away from her.[57]

Interlacing toward the worker gives the stitches on the surface of the item a downward inclination, but when the interlacing is away from the worker, it gives the stitches an upward direction. Almost all Aleut woven products had stitches sloping downward.

The direction of the weave spiral and the inclination of the stitch are interesting since they are traditional for particular ethnic groups. Among the Aleuts, we see deviation from this rule only in individual cases.

Study of the Aleut weaving technique allows several interesting features to be noted.

First of all, in the territory occupied by the Aleuts, Kodiak Islanders, Chugach, Tlingit, and Nootka, only the technique of twining on a vertical warp was used and the technique of sewing together on a circular (spiral) warp [coiling] was not used.[58] Within this indicated area almost all the above-mentioned types and variants of this [twining] technique are found. But individual groups gave preference to one or another technique [variation]. Thus, for example, the Tlingit widely employed the technique of diagonal weaving on vertical warps and three-strand twining, etc.[59]

In the territories adjacent to the area indicated above, on the Asiatic coast of the Pacific Ocean[60] and also on [mainland] Alaska, the Eskimos, except the Pacific Eskimos, and the Athabaskans used the technique of sewing together on a circular (spiral) warp [coiling] as well as the technique of weaving on a vertical warp. Relative to the Eskimos of Alaska, Mason expressed the opinion that they learned the technique of coiled basketry from the Athabaskan tribes of Alaska. The Alaskan Eskimos, except for the Pacific Eskimos, had a poor command of weaving. Thus, Mason writes that the Eskimos of the Yukon River, to judge by their rough and clumsy products, acquired the art of basket weaving only recently.[61] Among the central and eastern Eskimos there were no woven articles at all.

Second, it is curious that the imprints on ancient pottery discovered during the excavations on the mainland of North America are most similar to Aleut woven articles. Mason had pointed this out (based on the materials of W. Holmes).[62] He cites three specimens of imprints of weaving. One of them, loosely woven on divided warps, is exactly similar to Aleut weaving specimens. In the second specimen, the warps are placed diagonally, which Mason considers unusual for the Aleuts. However, at the same time, he notes the fine workmanship of the threads, so characteristic of Aleut articles. In the collections of the MAE, as we have already noted, there is an Aleut basket executed by the technique of diagonal weaving. The final specimen is simple loose weaving on parallel warps. On the basis of these data, Mason concluded that the technique of weaving on vertical warps and the art of making fine threads were well developed by the Aleuts long before they settled the Aleutian Islands.[63]

In another work, devoted to the imprints of weaving on articles discovered in the excavations of sites in the state of Missouri,[64] the technique of weaving on vertical warps, analogous to that of the Aleuts, is also noted. This technique is represented in similar variants: dense and loose twining on vertical and diverted [oblique, angled] warps and diagonal weaving on vertical warps.

It is possible that the Aleuts are the custodians of that ancient tradition of weaving on a vertical warp which was brought along by the peoples who settled America. For ecological reasons (the abundance of grasses for weaving and the shortage of other materials for the production of household articles), this cultural tradition among the Aleuts was perfected technically to a level [of excellence] which made Aleut woven articles famous among ethnographic materials (Figure 22). As was pointed out above, the western Aleuts surpassed the eastern in the art of weaving.

Any investigation of the ethnogenetic and ethnocultural relations of the Aleuts should take all these factors into consideration.

Clothing

Sources dating to the second half of the eighteenth and the very beginning of the nineteenth century make it possible to describe the traditional clothing of the Aleuts, while later sources already reflect the influence of Russian culture. From the early written reports and existing illustrations, we can obtain an idea of the general type of clothing and the material from which it was sewn. Museum collections assist us in defining more accurately the material and details of ornamentation, but the main thing is that they reveal the cut of [pattern for] the clothing.

The strict differentiation of clothing by particular territorial or social group did not exist among the Aleuts. There was no special difference according to usage, either. For convenience of description, only the following categories of clothing could be singled out: festive and everyday, hunting, belts, and footwear.

The principal everyday as well as festive garment of the Aleuts was the parka, a straight, closed garment, made from fur or bird skins, resembling a long shirt. The Siberian term "parka," used to designate that type of Aleut and Eskimo clothing, was in use in Alaska in the eighteenth and first half of the nineteenth century. It is also accepted in the literature. The Fox Aleut [eastern] term for clothing in general is *akhsiaq [hax̂sax̂]* and also *chukhtaqaq [chux̂taqax̂]*.[65]

In the pre-Russian period parkas were sewn from the skins of water birds—murres [*arry*],[66] horned puffins [*ipatki*],[67] tufted puffins [*toporki*][68]—and from the skins of sea mammals—sea otters, fur seals, and, rarely, from seal skins. Besides parkas of their own make, the Aleuts also used parkas which they obtained in trade from the Eskimos of mainland Alaska, bear skin and caribou parkas, and from the Kenaitsy

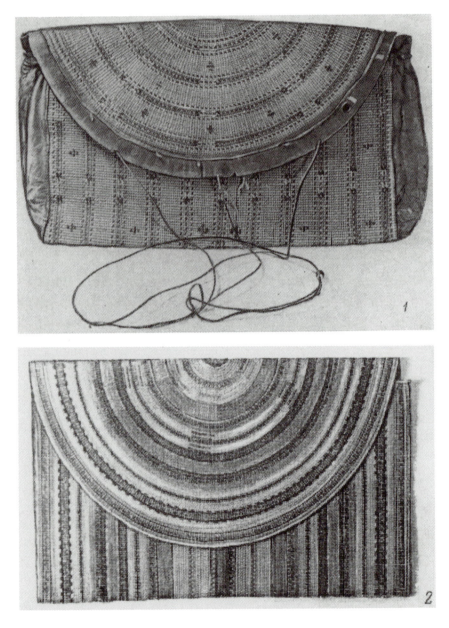

Figure 22. Woven articles (from the collections of the MAE). 1) flat bag, No. 337-1/5 (width 28 centimeters, height 17 centimeters); 2) purse-wallet, No. 633-12 (width 18 centimeters, height 11 centimeters).

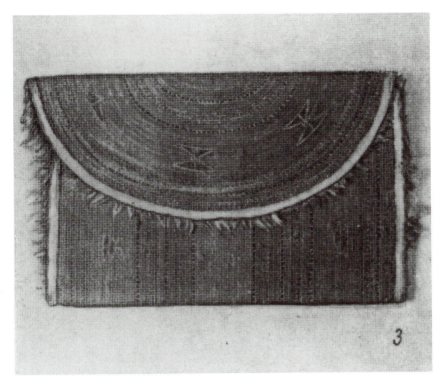

Figure 22 (continued). 3) purse-wallet, No. 2868-29 (width 14.5 centimeters, height 9 centimeters).

and Chugach, marmot parkas.[69] Women's and men's clothing differed only in material. Women's parkas were sewn from sea otter and fur seal skins and sometimes from seal or bird skins (Figure 23); men's parkas were made only from bird skins. The cut and ornamentation were almost identical.[m] When the Russians began to barter with the population of the islands for the skins of sea otter and fur seals as a valuable commodity, and later, when the hunting of these animals was carried on only for the Russian-American Company, the Aleuts, as can be seen in the sources

---

m. There were some important differences. For example, puffin beaks were not used to decorate men's parkas. Also, women's bird skin parkas in museums are of eider, but the men's parkas are never of this material—L. B.

Figure 23. Women from Unalaska Island. Drawing by P. N. Mikhailov. GIM ESSR. Published for the first time [in 1975].

of those years, stopped sewing parkas from sea otter skins, and later also from fur seal skins. In the last decade of the eighteenth century, fur seal parkas were still used, but sea otter parkas were by then not worn. Two decades later, both men's and women's parkas were made only from bird skins (the women's sometimes from seal skins) or from European materials (cotton). Fur was only used for the collar and for decoration in the form of hanging strips. Subsequently, the substitution of European clothing for Aleut [clothing] was all the greater.

Many authors have noted the excellent suitability of the parka to the conditions of life of the Aleuts. Cited here is a characterization provided by K. T. Khlebnikov:

> The bird parka was devised by them in their savage state, and nothing could be more comfortable than it in relation to the climate and to their way of life. These parkas are rather warm, and as they are worn with the feathers on the outside, the rain usually runs off and

does not soak through to the skin side, which is already treated with oil and does not permit quick absorption of humidity from the air and wetness. The wind also does not penetrate the skins; when [use of] the parka is combined with an intestine [gut] *kamleika*, the Aleut is able to withstand the wind, cold and wetness for a long time. If it happens that he gets rather chilly and the parka becomes wet, he enters the yurta, or if out of doors, he squats, places a saucer [lamp] with oil at his feet, lowers the parka tightly to the ground, and also closely covers his head. In an hour or less his entire body is warmed and his clothing is dry.[70]

I. Veniaminov also writes that the parka was an irreplaceable article for the Aleuts. It served as a bed, as a blanket, and even as a house, and with it they were not afraid of dampness, or frost, or wind. And until Veniaminov himself began using the parka during his journeys, he suffered greatly from the cold and winds, even wearing the warmest wool and fur clothing.[71]

Parkas of tufted puffin skins were considered to be the most durable.[72] Just the same, they only lasted a year or a maximum of two.

A parka required the whole skins of 60 horned puffins [or] 40 tufted puffins; the [number of] skins of arra (uril)[n] [required for a parka] was the lowest.[73] The parkas considered to be the smartest were made from bird bellies only, but parkas sewn solely from the necks of horned puffins, tufted puffins, and murres were prized most of all. Polonskii writes that they were the parkas of the "wealthy" and up to 150 necks went into them.[74, o]

Parkas of bird skins *(kulgudaq)* [*qulgudax̂*][75] were sewn from vertically placed bird skins (Figure 24, item 1). On the sleeves the skins were placed in the same way. Gussets were placed in the underarm. The skins were usually sewn with the head part upward, that is, so that water would roll down off their surface (neither penetrating between the feathers nor soaking the skin side). The length of the parka reached mid-calf or the

---

n. Sic. Arra (murre) and uril (cormorant) are not identical—L. B.

o. Polonskii errs. More were required—L. B.

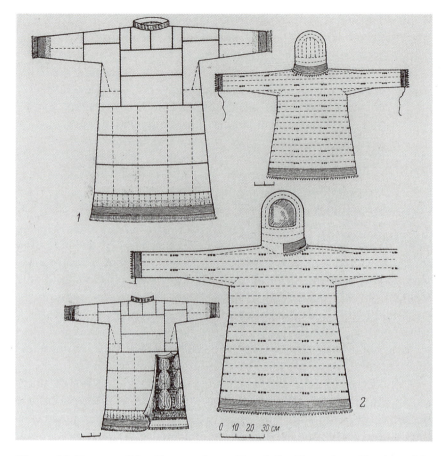

Figure 24. Pattern of the Aleut parka and kamleika (from the collection of the MAE). 1) bird parka, No. 593-17; 2) hunting kamleika, No. 593-24.

heels. The parka sleeve *(amgaq)* [*hamĝax̂*][76] was not set in, but of the kimono pattern. It narrowed somewhat at the wrist. The collar of the parka *(itgasiq)* [*itx̂aasix̂*][77] had a fairly wide cut. The collar was a standing one, seven to eight centimeters in width, with fur either on both sides or on one side only. The outer side was sometimes made of a band decorated with ornamental stitching,[78] and in later years from European cloth, sometimes with decorations of seed and [other types of] beads. Two bird skin parkas of the [above-described] type are in the MAE (Figure 25).

198

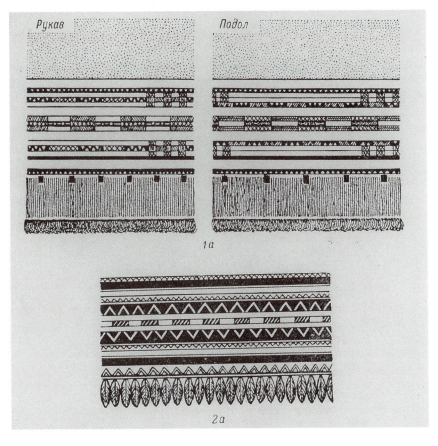

Figure 24 (continued). 1a) detail of "embroidery" of a bird parka (left: from sleeve; right: from hem); 2a) detail of "embroidery" of a kamleika.

Some parkas had more decorations on the feathered side, and some on the skin side. The character of the decorations in both cases was identical: ornamented bands on the collar, at the cuffs of the sleeve and on the hem, on the seams outlining the yoke front and back, and circular bands around the waist and sleeves. Besides that, the parkas were decorated with hanging thongs (fringes) made from sea lion esophagus or from sea otter or fur seal fur. At sleeve edges and at the hem a border of sea otter fur was sewn on *(atmikh [hatmix]*, "edging, trimming").[79]

There are descriptions of bird parkas with decorations on the wrong side (the skin side). On that side ornamental bands are sewn on the

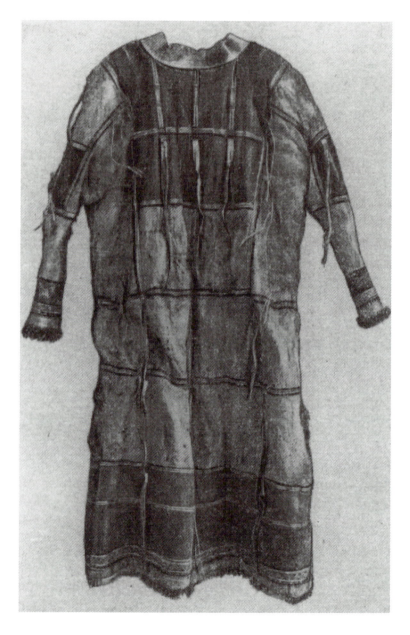

Figure 25. A parka of bird skin with the feathers turned inside (from collection of the MAE, No. 2888-86).

collar, sleeves, hem and along the waist; hanging thong strips, fringes, are attached to this side also. The flesh side of the skin of such parkas was dyed red with ocher. Sometimes the entire skin side of the parka was dyed, sometimes only stripes or other simple geometric designs were painted. Merck describes such a parka from Unalaska, noting that they wore it with the feathers inside. On the flesh side, he writes, the collar was painted with "red earth."[80] Sauer describes a similar parka; he points out that they sometimes wore them with the feathers outside, and sometimes inside. The flesh side they painted, writes Sauer, with red paint and decorated with hanging strips of hide, and the seams which outlined the overlapping yoke, they covered with thin strips of skin embroidered with white caribou hair, goat hair, and colored sinews of sea mammals.[81]

In museums, unfortunately, there is not a single example of a parka made from sea otter or fur seal skins, the traditional garment of the Aleut women. Judging by the descriptions in old sources, the cut of such a parka was the same as that of the bird skin parka and they were worn with the fur on the outside. Sarychev provides a description of such a parka: "The women's simple or everyday dress is identical in cut to those worn by men, only it is not made from bird skins, but from fur seal skins. The collar is usually standing, a hand palm in width, and wholly decorated with glass beads in various designs. At the front part of the collar are hung several long threads strung with seed beads and *korol'ki* [large beads] which hang down the garment. The hem of the parka and the end [cuffs] of the sleeves have a decorated edging [border]."[82] He also has illustrations. The best sketch of a "fur seal parka," however, is found in the album of Levashov (Figure 26).

Merck also describes in the category of women's garments a parka of fur seal skins. He writes that it was sewn from fur seal skins with the fur outside, with a standing collar. The sleeves ended in a wide border of the same fur, cut short with a woman's knife, in the form of longitudinal strips. The same edging was at the bottom of the parka. The collar was decorated with rows of glass beads, alternating in color: a row of white, two rows of blue, and across the rows, crosses of red [beads]. From the collar hung three or four strings of white beads five centimeters or more in length, with little amber tubes the quill of a feather in diameter. The amber, writes Merck, the Aleuts obtained by barter on Kodiak. From the

Figure 26. Woman of Unalaska Island in a fur seal skin parka. Beside her are wooden bowls, bone spoons, and a dancing belt. Drawing by M. D. Levashov. TsGAVMF.

shoulder to the elbow or to the wrist, several rows of free-hanging narrow skin strips were attached.

Besides the parka, capes woven from grass could also apparently be considered an everyday garment of the Aleuts. There are, though, only a few statements about them. For example, there is the report of S. Cherepanov, who writes that "when it was very cold during the winter, then on top of that bird skin garment they wore woven grass blankets."[83] Veniaminov also mentions capes woven from grass. Among the women's articles constituting valuable possessions he lists "spread [shawl, cover] of grass, neatly woven and resembling a cape *(chuguiuk)* [*chugaayux̂*]."[84] Iokhel'son provides a photograph[p] of an Aleut woman in a skillfully woven grass cape.[85]

During feasts (or plays [*igrushki*] as the Russians called them) the Aleuts wore festive dress, *chugukh* [*chugax*].[86] The same parkas served the purpose, but were newer and more richly adorned. Thus the men's festive bird skin parka had a high standing collar made from a strip of hide "embroidered" with ornamental stitching. The same kind of strips were sewn on the sleeves and hem. The entire parka was covered with hanging strips of fur. The women's festive parka was lavishly adorned with seed and large beads and caribou hair[87] and puffin beaks (which, apparently, were one of the principal distinctions of festive women's garments), and attached over the entire dress were strips of fur seal fur, skin, or esophagus.

The necessary accessories to the festive women's garments were necklaces, arm bracelets and anklets, and ornaments for the ears, lips and nose.

In an Aleut tale, recorded by Veniaminov, the festive finery of a girl is recounted: "She immediately ordered...to have herself dressed in the best outfit, that is, to put necklaces around her neck, bracelets on her arms, earrings in her ears and a pendant in her nose (of the best *tsukli* [dentalium shells]), etc....then she put on the best festive parka *(chugukh)* decorated with strips of fur seal skin, and puffin beaks, etc...."[88]

In I. Solov'ev's report, there is mention of a special dancing belt: "brought... from the local peoples, of the craftsmanship of the inhabit- ants of that island... one belt, which, according to their custom, is worn

---

p. The same photograph appears in T. A. Jaggar, "Journal of the technology expedition to the Aleutian Islands, 1907," *Technology Review* 10, no. 1—L. B.

when they dance."[89] Two sketches of such belts are in the album of M. D. Levashov (Figure 26), but the following description (though from a later time) defines these sketches more accurately: "The belt which the Aleuts tied on and wore during the dance to the drum is embroidered with hair, overcast with caribou hair, and with hanging tails cut from the skin of fur seals."[90] It apparently was a specially decorated men's "belt of modesty" [penis cover or sheath], as may be concluded from the report of I. Georgi: "Sometimes they cover their faces with wooden masks, which make them look like animals and are extremely ugly. In that case the men undress and only leave an apron or pouch in front of their genitals, the women remain clothed."[91]

Merck describes women's garments for dancing, made of the fur of the ground squirrel *(evrashka)*, which, as he writes, the Aleuts acquired from distant islands. Along the waist, this parka had four circular transversal strips of very fine embroidery, which were decorated with bundles of goat hair along the edges. The same kind of embroidered bands were on the collar, the cuffs and the hem. From the upper edges of these bands were hung short strands of beads with larger beads [*korol'ki*] at the ends. The same kind of bead strings were suspended from the lower edges of these bands; [these strings] also ended with a larger bead or a copper coin. To these strands of beads puffin beaks, with trimmed goat hair inserted in them, were attached. [Hanging] fur seal skin strips were sewn over the entire parka. On the shoulders, chest and back, strings of multicolored beads alternating in length were hung: on the back and chest, by threes, and on the shoulders, singly. The standing collar was decorated in the following manner: from the upper edge in the front were hung several rows of strings of beads alternating with puffin beaks; the lower edge was also hung [with such bead strings] along its entire length. From beneath [the collar's lower edge] strings of beads with large beads [at the ends] hung to the waist.

An indispensable addition to the hunting clothing of the Aleuts was the hooded kamleika[92] sewn from the intestines of sea mammals—sea lions, seals, harbor seals, whales —and also from the intestines of bears. The Aleut name for the kamleika is *chikhdaq* [*chigdax̂*] (from *chikhtak*, "drizzle").[93]

This type of Aleut clothing is excellently illustrated in museum collections, and this allows the formation of a clear idea about the original appearance of the Aleut kamleika, distinct from the kamleika of the Eskimos and the inhabitants of the northeastern coast of Asia.

The Aleut kamleikas were always sewn from horizontally placed strips of intestines (Figures 27 and 28). The body of the garment is straight. The strips from the back and chest are extended into the sleeves. The sleeve, therefore, is not set in, but is of a kimono pattern; sometimes it narrows toward the wrist. On the chest and back, gussets are put in from the neck opening. Gussets are also put in under the arms,

Figure 27. A festive intestine [gut] kamleika (from collection of the MAE, No. 4108-11).

205

Figure 28. Aleut in a hunting kamleika (on the left) and in a festive one (on the right). Drawn by P. N. Mikhailov. GIM ESSR. Published for the first time [in 1975].

in the front and back. The neck portion of the hood is sewn from circular horizontal strips of intestine, the nape from vertically placed strips of intestines, and the front from strips of intestines, either encircling or in a semi-circle, outlining the opening for the face.

Such a kamleika pattern was typical for the Aleuts, and its later modification signified a break with the traditional [style of its] cut.

Along the facial opening, a casing was made and a drawstring plaited from sinew was passed through it. Exactly the same kind of casing was made in the sleeves at the wrists. On some kamleikas at the bottom of the sleeves at the back of the hand, a loop made of skin or sea lion esophagus was attached, to which the sinew drawstring, used to tie and tighten the sleeve, was fastened. These devices prevented water from penetrating inside the kamleika.

In order to prevent water from getting into the baidarka, the hunter, while in it, obligatorily wore a drip skirt, *tsuki*, a special belt with the appearance of a short and wide skirt, sewn from horizontally placed strips of intestines. The term *tsuki* (or *suka*), in use among the Russian population of the islands and in the literature, comes from the Aleut (Fox dialect) *suk-kakh* [*sukax̂*].[94] The lower edge of the drip skirt closely fitted the figure of the hunter at the level of the chest, and over the left shoulder (if the hunter was not left handed) passed a strap or a sinew cord. The Aleut term (Fox dialect) for this cord, secured over the chest of the hunter, is *kan-nakh-akh-tusian*.[95] For fastening this cord which passed over the shoulder, a beautifully woven button was some-times attached. Sometimes the fastener was [in the form of] a loop made of a thong. Iokhel'son provides drawings of bone or stone rings, *ukamlux* [*ukamlux̂*], which served as fasteners; they were excavated by him.[96]

The seams on the kamleikas and drip skirts were always serged [*vyvorotnye*]. [They were formed by] first employing a running stitch, with stitches placed very close together, and then using an overcast stitch over it. The sinew thread (which the Aleuts used for sewing) swelled when damp, therefore the seams on kamleikas and drip skirts were absolutely waterproof.

For the decoration of the kamleikas, they used narrow strips of sea lion esophagus, undyed or dyed red or black, placed on the hood around the edge of the face opening, on the sleeves, and on the hem. Sometimes those strips were decorated by means of narrow decorative [appliqué]

207

stitching [made with] grass stems, caribou, horse and goat hair, but sometimes they simply alternated in color. Besides that, into the seams they inserted small feathers and long white hairs ("hair of old men" as Veniaminov writes). With the arrival of the Russians, the feathers were replaced with colored woolen threads *(stamedy)*.

They also sewed kamleikas from sea lion esophagi, but very rarely, since such garments were very expensive, even though they were very durable. Polonskii writes that the Russians preferred to wear these. They also sewed kamleikas from the membrane of the liver or tongue of a fresh whale.[97] The most widely used were gut kamleikas, of which the strongest were considered to be those made from sea lion and the most beautiful from bear intestines. The gut kamleikas were not noted for their durability. Veniaminov points out that "an active man required two or even three kamleikas per year." They smeared the kamleika with sea mammal oil (but not that of fish!) to better preserve it, and at the time of each wearing, they sprayed it with water.[98]

There is mention that sometimes kamleikas were worn over the naked body,[99] but this apparently refers only to those worn during festive dances.

The making of kamleikas, as well as all other clothing, was the occupation of women.

On the basis of studies of the kamleikas of the Aleuts and Eskimos (except the southern Pacific groups) in museums, it is possible to note the following difference in their pattern: in the Eskimo kamleika, the hood is cut out together with the back and both constitute a whole; in the Aleut kamleika, the hood is sewn on separately and is not linked with the body of the garment in the process of cutting. This is vividly apparent on kamleika No. 593-24, which has a wide circular ornamented strip in the neck portion (like the collar on the parka) to which the hood is sewn (Figure 24, item *2*).

The cut of the Aleut kamleikas, as we see, is analogous to the cut of the Aleut parka, which has no hood, while the Eskimo kamleikas are sewn according to the pattern of a *kukhlianka* [outer shirt], which is hooded. Thus, despite the complete similarity in appearance of the kamleikas of the Aleuts and the Eskimos, they differ in cut (Figure 29). It is also interesting to note the differences in the seams [construction]: all the seams on the Aleut kamleikas are on the inside and made with small running stitches, and then overcast; on those of the Eskimos, the seams are in the main external and made only with running stitches.

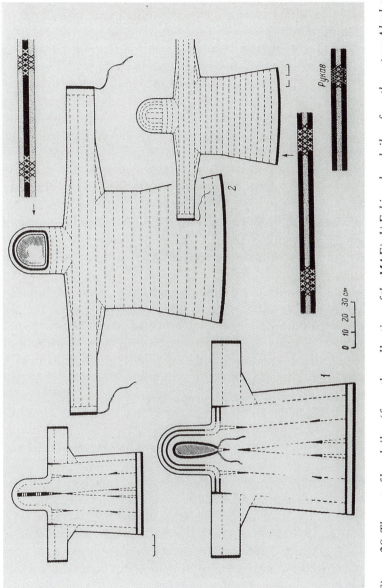

Figure 29. The cut of kamleikas (from the collection of the MAE). 1) Eskimo kamleika of northwestern Alaska, No. 2925–24; 2) Aleut hunting gut kamleika, No. 2868–69.

For sewing, the Aleuts used needles *(aliusiq)* [*haluusix̂*][100] made from the leg bones of gulls. Merck writes that, with broad iron knives, women split the bones of gulls, which they then ground on a porous type of volcanic rock until they were transformed into needles.[101]

In his book, Iokhel'son shows, together with awls he found during archaeological excavations, a piece of bone intended for the manufacture of awls and needles, with longitudinal incisions made with a stone knife.[102]

The needles were of very different sizes and thicknesses, depending on the material which was to be sewn. The finest were used for "embroidery," the thickest for sewing baidarka covers. The Aleut needles did not have eyes, [instead] the thread was tied at a knob made on the dull end. Sauer states that they attached thread to a carefully made notch at the dull end with such mastery that it "followed the needle without any hindrance."[103] Even when the Aleuts began to obtain metal needles from the Russians, as Sarychev writes, they always broke off the eye and ground the dull end on a stone, making a notch, in order to be able to tie on a thread.[104]

The threads, *idgitgan* [*idgitxax̂*],[105] were made from the sinews of sea mammals; the finest were made from caribou and fox sinews. For the splitting of sinews (and also grass) "each seamstress had on her index finger a longer fingernail sharpened like a little knife; with it she split not only grass, but also the sinew of sea mammals into thin fibers with which, with the fingers and without any equipment, she twisted thin, even, and clean threads."[106] Sauer writes that in this way they made thread of all sizes, from the thickness of a hair to the thickness of cords.[107]

The processing of bird skins and intestines for clothing, and the sewing of clothing and footwear *(uliukuk,* "sewing") was done by women. The bird skins were processed "for the most part through squeezing." They also used urine in the processing, and after that the skins were washed in fresh water. The animal skins were scraped with scrapers (Figure 15, items 2 and 3). [The skins] were cut with special women's knives, *ulu* (Figure 15, item 1).

Merck writes that women spent a lot of time on their needlework, especially fine sewing. A woman sewed a kamleika in a period of two months. Needlework was done for the most part after supper, by the light of an oil lamp. During the fall the main handiwork occupation of women was the preparation of thread.

210

The clothing of the Aleuts, particularly the festive, ceremonial headgear and belts, and also some kamleikas, are decorated with ornamental bands that give the impression of being skillfully embroidered. The names for such bands in the Fox dialect of the Aleut language are as follows: *atmiguasiq* [*hatmigasix̂*]—"the hem of the clothing," "embroidery bordering the hem" (a hem in general is *tuktin* [*tuxtin*]); *itgasiq* [*itx̂aasix̂*]—"collar of the dress."[108] Sarychev writes that these articles of Aleut women's manufacture are "made with such art and intricacy that not a single European gold embroiderer is able to compete with them... Instead of thread they use long goat hair; with it they fasten the hair from horses' tails to the skin, overstitching it with white caribou hair and silk of various colors so that their sewing resembles the finest strung seed bead work. With similar designs they embroider the men's festive parkas, small hats, belts and cuffs, used only during dances."[109]

When bartering with the Russians, the Aleuts willingly accepted fine needles, goat hair, and white horse hair, with which they not only decorated parkas and hoods, but also "embroidered." From the Eskimos they earlier obtained by trade the white hair from beneath the neck of the caribou that served as the principal material for "embroidery."

Since the material from which the Aleuts manufactured their clothing (intestines, bird skins, and fur) was not strong enough and not suitable for ornamentation, the Aleuts did their "embroidery" on a more durable base, on strips of sea lion esophagus. They dyed these strips red or black (occasionally blue or green) beforehand, and then with sinew thread they sewed on [even] narrower little strips of dyed sea lion esophagus with various decorative stitches made with hair. Sometimes these small strips were "plaited" [overcast] with hair by various methods. They also simply sewed on little strips without [decorative] stitches or overbraiding. Earlier they used caribou hair, but after the arrival of the Russians they used goat and horse tail hair. Sometimes, instead of hair, they used dried grass and very thin, small strips of sea lion esophagus.

As S. V. Ivanov notes in his work, the term "embroidery" is not suited for defining the technical methods used by the Aleuts for the ornamentation of these strips; it is rather more like appliqué. The various ornamental stitchings were sewn to the base with sinew thread.[110]

The simplest method of appliqué work was the sewing of dyed strips of sea lion esophagus to the base with longitudinal stitching with a running type of stitch. The most widely used was a decorative stitching [seam] in the form of a chain of ovals, formed by two locking

211

[crossing?] caribou hairs. Also frequently used were various ways of winding over the sea lion esophagus strips with two white caribou hairs. It was quite common to have a combination of various stitching types on one strip.

The ornamentation on these "embroidered" strips on the whole is a simple rectangular-geometric one, created by means of small strips dyed in various colors and arranged in chess-board pattern, and by decorative stitching in various designs.

It must be said that the art of "embroidery" was raised by the Aleuts to a very high technical and artistic level. The almost jewellike delicacy of the manufactured articles of the Aleut seamstresses points to the probability of a prolonged period of development of that type of art.

Belted clothing and footwear were not widespread among the Aleuts. A number of earlier authors note that the parka was their basic and almost sole garment; trousers and footwear were encountered but seldom. S. Cherepanov (1759–1762), for example, states that footwear was sometimes worn by the inhabitants of the Near Islands: "They do not have any pants and boots [*torbasy*] except for a small number who wear boots on their feet during the winter, sewn according to their own manner."[111] In the description by A. L. Tolstykh (1764) it is stated that the inhabitants of the Andreanof Islands do not have any other clothing besides the parkas and gut kamleikas.[112] In the "report" of I. Korovin (1766) it is also said that the Aleuts of Unalaska and Umnak do not have pants and boots [*torbasy*], but the latter were only seldom worn by some of them during the winter.[113]

Therefore, there is reason to suppose that, on the whole, it was not customary for the Aleuts to wear pants and footwear.[q] Hrdlička also noted that not one mummy found by him in caves had footwear.[114] It is possible that such a tradition [of wearing footwear?] began only under the influence of the Eskimos. It is also characteristic that in the reports dating to the nineteenth century one does not encounter categorical assertions about the absence of pants and footwear among the Aleuts. It is mentioned that they were worn, but only when outside the dwellings or not in the baidarkas.[115] Subsequently, under Russian influence, pants and boots became incorporated as common elements of men's clothing.

---

q. The absence of footwear is linked to the widespread use of kayaks at all times—L. B.

Pants were sewn mainly from strips of sea lion esophagus, and sometimes from smoked seal skins.[116] In length, the pants came to just below the knee. In the MAE there are several specimens of Aleut pants made of sea lion esophagus (No. 313-66v). Their cut is very similar to Eskimo pants of the same type.

The belt of modesty [penis sheath] among the men had the appearance of a belt [cord] with a pouch. Women did not wear any belts. They only periodically used sanitary belts—a strip of skin passing between the legs and fastened to a [narrow] skin belt; into this band they put soft moss which was changed several times a day.[117]

Aleut footwear, *torbasy*,[118] was sewn with tops [legs] made from sea lion esophagus and with soles of seal flippers, or with tops and soles both from seal skin, or with tops from sea lion esophagus and soles from seal skins. It was very strong. Langsdorff writes that it was manufactured in such a manner that people could walk in the swamp all day, but their feet did not get wet. The sinews with which it was sewn expanded when in contact with water and made the seams impervious to moisture.[119]

The most ancient Aleut boots *(uligik [uliigix]*, "all sorts of footwear, *torbasa*, boots, etc.")[120] resembled a sack (forming a wide leg) to which was sewn a cut out oval sole, gathered at the edge with tucks and bent upwards (in the form of *porshni*).[121]

Veniaminov writes that in his time they already sewed boots with uppers (vamps) of Russian worked leather. In other respects, the pattern remained the same. They sewed the legs from sea lion esophagus or the skins of sea mammals. The soles continued to be made either from Russian leather or, as before, from seal flippers and the skins of sea mammals. Veniaminov reports that sea lion flippers "being wrinkled" were very convenient for walking on stones and slippery places. But already in the 1830s, a number of men wore Russian boots and the women wore shoes.

Many specimens of Aleut boots are preserved in the MAE. Some of them represent the old type with a sacklike top, and others are already footwear with uppers (vamps).

The clothing of the Aleuts of the eighteenth and beginning of the nineteenth century may serve as evidence of great importance for the study of Aleut ethnogenesis. It is obvious that, together with the clothing of other Bering Sea Mongoloids (the Koriak, Itel'men, Chukchi, and Eskimo), it constitutes a single type. The main feature of such a unity is the fact that the garments are closed [lack front opening]. Conditioned by the peculiarities of the climate, that type of clothing is directly dependent on the type of economy, which determines both the selection of material and the design of the clothing. In the same way as the other inhabitants of the Bering Sea region, the Aleuts sewed their clothing from materials which sea hunting provided: skins, intestines, esophagi, sinews of sea mammals, and skins of sea birds. But the similarity of the clothing of the Aleuts, the Eskimos and the northeastern Paleo-Asiatics cannot be explained solely by the similarity of their economies. There are also, undoubtedly, indications of common ancient traditions. These can be discerned in the common principles of the cut and in the method of decorating clothing.

Besides the Bering Sea Mongoloids, the closed garment was characteristic also of the peoples of the Arctic region as a whole (from Eurasia to America). But in the clothing of the Aleuts, features testifying to common ancient ties, specifically to the clothing of the peoples of the circumpolar zone, are less pronounced than in the clothing of the other inhabitants of the Bering Sea. This also applies to the clothing of the Aleuts' neighbors, the Pacific Eskimo (the Kodiak Islanders, Chukchi [*sic*, Chugach], and Eskimos of southern Alaska). The clothing of all the other groups of Eskimos, in its pattern, clearly reveals similarity with the clothing of the peoples of the Arctic [circumpolar region]. This is the reason, it seems to us, for the differences that exist in the clothing of the Eskimos (aside from the Pacific Eskimo mentioned above) and the Aleuts. That these differences have deep roots is indicated by the differences in the traditions of the cut of Aleut parkas, Eskimo *kukhliankas* and the kamleikas of both peoples. As we were able to trace through museum materials, the Aleut kamleikas duplicate the pattern of the parka. The hood on the Aleut kamleika always constitutes a separate part. The Eskimo *kukhlianka*, on the other hand, is characterized by a hood which is cut of a piece with the body of the garment. The Eskimo kamleika repeats this pattern exactly, even in the material which had to be sewn together beforehand. This convinces us that among the Aleuts the hooded clothing was not aboriginal. Thus it is possible to hypothesize that the existence of differences in the clothing of the Aleuts and the Eskimos was conditioned, on the one hand, by the inclusion in Eskimo clothing of traditions coming from Asia by a northern route, and the inclusion in Aleut clothing of very ancient traditions coming via Kamchatka, and on the other hand, by the adaptation of each people to its ecological environment. In this context, we may mention an additional distinctive Aleut trait: it was not characteristic for them to wear pants and footwear.

In the method of clothing decoration with "embroidered" bands and fringes, however, the Aleuts do not differ from the Eskimos on the whole. It is also necessary to note that the high level of mastery in the execution of Aleut "embroidery" indicates a long period for its development and perfection. G. M. Vasilevich links the ornamentation of the clothing of the Eskimos and the Athabaskans of Alaska with the cut and ornamentation of the Tungus caftan, and assumes the possibility of ancient contacts of the ancestors of the northeastern Paleo-Asiatics and the Eskimos with the Tungus-speaking hunters of the mountainous taiga more to the south.[122]

Even more suggestive of possible ancient contacts is the similarity of the Aleut parka, decorated with "embroidered" bands (on the upper line of the armholes, on the yoke [extending over the shoulder in front and in back] and on the ends of the sleeves and hem) and fringes, with the clothing of some of the Indian tribes of North America (the Alaskan Athabaskans and the Plains Indians—the Crow, Mandan, and others).[123] We see here the analogous pattern of a closed garment without a hood, and the similar decorations of hanging fringes and ornamented bands, the design on which, though made with other material (porcupine quills), uses the same technique (placing and sewing of quills with sinew thread) and the same type of ornamentation. The closeness in character and technique of Eskimo-Aleut (and also northeastern Paleo-Asiatic) ornamental motifs of caribou [reindeer] hair to the design executed in porcupine quills by the North American Indians, was already noted by L. Ia. Shternberg.[124] Very interesting also is the conclusion of S. V. Ivanov, that the individual motifs of Eskimoid design, also typical of the ornamentation of Aleut clothing, can be traced in the Indian area.[125] Thus, he considers to be similar to that of the Eskimo the banded ornamentation of the northern Athabaskans (Kenaitsy) and the designs in the form of a concentric circle with one or several (as among the Koriak, Chukchi and Aleuts) tassels attached to its center, on the clothing of the Plains Indians of the Sioux group, the Assiniboin[126] and Mandan.[127]

The complete correspondence of Aleut men's and women's clothing in cut and ornamentation (it sometimes differs in material only) may serve as confirmation of the fact that the Aleuts did not experience changes in living conditions from very ancient times. It is usual that when a change in habitation occurs with a concomitant economic change, men's clothing undergoes changes, is adjusted to new conditions, but women's clothing remains the same. In such a way, a process of differentiation in men's and women's clothing among the peoples of Siberia often took place.[128] From the time of the Aleuts' arrival on the islands, their clothing apparently was preserved unchanged in its main features.

The fact of exclusive utilization of the skins of sea birds and sea mammals as material for traditional clothing, despite the availability of land animals (fox, arctic fox, and caribou) on the eastern islands close to the Alaska Peninsula, appears interesting to us and deserves to be mentioned. This points to a very stable tradition of economic orientation toward the maritime fauna characteristic of the islands.

Headgear

The traditional culture of the Aleuts had an interesting peculiarity—the absence of everyday headgear despite the severe climate. Children's hats were the only exception.[129] The Aleuts wore special headgear only when hunting at sea. Another form of headgear was worn during festivals. The Aleuts called the Russians *saligungin*, "the wearers of hats."[130]

The hunting hats were wooden, and richly decorated with polychrome paints, carved bone, and sea lion whiskers; they were conical (Figure 30, item 1) or open-crowned visors (Figure 30, item 2), which invariably had a greatly extended frontal part. The hoods cannot be considered as independent headgear; since they are tightly sewn to the kamleikas, they constitute a component part of the latter.

The festive-ceremonial headgear was hats of various forms, of skin and bird skins with decorations of bands, circles, and semicircles, all ornamented with patterned stitches. With festive-ceremonial headgear it is necessary also to include skin straps for the head, decorated with patterned stitches.

All the above-mentioned headgear was worn by men; women had none. Only during festivals when taking part in hunting scene performances, did women, imitating the male hunters, put on hats.

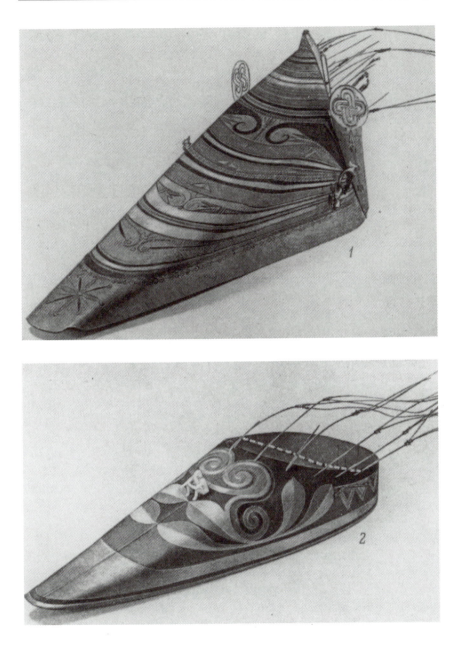

Figure 30. Wooden hunting hats (from the collection of the MAE). 1) conical hat, No. 4104-7; 2) visor, No. 4104-3.

With regard to the children's headgear discovered by A. Hrdlička on mummies, insofar as it is possible to judge from photographs published by him, they were closely fitted to the head, and from the sides to the top they had ear-like protrusions which gave them the appearance of an animal head.[131]

At the beginning of the nineteenth century, under the influence of the Russians, the Aleuts began to wear everyday headgear. These hats and caps were for the most part of a European type, and for women, kerchiefs [shawls].[132] But at the same time, until the middle of the nineteenth century, apparently both men and women sometimes wore headgear of intestines and bird skins, sewn roughly to the patterns of the earlier festive-ceremonial kind.

The traditional hunting and festive-ceremonial headgear went out of use among the Aleuts at the beginning of the twentieth century.

Museum collections provide the principal material for the study of Aleut headgear. The information in old sources, although in the form of brief remarks, is an extremely necessary supplement to [the former].

The MAE has a large collection of hunting headgear: conical hats and visors. Festive-ceremonial headgear is represented in the form of a set of diverse [different] skin hats. The particular value of this collection consists in the fact that it dates to the end of the eighteenth and beginning of the nineteenth century and in it are specimens executed with a mastery already lost in the articles of the second half of the nineteenth and beginning of the twentieth century.

The hunting headgear was studied in detail by S. V. Ivanov on the basis of museum collections.[133] He reached an interesting conclusion about its character and genesis, and also concerning the place occupied by Aleut art among the artistic creations of the Paleo-Asiatics and the Indians.

Hunting headgear. These hats constituted a part of the hunting equipment of the hunter. They were worn over the hood and fastened with sinew cord under the chin when going to sea in a baidarka. According to some sources, these hats protected the eyes of the hunter from the sun's reflection on the water, and according to others from the sea spray.

The hunting hats, as mentioned, were of two types: with a conical top (Figure 30, item 1) and with an open crown (visors; Figure 30, item 2). The hats of the first type were an attribute of the chiefs or of distinguished hunters and warriors, while visors were used by everyone of the rank and file hunters.[134]

Veniaminov cites the Aleut term for a wooden hat "decorated with long sea lion whiskers and various small stones," which apparently refers to the conical one—*kaiatgum tumgagigan aliukhsag inliat* [*qayaatx̂ux̂*].[135] The terms *tschachudak*[136] and *chugudak* [*chagudax̂*][137] Veniaminov defines as "wooden hat without a crown."[138]

The conical hats, particularly, were carefully made and richly decorated. Their manufacture required much time and materials which were scarce on the islands, and therefore they were very highly valued. Veniaminov writes that for such a hat one could receive from one to three slaves. The number of slaves among the Aleuts was, however, quite limited; even the wealthiest chiefs had no more than twenty.[139]

Construction of the body of a hat was a very prolonged, complex, and labor-intensive process. It began with a search for the required material. According to some of the reports, hats were made from small spruce boards, and according to others, from birch. Veniaminov states that the hats were made from any stump washed ashore.[140] Judging by the structure of the wood in the hats in the museums, they were hollowed out from whole pieces of wood. Langsdorff writes that often an Aleut was occupied for an entire week transforming a piece of wood into a [thin] board, which it was necessary then to bend in a certain way.[141] For this purpose it was "cooked" (steamed), either by putting hot stones into a container where it was placed, or it was shaped by direct application of hot stones and simultaneously pouring water on it.[142] When the board acquired the shape of a conical hat (or a visor) and the ends were linked at the back, a back seam was made with sinew threads. After that they started to paint it.

The conical hats, as is possible to observe in museum specimens, are striking in the perfection of their form, always scrupulously controlled. They have a greatly extended brim, the top of which initially is straight, then bends slightly inward, widening from the tip to the top of the head area (here reaching a width of approximately 10 to 12 centimeters), and narrowing slightly toward the edge. On the inside the center of this brim, along the central longitudinal line, was always thickened (the thickest part was about 1.5 centimeters) in comparison with the rest of the parts of the hat, which in the best specimens are very thin (2 to 3 millimeters thick). The length of the front part of the cone varied from 39 to 54.5 centimeters. On its sides, the frontal part merges via rounded corners with the [actual] sides of the hat which slant from the top at a small angle. The lower edges of the sides are also thickened (up to 1.5

centimeters); sometimes this thickening assumes the form of elongated strips. The occipital [back center] line with the seam is almost plumb, but not always strictly straight, and has some slope on the outside. The length of this line (the height of the hat) varies from 19.5 to 24 centimeters. In some specimens the occipital part is strengthened on the inside with a wooden semicircular strip.

On the inside surface of the hat sinew laces were fastened. Sometimes their upper ends were pulled through to the exterior surface of the hat and equipped with ornaments: beautifully braided cords, rings of bone, small carved clasps, and beads.

The hats were painted, principally with mineral paints [pigments], more seldom with vegetal paints. The Aleuts obtained most of the paints on their own islands, but some they received from mainland Alaska.[143] The paints were highly prized. They were considered objects of barter and valuable military trophies.[144] They were used to paint hunting weapons, baidarka frames, and strips of skin and sea lion esophagus, and to decorate clothing, wooden headgear, masks, and their faces. The paints were also used as ritual objects—as offerings to the spirits—and also for burials: they were placed with the deceased in the grave. The procurement and manufacture of paints was the responsibility of the women.[145] They also, apparently, were the guardians of the supply of paints, since it was women who presented paints as gifts to the first travelers.[146]

Merck lists the paints used by the Aleuts together with their local names, and indicates where they were obtained:[147] black *(kaktschichtyschk)* [*qaxchixtusix̂*], brought from mainland Alaska; white *(schawak)*, obtained from a volcano; green *(tschidgajak)* [*chidgi-*]; red *(clodak);*[148] and yellow, obtained from the crust of ocher covering the bottom of some ponds *(akundak, badaraguak)* [*akungax̂, madalaagnax̂*].[149] The last four paints are Unalaskan. They ground the green and black paint together in order to get blue—*unukugtan* [*unuqux̂tax̂*]—"double paint."[150] Lisianskii lists black, dark red, and green-blue as the Aleuts' favorite colors.[151] Veniaminov mentions clay of white, red, yellow (ocher), green, black, and blue colors.[152]

The Aleuts, like the Eskimos, gave wood an undercoat of thin white paint. This could be seen on the edges and parts of the hats not covered with other paints.

They ground the paints on stones. Such stones (grinding stones) are found in large quantities in archaeological investigations on the Aleutian Islands. When grinding the paints on the stone, the Aleuts used blood plasma as a binding substance which, according to numerous travelers, they obtained by means of scratching the inside of the nose with a dried grass stem.[153] Such paint was very durable. Sarychev write that it "may be so durable that neither rain nor salt water washes it off."[154] All the rich colors of the paints are still preserved on the hats in the museum [the MAE].

We see the following designs on the hats: bands of alternating colors, lines of dots, circles, semicircles, strokes, etc., and curvilinear designs—curlicues, double and s-like spirals, and rosettes of complex design. Besides that, they [sometimes] painted the hats with representational drawings.

After the hat was painted, it was decorated with carved bone plaques and figurines, and also with sea lion whiskers. These decorations were placed in strictly defined spots.

The bone plaques were secured to the back of the hat and on the sides. The back bone plaque covered the seam of the hat as if serving to strengthen the hat and as the base into which sea lion whiskers were inserted. It [the back plaque] was sewn to the hat with sinew threads. This plate was carved from a walrus tusk and had the shape of an elongated bar with a groove on the inside. It often represented the finest example of artwork: deep relief carving (high relief), consisting of two or three rods almost separate [from the plaque itself], and serrated or undulating projections at the edges and in the center. The surface of the plaque was covered with geometric engravings, rubbed with red, blue, black, or green pigments. On the top of the plaque, which also formed the top of the hat, a small figure of a bird or a sea otter was attached (or carved as one piece with the plaque). Sometimes entire hunting scenes were placed here.[155] Into the holes drilled into the plaque along its entire length, in two rows, were inserted long sea lion whiskers extending up to fifty centimeters. Each whisker, roughly ten to fifteen centimeters from the base, was doubled [in length] by adding another whisker which [at the juncture] was wound with sinew placed on birch bark. The juncture was often decorated with a bundle of small feathers. On many hats, large beads *(korol'ki)* of various colors were threaded here and there on these whiskers.

On the sides, at the temples and perpendicular to the surface of the hat, bone ear plates were attached. These plates were flat and usually shaped like a circle with an elongated triangular extension. Such a form, according to the interpretation of S. V. Ivanov, is a stylized image of the head of a bird. The place of attachment of the side plates is dictated by the form of the hat, which approaches [suggests] an animal head (the side plates mark the ears of the animal). Some side plates have the form of an elongated rectangle with cut-through designs in the form of rows of concentric circles with spurs, depicting birds' heads with beaks.[156] As a result of further stylization, such a plate on one of the hats in the collection of the MAE has been transformed into a cylindrical spiral.

Small figures of birds carved from bone are fastened on the tops of some side plates, and in one case, the small figure of a sea otter [is used]. On the plates themselves, geometric designs of lines and dotted circles rubbed in pigments are engraved. This stylized design on the triangular spur, that is, on the beak, apparently originates from the line of the maw of a bird's beak, and [the design] on the circle [apparently originates from] a bird's eye.[157] On the side plates, just as on the back plaques, sea lion whiskers were inserted.

Langsdorff states that the sea lion whiskers fastened to the hat served as an indication of the hunting merit of the wearer. Since a sea lion has only four long whiskers, a large number of whiskers on a hat signified a good hunter. Langsdorff writes that he had in his possession a hat decorated with the whiskers of thirty-seven sea lions and that it was correspondingly very expensive.[158]

The hats were made by men. There were apparently masters specializing in this occupation. P. Tikhmenev writes: "The old men work stones, slate, bone for spears...wooden hats and baidarka frames, many such articles...they carve taking great care, paint them with mineral paints and decorate...with painted designs." They were assisted in this by boys.[159]

There is considerably more information in the early sources about visors than about the conical hats—it was these that were primarily seen on the heads of the Aleut-hunters encountered by travelers at sea and ashore.

The first descriptions of such Aleut headgear were given by members of the Bering-Chirikov expedition.

In the log book of the *St. Paul* (A. I. Chirikov) [the following] is reported about the inhabitants of Adak Island: "On their heads they have instead of hats little encircling bands made of thin birch boards, which are painted with various colors and affixed with feathers, and on some, bone figures are fastened at the top."[160]

222

A. Tolstykh writes about the headgear of the inhabitants of the Andreanof Islands: "... on their heads the men wear instead of caps bent wooden rims, glued together with blood obtained from their noses; it looks like a hat with a brim extending over the eyes, the wood is colored with local mineral paints."[161]

Levashov reports that the Aleuts of Unalaska "wear on their heads wooden hats inset with feathers and sea lion whiskers and decorated with large beads [*korol'ki*] of various colors and with small figurines made from bone or soft white stone."[162] There is an illustration of such a hat in his album (Figure 2).

The visors were made approximately in the same way as the conical hats. The center of the elongated frontal part of the cone and the lateral edges were also made thicker. There were no bone plaques at the back of the visors and there were seldom any side plates. On the top of the frontal part of the visors, seated human figurines of bone were fastened.

The oldest specimens in the collection of the MAE are made from a single piece of wood; the later ones are made from two or even three pieces. The seams are thoroughly glued and reinforced (stitched) with sinew threads. The technique of joining the parts is by placing the thinned end of one strip on another, which is also thinned.

The painting of some of the specimens is of one color; on others we see bands, curlicues, spirals, and rosettes.

Ornamentation in the form of long sea lion whiskers, according to Veniaminov, was arranged only on the left side "in order that they would not interfere with the throwing of spears, but if one is left-handed, the sea lion whiskers are attached to the right side."[163] On all existing visors in collections they [sea lion whiskers] are inserted into the left side on the upper edge, beginning at the front.

The hunting headgear of the Aleuts is not only evidence of the high artistic capabilities and great skill of their makers, the Aleuts, but also discloses some features of the distinctive culture of that people, connected with the conditions of its formation.

Of utmost importance is the determination of what conditioned the unusual form of these hats, their coloration, the obligatory details such as plaques and whiskers, and also the presence of a conical tip.

These questions were investigated by S. V. Ivanov.[164] The prevailing opinion about the protective function of the hunting headgear is refuted even by Veniaminov's statement that during strong winds such a hat could have caused the death of a hunter, for the wind, a blast hitting under the hat, could overturn the baidarka. Besides that, the protective goggles known to all Eskimos could serve as protection from the brightness of the sun and the spray. It follows that merely the utilitarian function of these hats does not explain their wide usage.

Ivanov came to the conclusion that the origin of the above mentioned headgear was connected with certain hunting concepts. This conclusion was drawn on the basis of comparative studies of Aleut hats, analogous to the hats of the northwestern and Pacific Eskimos, and also the hats and masks of the Indians of the northwest coast of America.

The hats of the Eskimos, being in basic details similar to those of the Aleuts, display a clearly apparent resemblance to an animal head. The details of ornamentation of the Aleut hats are not fortuitous, just as the strict regularity in the placement of the ornamentation is not. It [the ornamentation] marks the locations of the nose, ears, eyes and mouth of the animal.

Ivanov came to the conclusion that wooden hunting hats were descended from zoomorphic headgear worn during hunting. This proposition is based on the following data. In the first place, the Aleuts, the Eskimos, and the Indians of the northwest coast of America used zoomorphic masks personifying game. Secondly, masks and wooden hats in the form of animal heads were worn for the performance of ritual hunting dances during winter festivals. Thirdly, among the Kodiak Islanders and northwestern Eskimos, the hats in the form of the head of a sea mammal were used only during the hunt for marine game. And fourthly, the wooden hunting hats of the Aleut-Eskimo region, when examined in detail, are shown to be none other than those very same heads of animals, somewhat altered in form.

Of especial interest is the fact that the tips of the Aleut conical hats were usually painted with alternating bands. The conical pointed tip and bands on it cannot be explained by postulating descent from the head of an animal. The Kodiak Islanders, who are in this case the connecting link between the Aleuts and the Tlingit, have cone-shaped hats woven from the roots of trees and from grass. Some of them have a split cylindrical top. Such hats were adapted from the Tlingit, among whom the wearing of a hat with a cylindrical top is the privilege of only the chiefs and nobles. The top here is a sign of honor. Ivanov cites for comparison a wooden dancing hat of the Haida Indians; it portrays a beaver and has a cylindrical top, split into sections. Consequently, the upper part of the Aleut hat can also be viewed as a distinctive sign which earlier was secured to the head of an animal and later became a part of the hat. A significant distinction between the conical hats of the Aleut type and the Indian types is the narrowing which extends to the very top. However, on some Tlingit totem poles, hats with the very same pointed tip, divided into sections, are reproduced.

An analysis of the decorations also indicates the long evolution of the headgear. But if the genesis of the headgear on the whole reveals ancient links with the Indians, in ornamentation features of an Eskimo character are present.[165] First of all this is true for the greater part of the carved walrus ivory decorations. The art of ivory carving had reached the highest development in Alaska, among the northwestern Eskimos, and close to the same development among the Paleo-Asiatics of the Pacific coast.

The ivory carving on headgear, which we discussed above, reflects only part of that form of art among the Aleuts. We know that besides the ivory plaques and small figurines on the headgear, the Aleuts carved separate human figures,[166] zoomorphic figurines for baidarkas and amulets,[167] and also decorated by engraving the bone foreshafts "of sea otter spears."[168]

Examining the Aleut small seated human figurines found in the collections in the MAE and GME [State Museum of the Ethnography of the Peoples of the USSR], Ivanov concluded that they are close not only to Eskimo and Asiatic, but also to Indian sculpture.

Their seated posture with arms crossed on the chest argues in favor of the latter, as [such a posture] is a deeply ingrained tradition in Indian art.[169]

In such a way, an analysis of the form and ornamentation of the hunting headgear of the Aleuts allows one to speak of the deep ancient connections of the Aleuts not only with the Eskimos, but also with the Indians and the Paleo-Asiatics. Departure from the animal prototype, the stylization of the Aleut headgear, suggests the latter's long evolution under conditions of isolation. The amazing perfection of the technique of making hats also indicates this. We note here that the headgear examined was equally characteristic of the culture of the western and eastern Aleuts.

Festive-ceremonial headgear. These hats, together with masks, headbands and other attributes, constituted an integral part of the Aleut ceremonial garments used in performance or hunting rites. Such rites were the basis of Aleut festivals *(igrushki)* conducted in winter after the completion of one hunting season and before the beginning of the next. They were held by turns, first in one settlement, then in another. The inhabitants of the settlement where the current "performance" took place performed scenes with songs and arranged for the feasting.[r] The inhabitants of the other settlement were the guests and spectators.[170]

The character of such festivities, dedicated to the spirit protectors of the hunt, is attested by the information of G. A. Sarychev, who witnessed one of the festivals on Unalaska in 1791. "The beginning of these festivities," he writes, "they say, originated with the shamans who assured the Aleuts that the spirits who served them were fond of these entertainments and promised to wash ashore whales for them."[171]

In these pantomime performances, they represented the successful hunt for sea mammals and birds, the myths and legends of the Aleuts, and glorified the military exploits of ancestors, etc.

As is evident from Sarychev's record, it is obligatory that ritual headgear be worn by the participants in the performance:

> In that yurta where I stayed, the Aleuts once made an *igrushka*...When the guests were seated in their places, the dance began in the usual manner: at first naked boys and adult men wearing *small embroidered hats*,[172] belted with belts and having bands on the hands and feet, with drums in their hands hopped one after the other. Then the women came out by twos in a row wearing bands [*poviaźki*] embroidered and decorated with goat hair...When all the women finished their dances, then the men came out one after another wearing various masks...Here were several Aleuts from the Andreanof Islands. They also demonstrated their own dance[s]... Men, taking off their parkas, only in shirts and trousers, dance one at a time. On the head they place *an embroidered hat with a long and narrow top, extending far in front, bent somewhat upward, and decorated all around with goat hair.*[173]

---

[r]. Food is meant here—L. B.

Putting aside analysis of the Aleut igrushkas as a whole, we shall focus on the headgear worn during such festivals.

Together with the other headgear, the early visitors saw among the Aleuts hats made from the entire skin of a bird, with the wings and tail. I. Solov'ev, for example, speaks of such a hat.[174] According to the description given by I. Georgi, they were made from the skin of *pegankas*[175] "which they skin and dry in such a manner that the head goes into the belly of the bird, while its neck, wings and tail remain as before in their places."[176]

But the information concerning the use of such headgear is contradictory. Georgi described such headgear as a winter hat as opposed to the wooden hunting headgear, which he describes as summer hats.

Georgi also has a description of another hat made from the skin of the *peganka*: "The most splendid of their feather hats are made from *pegankas*. At the neck they attach a narrow springy [elastic] strip consisting of a skin doubled, two fingers in width, which is decorated with fine sewing on the top and bottom, and along the edges hair fringes the length of a finger are attached. Instead of the bird's head, they attach to that kind of a curved strip the lower jaw of an arctic fox. It is embroidered on the back and decorated with fringes."[177]

It became possible to explain the connection between the hats described by Georgi and Sarychev, and also the character of the ceremonial headgear of the Aleuts as a whole, by examining the Aleut collection in the MAE. The comparison of these various and initially strange-looking forms of skin headgear, allowed definition of one common feature: all were representations of birds, some more realistic than others. It was also possible to trace the process of stylization and the gradual deviation from the prototype. Thanks to this, it is possible to see the same bird (duck) in the headgear already very divergent from a realistic representation.[s]

Hat No. 4104-9 (Figure 31) corresponds almost [exactly] to the second hat described by Georgi (the one with attached "neck"), though it is made not of bird skin but of seal skin. By its form, that hat reproduces the body of a bird, and the extension in the form of an embroidered band stretching upward and forward [reproduces] its neck

---

s. Liapunova follows the evolutionary notion accepted as a given that abstract forms evolve from naturalistic representations—L. B.

Figure 31. A ceremonial hat of the western Aleuts made of seal skin and decorated with strips of "embroidered" leather and sea lion esophagus (from collection of the MAE, No. 4104-9).

and head (inside the band is a baleen strip which provides for the band's rigidity). The tail of the bird is represented by means of long fringes of leather strips attached at the back to the lower rim of the hat. We note here that ornamented bands extend from the base of the "neck" forward along the lower edge of the hat and back to the "tail." These details are preserved in some hats where the "neck," "head" and "tail" are absent. Such is hat No. 2868-232 (Figure 32, item 2). Hats Nos. 2868-234 and 536-22 are types of pointed hoods (Figure 32, item 1); however, a series of details point to their genetic link with the hats analogous to No. 4104-9 (Figure 31). In those pointed hoods the frontal ornamented band stretches upward jointly with the back (dorsal) ornamented band and with the sides of the hat. The "neck" as such is lost, but the very top of the hood has decorations of small birds' beaks on sinew strings. The frontal ornamented band remained vertical but the rear slanted, preserving the line of the back of the bird. At the back of the bottom, several short pieces of thong are attached—this is the remains of the "tail." For the sake of convenience, we will designate all these hats as type I.

In another set of hats (let us call it type II), the manner of representation is different, although the protrusion of "neck" and "tail" are also present here. The closest to the image of a bird is hat No. 313-17. Here the body of a bird, that is, the body of the hat, consists of an oval top and rim, which narrows toward the back, where the "tail" of skin fringes is attached. The "neck" has the form of a long tongue framed with feathers, which is sewn onto the front of the upper end of the rim. This form, but with a shorter "neck" and round top, is illustrated by hat No. 536–14 (Figure 32, item 4). On hat No. 2868-233 the "neck" is completely absent, but the "tail" remains (Figure 32, item 3). The rest of the hats have already lost all features of birds, but are similar in form to the hats mentioned above as they retained these features.

In that way, it becomes clear which hats are referred to by the early authors in their reports. For example, in Georgi: "Men wear such bowling pin shaped [conical] hats over a handspan in height, of which the edges [rims] and the two opposite seams are [decorated] with various designs [*vychury*].[t] These have, at the edges, hair fringes about a palm wide. The top has strings of shells [*ulitka*]. On some islands they wear flatter hats, very near resembling our foot messengers' [hats]. The upper

---

t. *Vychury*—specifically, designs used as edging—L. B.

229

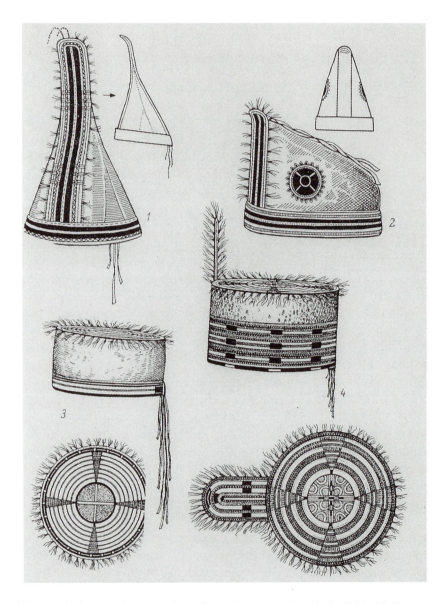

*Figure 32. Ceremonial hats (from the collection of the MAE). 1) No. 2868–234;
2) No. 2868-232; 3) No. 2868-233; 4) No. 536-14 (items 1 and 2 from the
western Aleuts; items 3 and 4 from the eastern Aleuts).*

seam of those hats is also decorated with long hair fringes; the edges and sides are adorned with [fanciful] designs and feathers."[178] It is clear that the first of these hats refers to those we classified as type I and the second to those of type II.

Information contained in various sources about the differences in the form of the headgear of the two subdivisions of Aleuts, the eastern (Fox Islands) and western (Andreanof Islands), from our point of view, expresses only the presence of diverse variants of stylization of a bird image. It is necessary to note that the degree of stylization among the eastern Aleuts was greater and that the hats of type II were typical for them, while type I was characteristic of the western Aleuts.

Why did the ritual hats among the Aleuts resemble a bird (specifically waterfowl)?

As is apparent from the early reports, a quite important role was allotted to the bird in the religious beliefs of the Aleuts. The skins of birds were considered the embodiment of their familiar spirit-guardians. Birds' feathers, bird skins, and bird images were associated with certain magic rituals. Thus, offerings to the spirits were made of bird feathers or of whole skins. According to Veniaminov, they offered the idols sacrifices, among which was also the skin of a hawk.[179] The offerings to the invisible spirits consisted of feathers from the tail of the murres and the variegated feathers of the [screech] owl, which were dipped in paint and scattered in all directions.[180] During the hunting rituals summoning an animal, feathers, bones, and images of birds also played a large role. Merck, for example, writes that to assure the successful hunt for sea otter, falcon feathers were inserted into the sides of the boat. It was believed that the sea otters approached the boats by themselves. But, not many Aleuts possessed such feathers because they were very fearful of killing a falcon.[181] They also attached bone [ivory] bird figurines to the boats.[182] On the hunting hats bone [ivory] figures of birds were often placed.[183] Besides that, in the painting [decoration] of these hats, as we saw, the motifs of birds' heads and beaks can be discerned.

The evidence cited indicates the fact that birds undoubtedly were among the spirit-protectors of hunting, together with other animals. But apparently this was not their only role in the religious concepts of the Aleuts.

Religious beliefs, traditional ritual practices, together with their attributes, are extremely tenacious and conservative [phenomena]. As A. P. Okladnikov notes when speaking of the art of the Neolithic cultures of northern Asia, a fundamental change in world view [ideology] (the reflection of which is both art and religious concepts) occurs only with a change in the entire economic mode, for example, with the transition from a hunting-fishing way of life to agriculture and cattle breeding.[184] The Aleuts remained hunters, fishermen, and gatherers up to the eighteenth century. Moreover, it is necessary here to recall the stability of the Aleut culture, indicated by the data of archaeological investigations which testify to a long period of their presence on the Aleutian Islands (and in a condition of isolation). It is fully possible that the combination of all these factors permitted the preservation of the ancient features of their religious concepts, possibly originating in Paleolithic times and in their original Asiatic homeland. It appears probable that in their form the ritual hats of the Aleuts reflected those early religious ideas which were formed on the basis of ancient totemic beliefs.[u] We recall that the ritual hats of the Aleuts represented not simply a bird, but a duck, *peganka*.[v]

Now let us turn our attention to those ancient cultures among which the search for the roots of the cultures of the North Pacific basin (including the ancestors of the Eskimos and Aleuts) continues. At both the Siberian Paleolithic sites of Mal'ta[185] and Buret',[186] images of waterfowl were found. These regions, tundra and forested tundra at that time, teemed with waterfowl. A. P. Okladnikov, speaking about elements of Paleolithic art preserved among the [arts of the] Neolithic tribes of Siberia, specifically notes as a very interesting fact that in the Neolithic art there appears, firmly surviving in its age-old form, such a characteristically Siberian Paleolithic motif as waterfowl—duck or loon. Paleolithic carved images of birds from Mal'ta and Buret' find a direct reflection [continuation] in the small figurines of birds from Neolithic burial sites near Karsnoyarsk and from Yaisk burial ground on the Tom'. And furthermore, echoes of that motif are also found in folklore. Okladnikov cites a very interesting example. Not only the western

---

u. Here Liapunova follows the standard evolutionary concept of religion, evolution from animism to totemism, etc.—L. B.

v. See editor's addendum to note 175.

Siberian Neolithic tribes and inhabitants of the Urals, but also the Finno-Ugrian peoples, are traced to the large ethnographic group of the Stone Age, the Ural group. In the folklore and mythology of the Finno-Ugrian peoples it is possible to see, Okladnikov believes, the reflection of the concept regarding the special place of birds in their ideology. According to the cosmogonic concepts of the Finno-Ugrians, the world originated from an egg laid in the sea by a gigantic duck.[187]

We do not know of a similar motif in Aleut mythology, but the fact that the ceremonial hats of the Aleuts represent a duck, indicates the deep roots of the concept of the special role of these birds.[188]

Referring to the ethnographic material concerning the Eskimos of Alaska, we also find a basis for the assumption of ancient aboriginal beliefs about the special role of waterfowl. The fact that a great number of anthropomorphic masks of the Eskimos of Alaska have a perfectly definite configuration, namely the configuration of waterfowl, appears to be very interesting.[189]

The possibility of an ancient cultural and genetic connection of the ancestors of the Aleuts and Eskimos with the Paleolithic cultures of the Baikal region (Cisbaikalia) is not in disagreement with present beliefs about the ancestral cultures of the Aleuts and Eskimos.[190]

* * *

When discussing the headgear of the Aleuts as a whole, it is necessary to note some curious regularities. The Aleuts had no everyday hats, but only the hunting and festive-ceremonial ones. In this the Aleuts display a certain resemblance to the Indians for whom headdresses were not articles of everyday clothing, but were only attributes carrying a definite ideological load [significance] (social or religious).[191]

The wooden headgear of the Aleuts represented the essential part of the hunting outfit of the hunter. In this respect, the hat had the primary function of fulfilling the role of a hunting helper. This follows from the genesis of the hunting hats' forms, originating in the zoomorphic hats representing the animal-protectors and helpers in hunting. The details of the decorations, which represent such animals and birds, also testify to this. As convincingly demonstrated by S. V. Ivanov, the hunting hats have much in common not only with the hats and masks of the western Eskimos, but also with the zoomorphic masks and hats of the Indians of the Northwest Coast.[192]

233

The ceremonial hats also, apparently, reflect the beliefs of the Aleuts about the influence of the guardians on the success of hunting. The ritual festivals preceding the hunting season were to guarantee success in the future hunt. Both the guardian spirits of the hunt and the objects of the hunt participated in the performed pantomimic presentations. A special role was allotted to the bird, which apparently occupied a significant place in the religious beliefs of the Aleuts. A specific bird (duck), as it was possible for us to establish, was represented by their ceremonial hats. Besides the indication of the possibility of ancient ties with the Paleolithic cultures of Cisbaikalia, the Aleut hats in the shape of a bird and the utilization of feathers in decoration point to ties with the Indians. In details of decorations, on the other hand, both the hunting and the festive-ceremonial hats have many elements of the Eskimo type.

Thus, the study of Aleut hats permits us to postulate not only a possible Eskimo-Aleut unity in the distant past (perhaps linked to the Paleolithic of Cisbaikalia), but also some cultural contacts between the Aleuts and American Indians, also in the distant past.

CITATIONS AND NOTES

1. Russian promyshlenniki, and later the administration of the Russian-American Company, wishing to take stock of the number of able hunters, first of all found out the number of baidarkas in the settlement, that is, the number of potential fur hunters.

2. To the number of male hunters Veniaminov added the rest of the population—old men, women, and children (I. Veniaminov, *Zapiski ob ostrovakh Unalashkinskogo otdela* [Notes on the islands of the Unalaska district], vol. 2, St. Petersburg, 1840, p. 177).

3. Shells, bones and other organic refuse, which accumulated over a long period of time, served as fertilizer for the soil for a long time (W. I. Jochelson, *Archaeological Investigations in the Aleutian Islands, Carnegie Institution of Washington Publication* 367, Washington, 1925, p. 21).

4. W. I. Jochelson, *Archaeological Investigations...*, p. 23.

5. It should be taken into account, however, that the first discoverers of the islands—merchants and promyshlenniki—often overstated the number of inhabitants.

6. A baidara held roughly up to forty persons, consequently, in the settlement there were five baidaras.

7. *Russkie otkrytiia v Tikhom okeane i Severnoi Amerike v XVIII v.* [Russian discoveries in the Pacific Ocean and North America in the eighteenth century], ed. A. I. Andreev (Moscow, 1948), pp. 123, 125, 126.

8. TsGAVMF, f. 172, op. 1, d. 131, l. 326 ob.

9. After K. T. Khlebnikov, "Zapiski o koloniiakh v Amerike" [Notes on the colonies in America], part 3, ALOII, koll. 115, d. 344, l. 16.

10. G. A. Sarychev, *Puteshestvie po severo-vostochnoi chasti Sibiri, Ledovitomu moriu i Vostochnomu okeanu* [Voyage to the northeastern part of Siberia, the Arctic Sea, and the Eastern Ocean] (Moscow, 1952), p. 212.

11. I. Veniaminov, *Zapiski ob ostrovakh Unalashkinskogo otdela*, vol. 1 (St. Petersburg, 1840), pp. 172-189.

12. Ibid.

13. Ibid., pp. 135-158, 189-254.

14. *Russkie otkrytiia...*, 1948, p. 115.

15. After L. S. Berg, "Iz istorii otkrytiia Aleutskikh ostrovov" [From the history of the discovery of the Aleutian Islands], *Zemlevedenie*, t. 26, v. 1-2 (1924), pp. 123- 125.

16. Noted among the western Aleuts in that period was the existence of small families, while among the eastern Aleuts there were large extended family communities (see below, pp. 166-167).

17. K. T. Khlebnikov, "Zapiski o koloniiakh v Amerike," part 4, ALOII, koll. 115, d. 344, ll. 117 ob., 143 ob., 144 ob., 145.

18. *Russkie otkrytiia...*, 1948, pp. 115-117.

19. After L. S. Berg, "Iz istorii otkrytiia...," p. 13.

20. *Russkie otkrytiia...*, 1948, pp. 123-126.

21. Ibid., pp. 142-143.

22. Ibid., pp. 168, 169.

23. This is, apparently, information about the sizes of dwellings of the eastern Aleuts.

24. Georgi probably has the western Aleuts in mind here.

25. This apparently relates to the eastern Aleuts.

26. I. Georgi, *Opisanie vsekh obitaiushchikh v Rossiiskom gosudarstve narodov* [Description of all the peoples living in the Russian state], part 3 (St. Petersburg, 1799), p. 90.

27. TsGAVMF, gidrograficheskii, f. 1331, op. 4, d. 702, d.[*sic*] 24, 26, 28.

28. James Cook, *A Voyage to the Pacific Ocean*, vol. 3 (London, 1785), p. 108.

29. G. A. Sarychev, *Puteshestvie...*, p. 212.

30. After A. Jacobi, "Carl Heinrich Mercks ethnographische Beobachtungen über die Völker des Beringsmeers, 1789-1791," *Baessler-Archiv*, 1937, Bd. 20, Hf. 3-4, p. 118.

31. I. Veniaminov, *Zapiski...*, vol. 2, pp. 199-200.

32. I. Veniaminov, *Zapiski...*, vol. 2, p. 204. This is connected, apparently, with special reverence of the East among the Aleuts. In the eastern part of a dwelling, the toion took his seat.

33. I. Veniaminov, *Zapiski...*, vol. 2, p. 207.

34. Ibid., p. 208.

35. Ibid., pp. 207-208.

36. V. I. Iokhel'son, "Drevnie i sovremennye podzemnye zhilishcha plemen Severo- vostochnoi Azii i Severo-zapadnoi Ameriki" [Ancient and contemporary subterranean dwellings of the tribes of Northeast Asia and northwestern America], in *Ezhegodnik Russkogo antropologicheskogo obshchestva* [Annual of the Russian Anthropological Society], vol. 2 (1905-1907) (St. Petersburg, 1908).

37. W. I. Jochelson, *Archaeological Investigations...*, p. 125.

38. W. S. Laughlin, "Human migration and permanent occupation in the Bering Sea area," in *The Bering Land Bridge*, ed. D. M. Hopkins (Stanford: Stanford University Press, 1967); N. N. Dikov, "Paleoliticheskoe zhilishche na kamchatskoi stoianke Ushki IV" [Paleolithic dwelling in Kamchatka's Ushki IV site], in *Sibir' i ee sosedi v drevnosti* [Siberia and its neighbors in antiquity] (Novosibirsk, 1970); A. P. Derevianko, *Priamur'e v drevnosti* [The Amur region in antiquity], Synopsis of doctoral dissertation (Novosibirsk, 1971). [See also A. P. McCartney "Prehistory of the Aleutian region," in *Handbook of North American Indians*, vol. 5, *The Arctic*, ed. D. Damas (Washington: Smithsonian Institution, 1984), p. 122—L. B.].

39. A. Hrdlička, *The Aleutian and Commander Islands and their Inhabitants* (Philadelphia: Wistar Institute of Anatomy and Biology, 1945), p. 374.

40. W. S. Laughlin, "Aleutian studies: Introduction," *Arctic Anthropology* 3, no. 2 (1966), pp. 23–27.

41. The weaving of the American aborigines is most completely investigated by O. T. Mason in "American aboriginal basketry," *Report of the United States National Museum for 1902* (1904), pp. 171–548, and "Basket-work of the North American aborigines," *Report of the United States National Museum for 1884*, part 2 (1885), pp. 291–306. [More recent studies of Aleut basketry are R. L. Hudson, "Designs in Aleut basketry," in *Faces, Voices and Dreams*, ed. P. L. Corey (Sitka, Alaska: Division of Alaska State Museum and Friends of Alaska State Museum, 1987), pp. 63-92; and A. T. Shapsnikoff and R. L. Hudson, "Aleut basketry," *Anthropological Papers of the University of Alaska* 16, no. 2 (1974), pp. 41-69—L. B.]

42. The Aleuts, when doubling the warp, do not place one element of the warp behind another, as did the Tlingit, but alongside. This makes it possible for the weavers to change the technique in successive rows [O. T. Mason, "American aboriginal...," p. 403].

43. O. T. Mason, "American aboriginal...," pl. 143.

44. A. Hrdlička, *The Aleutian and Commander...*, pp. 598-599.

45. That type of weaving can be viewed as a variant of weaving on a lattice warp (our type IV).

46. P. Gebhard and K. P. Kent, "Some textile specimens from the Aleutian Islands," *American Antiquity* 7, no. 2 (1941), pp. 171-176.

47. Together with the technique of twining the vertical warp with weft (twined work) and the circular (coiled) technique, some researchers (G. Weltfish, "Prehistoric North American basketry techniques and modern distribution," *American Anthropologist* 32, no. 3, pt. 1, 1930) single out chessboardlike or matting (checker), and diagonal (twill) weaving as a special type designated by the term "plaiting," based on the fact that in it there is no distinction between the warp and weft, since both of those elements are equal in degree of activity and position.

48. P. Gebhard, and K. P. Kent, "Some textile...."

49. In some works (A. Hrdlička, *The Aleutian and Commander...*, pp. 598-599) this type of ornamentation is designated by the term "overlay"—"twined with a covering strand." But the latter is a different technique (see O. T. Mason, "American aboriginal...," pp. 306-308; R. Underhill, *Indians of the Pacific Northwest,* Washington, 1953, p. 99; G. Weltfish, "Prehistoric North...," pp. 477–478). This method of ornamentation consists in that a decorative strand is added to each strand of weft of the warp structure. In twining, the decorative

strand is either covered with a strand of the warp structure, or covers the warp structure itself, forming on the surface stitches of another color and quality. Thus they create ornamental figures on the surface of an article. We did not find this technique of ornamentation on Aleut articles.

50. O. T. Mason, "American aboriginal...," p. 408.

51. W. I. Jochelson, *History, Ethnology and Anthropology of the Aleut, Carnegie Institution of Washington Publication* 432 (Washington, 1933), p. 62.

52. M. L. Kissel, "An Aleutian basket," *American Museum Journal* 7, no. 8 (1907), pp. 133-136.

53. P. Gebhard, and K. P. Kent, "Some textile...," p. 171.

54. A. Hrdlička, *The Aleutian and Commander...*, p. 610.

55. W. I. Jochelson, *Archaeological Investigations...*, p. 44. In this way, on a little post, the Haida too weave baskets.

56. P. Gebhard, and K. P. Kent, "Some textile...," p. 173.

57. In weaving, the basket is turned so that the part where the interlacing is, is always to be found directly in front of the weaver.

58. See O. T. Mason, "American aboriginal...," pp. 266, 253; G. Weltfish, "Prehistoric North...," pp. 454-495. The same technique of weaving was used among the tribes of northern California (P. M. Kozhin, "Pletenye sosudy indeitsev Kalifornii" [Woven vessels of the Indians of California], *Sbornik Muzeia antropologii i etnografii im. Petra I*, t. 24, 1967).

59. R. S. Razumovskaia, "Pletenye izdeliia severo-zapadnikh indeitsev" [Woven articles of the northwestern Indians], *Sbornik Muzeia antropologii i etnografii im. Petra I*, t. 24 (1967), p. 96; G. T. Emmons, "The basketry of the Tlingit," *Memoirs of the American Museum of Natural History* 3, pt. 2 (1903), pp. 229-277; O. T. Mason, "American aboriginal..."; idem, "Basket-work...."

60. Thus, the Koriaks, according to Iokhel'son, used both the technique of weaving on vertical warps and that of coiled weaving, but their work is better and their methods more varied than among the Eskimo. About the Koriak's technique of coiled weaving, Iokhel'son writes that it, like that of the Eskimo, is identical to that of the Athabaskans (W. I. Jochelson, "The Koryak," *The Jesup North Pacific Expedition*, vol. 6, *Memoirs of the American Museum of Natural History*, 1905–1908, pp. 631, 634). The similarity between Koriak woven baskets executed by the technique of weaving on vertical warps, and Aleut ones attracts attention (see A. A. Popov, "Pletenie i tkachestvo u narodov

Sibiri XIX i pervoi chetverti XX stoletiia" [Basketry and weaving among the peoples of Siberia in the 19th and the first quarter of the 20th century], *Sbornik Muzeia antropologii i etnografii im. Petra I,* vol. 16, 1955, pp. 41-46).

61. O. T. Mason, "American aboriginal...," pp. 287, 295.

62. W. H. Holmes, "Use of textiles in pottery making and embellishment," *American Anthropologist,* n.s., vol. 8 (1901), pp. 397–403.

63. Mason believed that the settling of the Aleutian Islands took place from America (O. T. Mason, "American aboriginal...," p. 385).

64. P. Munger, and R. A. McCormick, "Fabric impressions of pottery from the Elizabeth Herrel site, Missouri," *American Antiquity* 7, no. 2, pt. 1 (1941), pp. 166-171. This early site is attributed to the middle Mississippian phase of the Mississippian style.

65. I. Veniaminov, *Opyt grammatiki aleutsko-lis'evskogo iazyka* [Tentative grammar of the Aleut-Fox language] (St. Petersburg, 1846), pp. 24, 70. Sauer gives the following terms for parkas: women's—*tshaktakut* and men's—*iash* (M. Sauer, *An Account of a Geographical and Astronomical Expedition to the Northern Part of Russia, Performed by Commander Joseph Billings in the Year 1785,* London, 1802, p. 155).

66. Arry (ary) or murre *(Uria aalge inoraata),* of the family Alcidae.

67. Ipatki *(Fratercula corniculata)* [horned puffin], of the family Alcidae.

68. Toporki *(Lunda cirrhata)* [tufted puffin], of the family Alcidae.

69. A. Polonskii, "Promyshlenniki na Aleutskikh ostrovakh (1743-1800 gg.)" [Promyshlenniki on the Aleutian Islands (1743-1800)], AGO, r. 60, op. 1, d. 3, l. 30.

70. K. T. Khlebnikov, "Zapiski o koloniiakh v Amerike," part 2, LOAAN, r. 2, op. 1, no. 275, l. 39 ob., 40.

71. I. Veniaminov, *Zapiski...,* vol. 2, p. 212.

72. "No other bird was more difficult for us to shoot with shot than the toporok [puffin]; its feathers are so thick that the shot slides off" (G. A. Sarychev, *Puteshestvie...,* p. 154).

73. A. Polonskii, "Promyshlenniki na Aleutskikh ostrovakh...," l. 30; I. Veniaminov, *Zapiski...,* vol. 2, p. 214.

74. A. Polonskii, "Promyshlenniki na Aleutskikh ostrovakh...," l. 30.

75. I. Veniaminov, *Opyt grammatiki...,* p. 45.

76. Ibid., p. 13.

77. Ibid., p. 34.

78. About the ornamented strips, see below, pp. 209–210.

79. I. Veniaminov, *Opyt grammatiki...*, p. 21.

80. A. Jacobi, "Carl Heinrich Mercks...," p. 117.

81. M. Sauer, *An Account...*, p. 155.

82. G. A. Sarychev, *Puteshestvie...*, p. 140.

83. *Russkie otkrytiia...*, 1948, p. 117.

84. I. Veniaminov, *Zapiski...*, vol. 2, p. 239.

85. W. I. Jochelson, *History, Ethnology and Anthropology...*, p. 60.

86. I. Veniaminov, *Zapiski...*, vol. 2, p. 295.

87. Goat hair was brought from Kamchatka by the Russians.

88. I. Veniaminov, *Zapiski...*, vol. 2, p. 295.

89. *Russkie otkrytiia...*, 1948, p. 169.

90. M. M. Bulgakov Collection, AVPR, f. 339, op. 808, d. 733, l. 1, 2.

91. I. Georgi, *Opisanie...*, p. 95.

92. Siberian and Kamchatkan nineteenth-century terms for designating garments of intestines and sea lion esophagi.

93. I. Veniaminov, *Opyt grammatiki...*, p. 68.

94. I. G. Voznesenskii Archive, LOAAN, f. 2, 1845, No. 12.

95. Ibid.

96. W. I. Jochelson, *Archaeological Investigations...*, p. 100.

97. A. Polonskii, "Promyshlenniki na Aleutskikh ostrovakh...," l. 30-30 ob.

98. I. Veniaminov, *Zapiski...*, vol. 2, p. 180.

99. I. Georgi, *Opisanie...*, p. 89.

100. I. Veniaminov, *Opyt grammatiki...*, p. 11. On page 33 Veniaminov provides another name for needle, *inukak* [*hinguqax̂*], with the additional meaning *prodeto* ["pass" or "through"].

101. After A. Jacobi, "Carl Heinrich Mercks...," p. 121.

102. W. I. Jochelson, *Archaeological Investigations...*, p. 91, Figure 66, plate 28.

103. M. Sauer, *An Account...*, pp. 156, 157.

104. G. A. Sarychev, *Puteshestvie...*, pp. 138, 139.

105. I. Veniaminov, *Opyt grammatiki...*, p. 28.

106. G. A. Sarychev, *Puteshestvie...*, p. 138.

107. M. Sauer, *An Account...*, pp. 156, 157.

108. I. Veniaminov, *Opyt grammatiki...*, pp. 21, 34, 58.

109. G. A. Sarychev, *Puteshestvie...*, p. 140.

110. S. V. Ivanov, "Ornament narodov Sibiri kak istoricheskii istochnik" [Ornamentation of the peoples of Siberia as a historical source], *Trudy Instituta etnografii,* n.s., 81 (1963), pp. 196-202.

111. *Russkie otkrytiia...*, 1948, p. 143.

112. After L. S. Berg, "Iz istorii otkrytiia...," p. 130.

113. Ibid., p. 117.

114. A. Hrdlička., *The Aleutian and Commander...*, p. 78.

115. M. Sauer, *An Account...*, p. 155; G. H. Langsdorff, *Voyages and Travels in Various Parts of the World during the Years 1803–1807,* vol. 2 (London, 1814), pp. 36–37.

116. G. A. Sarychev, *Puteshestvie...*, p. 140; G. H. Langsdorff, *Voyages and Travels...*, pp. 36-37; M. Sauer, *An Account...*; A. Jacobi, "Carl Heinrich Mercks...," p. 117.

117. A. Jacobi, "Carl Heinrich Mercks...," p. 121.

118. This Siberian term entered the literature for the designation of an Aleut boot type of footwear.

119. G. H. Langsdorff, *Voyages and Travels...*, pp. 36-37.

120. I. Veniaminov, *Opyt grammatiki...*, p. 63.

121. Porshni—a type of bent [rather than sewn] footwear known to many peoples, made from a scrap of rawhide on a cord [a type of sandal].

122. G. M. Vasilevich, "Tungusskii kaftan" [The Tungus caftan], *Sbornik Muzeia antropologii i etnografii im. Petra I,* t. 18, 1958.

123. C. Wissler, "Indian costumes in the United States," *American Museum of Natural History Guide Leaflet Series* 63, (1931), pp. 1-32; F. W. Hodge, ed., *Handbook of American Indians North of Mexico,* vol. 1, *Smithsonian Institution, Bureau of American Ethnology Bulletin* 30 (1912), pp. 310–313.

124. L. Ia. Shternberg, "Ornament iz olen'ego volosa i igl dikobraza" [Ornamentation out of caribou hair and porcupine quills], *Sovetskaia etnografiia,* 1931, no. 3-4.

125. S. V. Ivanov, "Ornament narodov Sibiri...," p. 238.

126. C. Wissler, "Indian costumes...," p. 133 (Figure).

127. V. Bailey, "Maximilian's travels in the interior of North America, 1832 to 1834," *Natural History* 23, no. 4 (1923), p. 342.

128. *Istoriko-ethnograficheskii atlas Sibiri* [Historical-ethnographic atlas of Siberia], ed. M. G. Levin and L. P. Potapov (Moscow and Leningrad, 1961), p. 236.

129. Bird skin children's hats were discovered by A. Hrdlička in the Kagamil mummy cave (A. Hrdlička, *The Aleutian and Commander...,* pp. 80, 422, Figure 171).

130. I. Veniaminov, *Zapiski...,* vol. 2, p. 215. In his dictionary Veniaminov provides a general term for headgear, *shaliguk [saligux̂],* while *shaligugik [saliguĝix̂]* means "person wearing a hat, a Russian" (I. Veniaminov, *Opyt grammatiki...,* p. 71).

131. A. Hrdlička, *The Aleutian and Commander....*

132. I. Veniaminov, *Zapiski...,* vol. 2, p. 215.

133. S. V. Ivanov, "Aleut hunting headgear and its ornamentation," *Proceedings of the International Congress of Americanists* 23 (1928), (New York, 1930); idem, "Materialy po izobrazitel'nomu iskusstvu narodov Sibiri XIX - nachala XX v." [Materials on the depictive art of the peoples of Siberia in the nineteenth and early twentieth century], *Trudy Instituta etnografii,* n.s., 22 (1954), pp. 483– 504; idem, "Ornament narodov Sibiri...," pp. 163–248.

134. I. Veniaminov, *Zapiski...,* vol. 2, p. 218.

135. Ibid., p. 239.

136. A. Jacobi, "Carl Heinrich Mercks...," p. 117.

137. Iu. F. Lisianskii, *Puteshestvie vokrug sveta na korable* Neva *v 1803–1806 gg.* [Voyage round the world on the ship *Neva* in 1803–1806] (Moscow,1947), p. 201.

138. I. Veniaminov, *Opyt grammatiki...*, p. 66.

139. I. Veniaminov, *Zapiski...*, vol. 2, pp. 218, 239.

140. Ibid., p. 218.

141. G. H. Langsdorff, *Voyages and Travels...*, pp. 38–39.

142. A. Jacobi, "Carl Heinrich Mercks...," p. 117.

143. See I. Veniaminov, *Zapiski...*, vol. 2, p. 45; I. Georgi, *Opisanie...*, p. 90; A. Jacobi, "Carl Heinrich Mercks...," p. 117.

144. I. Veniaminov, *Zapiski...*, vol. 2, p. 94.

145. S. V. Ivanov, "Materialy...," p. 484.

146. The navigator M. Nevodchikov saw on the island of Agattu (in 1745), how an elderly woman "in common with other savages of both sexes danced to a drum and presented them with pigments" (P. S. Pallas, *O rossiiskikh otkrytiiakh na moriakh mezhdu Aziei i Amerikoi. Sobranie sochinenii vybrannykh iz mesiatseslovov* [On Russian discoveries in the seas between Asia and America. A collection of works, selected from *Mesiatseslov*], vol. 4, St. Petersburg, 1790, p. 298).

147. After A. Jacobi, "Carl Heinrich Mercks...," p. 117.

148. According to Veniaminov, *uliudaq* [*uluudax̂*] means red (*Opyt grammatiki...*, p. 63).

149. According to Veniaminov, *akunaq* [*akungax̂*] means yellow pigment, ocher (*Opyt grammatiki...*, p. 9).

150. A. Jacobi, "Carl Heinrich Mercks...," p. 117.

151. Iu. F. Lisianskii, *Puteshestvie...*, p. 149.

152. I. Veniaminov, *Zapiski...*, vol. 1, p. 45.

153. A. Jacobi, "Carl Heinrich Mercks...," p. 117. Sarychev writes the same: "The Aleuts obtain the blood for this purpose from their own noses, putting a straw inside the nose and picking with it until the required amount of blood flows out" (*Puteshestvie...*, p. 171).

154. G. A. Sarychev, *Puteshestvie...*, p. 214.

155. R. G. Liapunova, "Zoomorfnaia skul'ptura aleutov" [Zoomorphic sculpture of the Aleuts], *Sbornik Muzeia antropologii i etnografii im. Petra I*, t. 24 (1967).

156. S. V. Ivanov, "Aleut hunting...," pp. 486–489, 494–495.

157. Ibid., p. 495.

158. G. H. Langsdorff, *Voyages and Travels...*, p. 39.

159. P. Tikhmenev, *Istoricheskoe obozrenie obrazovaniia Rossiisko-Amerikanskoi kompanii* [Historical review of the formation of the Russian-American Company], part 2 (St. Petersburg, 1863), p. 369.

160. *Russkie otkrytiia...*, 1948, p. 109.

161. After L. S. Berg, "Iz istorii otkrytiia...," p. 128.

162. After A. P. Sokolov, "Ekspeditsiia k Aleutskim ostrovam kapitanov Krenitsyna i Levashova, 1764–1769 gg." [Expedition by captains Krenitsyn and Levashov to the Aleutian Islands, 1764–1769], *Zapiski Gidrograficheskogo departamenta Morskago ministerstva,* part 10 (1852), p. 99.

163. I. Veniaminov, *Zapiski...*, vol. 2, p. 218.

164. In view of the extreme interest this research (S. V. Ivanov, "Aleut hunting...") holds for the present work, we will dwell on his principal propositions.

165. S. V. Ivanov, "Aleut hunting...," p. 492.

166. S. V. Ivanov, "Sidiachie chelovecheskie figurki v skul'pture aleutov" [Seated human figures in Aleut sculpture], *Sbornik Muzeia antropologii i etnografii im. Petra I,* t. 12 (1949).

167. R. G. Liapunova, "Zoomorfnaia skul'ptura aleutov."

168. R. G. Liapunova, "Orudiia okhoty aleutov" [Aleut hunting implements], *Sbornik Muzeia antropologii i etnografii im. Petra I,* t. 21 (1963).

169. S. V. Ivanov, "Sidiachie chelovecheskie figurki...."

170. I. Veniaminov, *Zapiski...*, vol. 2, pp. 85-93.

171. G. A. Sarychev, *Puteshestvie...*, p. 200.

172. Here and farther the emphasis is ours.

173. G. A. Sarychev, *Puteshestvie...*, pp. 201-202.

174. W. Coxe, *Account of the Russian Discoveries between Asia and America* (London, 1803), p. 227.

175. *Peganka khokhlataia (Tadorna cristata)* in biological relation represents the transition from goose to duck. It was widespread in the northern part of the Pacific Ocean. Now the bird is close to extinction. [According to the *Russian-English Bird Glossary* (J. M. MacLennan, Ottawa: Department of Northern Affairs and Natural Resources, 1958), the term *peganka* refers to shelldrake or shellduck. According to *Entsiklopedicheskii slovar'* (F. A. Brokgauz and I. A. Efron, St. Petersburg, 1890–1904), *peganka* refers to birds of the genus *Tadorna*. Species of that genus are not listed in guides to Western birds, but in some books on avifauna, mergansers seem to be equated with shellducks or *Tadorna* species—L. B.]

176. I. Georgi, *Opisanie...*, p. 90.

177. Ibid.

178. Ibid.

179. I. Veniaminov, *Zapiski ob ostrovakh Unalashkinskogo otdela*, vol. 3, (St. Petersburg, 1840), p. 3.

180. I. Veniaminov, *Zapiski...*, vol. 2, pp. 122-123.

181. After A. Jacobi, "Carl Heinrich Mercks...," p. 120.

182. R. G. Liapunova, "Aleutskie baidarki" [Aleut bardarkas], *Sbornik Muzeia antropologii i etnografii im. Petra I*, vol. 22 (1964).

183. R. G. Liapunova, "Zoomorfnaia skul'ptura aleutov."

184. A. P. Okladnikov, "O paleoliticheskoi traditsii v iskusstve neoliticheskikh plemen Sibiri" [On the Paleolithic tradition in the art of the Neolithic tribes of Siberia], in *Pervobytnoe iskusstvo* [Primitive art] (Novosibirsk, 1971).

185. M. M. Gerasimov, *Mal'ta—paleoliticheskaia stoianka* [Malta: A Paleolithic site] (Irkutsk, 1931).

186. A. P. Okladnikov, *Istoriia Iakutii* [History of Yakutia], vol. 1 (Yakutsk, 1941), pp. 37, 48; idem, "Paleoliticheskie zhilishcha v Bureti (po raskopkam 1936-1940 gg.)" [Paleolithic dwellings at Buret' (from the excavations of 1936-1940)], *Kratkie soobshcheniia Instituta istorii material'noi kul'tury* 10 (1941).

187. A. P. Okladnikov, "O paleoliticheskoi traditsii...."

188. The origin of the closed garment with a hood, typical of the Ural, Paleo-Asiatic, and Eskimo groups of peoples, is connected with the Paleolithic of Cisbaikalia, which the famous statuette from Buret' showed quite convincingly (A. P. Okladnikov, "Paleoliticheskaia statuetka iz Bureti" [The Paleolithic statuette from Buret'], *Materialy i issledovaniia po arkheologii SSSR*, 1941, no. 2).

189. H. Hipszer, "Quelques Masques de Hiboux et de Corbeaux," *Anthropos* (1967), pp. 68-88.

190. R. S. Vasil'evskii, *Drevnie kul'tury Tikhookeanskogo Severa* [Ancient cultures of the North Pacific] (Novosibirsk, 1973), pp. 126-148.

191. C. Wissler, "Indian costumes...," p. 8.

192. S. V. Ivanov, "Aleut hunting...."

CONCLUSION

The ethnographic material discussed in this [the present] work illustrates in detail first of all the economic mastery by the Aleuts of their severe and ecologically distinctive region. Their implements and means of hunting are indicative of a long and independent path of development of the basic focus of their economy—sea mammal hunting—and of the high level of its specialization. These materials allow determination of the specifics of the Aleut maritime enterprise in comparison with the Eskimo; on the basis of such a determination, it is possible to propose that prior to the separation of the Aleuts and Eskimos, that single unified ethnic group did not have an economy oriented to sea mammal hunting.

The hunting-fishing-gathering economy of the Aleuts, despite its foraging character, was highly specialized and therefore resulted in a significant [level of] productivity. This facilitated the development of productive forces of a significantly high level, and correspondingly, of the relations of production specific to the decaying primitive communal formations (which were observed among the Aleuts in the eighteenth century). The comparatively high level of the economy with the corresponding socio-economic relations and social institutions could be the result only of a long period of mastery by the Aleuts of their territory.

The material culture of the Aleuts reflects certain traditions which point to the genetic and ancient cultural-historical ties of this people, beginning from the original Asiatic cultures and up to the Eskimo, Paleo-Asiatic and Indian [cultures]. Such a specific character of Aleut culture is the result of great antiquity (according to archaeological data, up to ten thousand years ago) of the settling by the Aleuts of the Aleutian Islands and their consequent geographic isolation in insular conditions.

Analysis of the ethnographic material leads to the conclusion that the culture of the Aleuts has all the indications of an extremely long period of development in the given ecological conditions. In all probability, the formation of the culture, as well as of the physical type and linguistic features of the Aleuts, occurred in the same territory they occupied at the time of their discovery by the Europeans.

These essays do not exhaust all the ethnographic material which could be used in the investigation of the problem of the ethnogenesis of the Aleuts. The full-scale study of ethnographic material (including the spiritual culture) will provide further illumination of the questions raised here.

INDEX

A

Academy of Sciences, 27, 30
Adak Island, 24, 25, 49, 167
Admiralty College, 26
Agattu Island, 24, 48, 61
Aglegmiut, 117
Aigner, J. S., 57
Ainu, 66
Akun Island, 165
Akutan Island, 65
Alaska
sale to United States, 32
Alaska Peninsula, 24, 42, 47, 54,
58, 60, 66, 71, 106, 150, 161,
166, 216
Aldan, 13
Aleutian Islands, 1, 10, 11, 13, 24,
27, 29, 35, 37, 38–39, 41, 42,
44, 45, 59, 61–62, 66, 67, 69,
71, 86, 91, 106, 107, 161,
162, 179
discovery, 23
excavations, 3334, 47, 49
map, 25
settlement, 49
Aleut
ancestors, 13
culture, 1, 7, 30, 37, 52
discovery, 23
early history, 14, 42
ethnography, 30
first contact, 24

history, 30
Neo-, 51, 52–53, 55–56, 70
origin, 31, 36, 46, 63–65, 67, 71
physical features, 37
Paleo-, 6, 11, 51, 52–53, 55–56,
61, 65–66, 70
Alutiiq, 8
Amak Island, 166
Amaknak Island, 40, 43, 44, 62,
164
Amchitka Island, 40, 168
Amur, 13
Anangula, 9–13, 16, 50, 51, 54–57,
60, 61, 62, 67, 179
Andreanof Islands, 3, 24, 142, 161,
167, 168, 212, 223
Andreev, A. I., 26
Angara, 13
Araya, 13, 55
Art, 45–46
decorative, 43
ivory carving, 225
on expeditions, 30
paints, 221
See also Ornamentation
Arutiunov, S. A., 8
Athabaskan, 36, 53, 192, 215
clothing, 215
Atka Island, 49, 70, 107, 161, 167
Attu Island, 4, 24, 34, 70, 167, 168
Avatanak Island, 165
Averkieva, Iu. P., 151, 153